Early Learning and Teaching of English

SECOND LANGUAGE ACQUISITION

Series Editor: Professor David Singleton, *University of Pannonia, Hungary* and Fellow Emeritus, *Trinity College, Dublin, Ireland*

This series brings together titles dealing with a variety of aspects of language acquisition and processing in situations where a language or languages other than the native language is involved. Second language is thus interpreted in its broadest possible sense. The volumes included in the series all offer in their different ways, on the one hand, exposition and discussion of empirical findings and, on the other, some degree of theoretical reflection. In this latter connection, no particular theoretical stance is privileged in the series; nor is any relevant perspective – sociolinguistic, psycholinguistic, neurolinguistic, etc. – deemed out of place. The intended readership of the series includes final-year undergraduates working on second language acquisition projects, postgraduate students involved in second language acquisition research, and researchers and teachers in general whose interests include a second language acquisition component.

Full details of all the books in this series and of all our other publications can be found on http://www.multilingual-matters.com, or by writing to Multilingual Matters, St Nicholas House, 31–34 High Street, Bristol BS1 2AW, UK.

SECOND LANGUAGE ACQUISITION: 86

Early Learning and Teaching of English

New Dynamics of Primary English

Edited by
Jelena Mihaljević Djigunović and
Marta Medved Krajnović

MULTILINGUAL MATTERS
Bristol • Buffalo • Toronto

Library of Congress Cataloging in Publication Data
Early Learning and Teaching of English: New Dynamics of Primary English/Edited by
Jelena Mihaljević Djigunović, Marta Medved Krajnović
Second Language Acquisition: 86
Includes bibliographical references and index.
1. English language—Study and teaching (Primary)—Foreign speakers. 2. Second language acquisition. 3. Bilingual, Education. I. Djigunović, Jelena Mihaljević, editor. II. Krajnović, Marta Medved
PE1128.A2E223 2015
428.0071–dc23 2014044404

British Library Cataloguing in Publication Data
A catalogue entry for this book is available from the British Library.

ISBN-13: 978-1-78309-338-0 (hbk)
ISBN-13: 978-1-78309-337-3 (pbk)

Multilingual Matters
UK: St Nicholas House, 31–34 High Street, Bristol BS1 2AW, UK.
USA: UTP, 2250 Military Road, Tonawanda, NY 14150, USA.
Canada: UTP, 5201 Dufferin Street, North York, Ontario M3H 5T8, Canada.

Website: www.multilingual-matters.com
Twitter: Multi_Ling_Mat
Facebook: https://www.facebook.com/multilingualmatters
Blog: www.channelviewpublications.wordpress.com

Copyright © 2015 Jelena Mihaljević Djigunović, Marta Medved Krajnović and the authors of individual chapters.

All rights reserved. No part of this work may be reproduced in any form or by any means without permission in writing from the publisher.

The policy of Multilingual Matters/Channel View Publications is to use papers that are natural, renewable and recyclable products, made from wood grown in sustainable forests. In the manufacturing process of our books, and to further support our policy, preference is given to printers that have FSC and PEFC Chain of Custody certification. The FSC and/or PEFC logos will appear on those books where full certification has been granted to the printer concerned.

Typeset by Techset Composition India(P) Ltd., Bangalore and Chennai, India.

Contents

	Contributors	vii
	Introduction	ix
1	Context and Structure of the Study Jelena Mihaljević Djigunović	1
2	Individual Differences Among Young EFL Learners: Age- or Proficiency-Related? A Look from The Affective Learner Factors Perspective Jelena Mihaljević Djigunović	10
3	Croatian Primary School Pupils and English Pronunciation in Light of the Emergence of English as a Lingua Franca Višnja Josipović Smojver	37
4	Acquisition of Markers of Definiteness and Indefiniteness in Early EFL Lovorka Zergollern-Miletić	66
5	Present Tense Development in 11- to 13-Year-Old EFL Learners Marta Medved Krajnović and Irena Kocijan Pevec	80
6	Associating Temporal Meanings with Past and Present Verb Forms Smiljana Narančić Kovač and Ivana Milković	110
7	What Vocabulary Networks Reveal about Young Learners' Language Renata Geld	149
8	Receptive Skills in the Linguistic and Non-linguistic Context of EFL Learning Renata Šamo	174

9 Early EFL Development from a Dynamic Systems Perspective 191
   Stela Letica Krevelj and Marta Medved Krajnović

Afterword 214
Appendix 219
Index 220

Contributors

Renata Geld is Assistant professor at the Department of English, University of Zagreb. She has done research on cognitive learning strategies as instances of general cognitive processes, such as attention and perspective. She has also conducted studies on meaning construal in blind users of English (both L1 and L2). Her main areas of interest are: applied cognitive linguistics and cognitive science.

Višnja Josipović Smojver is Chair of the Linguistics Section of the Department of English, Faculty of Humanities and Social Sciences, University of Zagreb. Her main areas of research include phonetics and phonology, varieties of English, and *English as a Lingua Franca*. Her current focus of interest is the phenomenon of foreign accent.

Irena Kocijan-Pevec works as a teacher of English at a grammar school in Varaždin, Croatia. Her main research areas include spoken and written language production in the acquisition of English as L2. She has been involved in two research projects: *Zagreb Project with Fifth Graders* and *The Acquisition of English Language from an Early Age: Analysis of the Learner's Interlanguage*.

Stela Letica Krevelj is a senior teaching and research assistant at the Department of English, Faculty of Humanities and Social Sciences, University of Zagreb. Her research interests include second and third language acquisition and processing, crosslinguistic interaction and teaching English as a foreign language. She has published on second language development, crosslinguistic interaction and metalinguistic reflection in second and third language acquisition.

Marta Medved Krajnović holds the position of Associate Professor at the University of Zagreb's Department of English. From 2003-2007 she was Secretary of EUROSLA, and was Director of Studies of Zagreb University's doctoral programme in FL education between 2010–2013. Currently Director of Stockholm International School, she is leading the school's strategic development. Her main research interests centre around dynamism and complexity of multilingual development in both children and adults.

Jelena Mihaljević Djigunović works as a Professor of SLA and TEFL at Zagreb University. Her main research interests centre around teaching modern languages to young learners and affect in language learning. She has been involved in a number of large scale research projects, the latest one being the *Early Language Learning in Europe* (ELLiE). Her publications include two research books on affective learner factors and over 100 papers. She has co-edited several research volumes.

Ivana Milković is a Research and Teaching Assistant at the Faculty of Teacher Education in Zagreb. She has participated in several research projects. Her main research interests are Croatian and English children's literature and their literary connections, as well as using literature in EFL teaching. She is currently completing her PhD thesis.

Smiljana Narančić Kovač is an Assistant Professor at the Faculty of Teacher Education, University of Zagreb. Her research interests include the narrative, children's literature, literature and culture in foreign language learning, and teaching English to young learners. She has participated in several research projects and published studies in the areas of comparative literature, children's literature, teaching methodology and applied linguistics. She is Editor-in-Chief of the *Libri & Liberi* journal.

Renata Šamo is an Assistant Professor at the Faculty of Teacher Education, University of Zagreb. Her research interests focus primarily on the psycholinguistic perspective of L2 acquisition, the age factor, the theory and methodology of L1/L2 reading. She recently published the book *From Reading to Cognition, from Cognition to Reading*, the first of this type in Croatian so far.

Lovorka Zergollern-Miletić is an Assistant Professor at the Faculty of Teacher Education, University of Zagreb. She has participated in two longitudinal projects focusing on learning and teaching of English. Her publications deal with both linguistic and applied linguistic topics, and cultural studies. Her main research interests focus on expressing in/definiteness in different languages. In 2014 she published the book *English Articles and Speakers of Croatian*.

Introduction

The world has changed dramatically in the last few decades. We live in a connected society with an enormous amount of data in different languages so easily accessible that knowing foreign languages has become of interest and need to a large number of individuals and societies. In line with these developments, programmes in foreign language learning have spread to practically all corners of the world and across all age groups. However, we still lack a sufficiently solid and comprehensive foundation to base these programmes on. In this book we will focus on the early acquisition of foreign languages and the teaching of young learners. In spite of the increasing number of studies that deal with these processes, it would be fair to say that some of the key issues in the field have not yet been resolved.

Without doubt, English is the most popular choice for the first foreign language in most contexts, as well as the most researched language from both the second language acquisition perspective and from the point of view of language teaching. Nevertheless, the existing evidence related to the early learning and teaching of English seems to indicate that new and deeper insights are needed, and all this for several different reasons. First, the status of English in the world has been changing in the last few decades to such an extent that some basic issues need to be reconsidered. One example is the issue of whether English should be taught as a foreign language (EFL), or as a lingua franca (ELF). This is not just an academic question. The perspective we take determines, in fact, why and how the language should be taught, and why and how it will be learned. Second, the increasing (omni)presence of English in the everyday lives of many young learners nowadays changes the role of classroom teaching, causing out-of-school exposure to English to feature as an important factor that researchers and practising teachers alike need to take into account. What also has to be taken into account is that learners bring into the classroom not only linguistic but also new digital skills, different learning strategies and sensibility that the teachers and teaching materials should start accommodating. Third, teachers of young learners have changed as well and many have embraced the philosophy of life-long learning. The growing body of knowledge about such relevant factors as learner characteristics, teacher beliefs and attitudes, impact of teachers on learner motivation, to name only a few, needs to be incorporated into how we go about the early learning and teaching of English today. Fourth, the number of stakeholders in the early learning of English has increased. Besides national and local official policy makers, parents have taken on an increasingly strong role in key decision making concerning their children's learning of English. Popular (and often erroneous) beliefs of how easy it should be to learn a foreign language at an early age put additional pressure on teachers and researchers alike.

This book looks into what we consider to be a new dynamic characterising the learning and teaching of English at the primary level that has emerged as a result of all these new developments. Its chapters focus on longitudinal research into how English is learned by Croatian young learners within the Croatian socio-educational context. The Croatian setting is very interesting and relevant for this topic for two main reasons. Firstly, as it will be seen in Chapter 1, Croatia has a very long and internationally-recognized tradition of research into the process of early foreign language learning and teaching. The research presented in this book will be drawing, explicitly and implicitly, on the knowledge and findings accumulated during almost five decades. Secondly, although specific in the way that any setting is, Croatia shares many features with any context where English is learned as a first foreign language. Hence our findings, we believe, are of relevance both to most settings in the world and to the field of second language acquisition in general. As shown in previous international research that included Croatian learners (e.g. Enever, 2011; Mihaljević Djigunović *et al.*, 2008; Moon & Nikolov, 2000; Szpotowicz *et al.*, 2009), Croatian young EFL learners share all the main characteristics, individual and contextual, that determine the processes of the early learning and teaching of English across Europe and wider (see also Chapter 2).

Briefly about the Structure of the Book

This volume comprises nine chapters and an afterword. They describe, present and interpret some of the findings of the Croatian national five-year long research project *Learning English from an Early Age: Analysis of Learner Language*.

The opening chapter offers an overview of the context in which the study was carried out, presenting a background against which readers can more easily understand and follow the rest of the book. Chapter 2 is devoted to individual differences among young learners that impact their early learning of English. Here, using a mixed-method approach, Jelena Mihaljević Djigunović shows how young learners' individual differences, in particular their affective processes during early EFL learning, are related to age and EFL proficiency.

Each of the next five chapters focuses on young learners' acquisition of English at a specific language level. In Chapter 3, Višnja Josipović Smojver presents a detailed analysis of young learners' pronunciation in an attempt to see which 'core' and 'non-core' features of ELF are characteristic of their oral production. Then, in Chapter 4, Lovorka Zergollern-Miletić looks closely into what means young learners use to express definiteness and indefiniteness in English, and how their interlanguage develops over a four-year period with respect to expressing these categories. The next two chapters focus on expressing present and past temporal meanings. Marta Medved Krajnović and Irena Kocijan Pevec analyse in Chapter 5 how 11- to 13-year-old EFL learners master the linguistic means for expressing the present in English, and how the lexical and morphosyntactic components of their interlanguage develops over time. In Chapter 6, Smiljana Narančić Kovač and Ivana Milković show how young learners develop a contextual understanding of general and temporal meanings of English verbs, and how reliance on this understanding directs their learning. Chapter 7 is devoted to the lexical level. Here Renata Geld offers evidence, based on free and thematically stimulated vocabulary production, of young learners' conceptual preferences in forming meaning relations.

In Chapter 8, Renata Šamo focuses on the receptive skills of listening and reading. She considers the development of these skills in young EFL learners by taking into account individual learner differences as well as contextual factors.

In Chapter 9, Marta Medved Krajnović and Stela Letica Krevelj look at the broader picture of young EFL learners' development. They offer an interpretation of this development from a dynamic systems perspective.

Based on the evidence presented in the chapters outlined above, and based on the already mentioned new dynamics that we think is or should be permeating the EFL classrooms, in the Afterword we offer a model of early EFL learning that – we believe – can inform EFL teaching across any contemporary primary context.

The Purpose of the Book

What existing literature has offered to date are mostly insights into fragments of the processes involved in learning English, while the 'big picture' that could form a framework for designing a modern, dynamic approach to learning and teaching English in the world of today is still missing.

To create the 'big picture', or at least a larger and fuller picture, learner EFL development is analysed and discussed in this volume from different theoretical perspectives. This development is also considered taking into account the key learner characteristics that are relevant to early foreign language learning: affective, cognitive, social, and linguistic. In addition, and as a special feature of the approach taken, classroom-based factors (which unfortunately are missing from most of the existing published work on foreign language learning at the primary level) are included as well.

We hope that this book will be informative and thought and dialogue provoking for both researchers and teachers dealing with the early acquisition of any foreign language, and English in particular.

The editors

References

Enever, J. (ed.) (2011) ELLiE: *Early Language Learning in Europe*. London: The British Council.

Mihaljević Djigunović, J., Nikolov, M. and Ottó, I. (2008) A comparative study of Croatian and Hungarian EFL students. *Language Teaching Research* 12 (3), 433–452.

Moon, J. and Nikolov, M. (2000) (eds) *Research into Teaching English to Young Learners*. Pécs: University Press Pécs.

Szpotowicz, M., Mihaljevic Djigunovic, J. and Enever, J. (2009) Early language learning in Europe: a multinational, longitudinal study. In J. Enever, J. Moon and U. Raman (eds) *Young Learner English Language Policy and Implementation: International Perspectives* (pp. 141–147). Kent: IATEFL.

1 Context and Structure of the Study

Jelena Mihaljević Djigunović

An Overview of Research into the Processes of Early English as a Foreign Language (EFL) Learning in Croatia

Early studies

The project *Learning English from an Early Age: Analysis of Learner Language*, whose findings are presented and discussed in the following chapters, did not start from scratch. It relied on decades of research on early learning of foreign languages (FLs) that was initiated during the 1970s by Mirjana Vilke of Zagreb University. Her interest in the role of the critical period, together with her wish to find the optimal starting age for the introduction of FL into the primary curriculum, resulted in several projects. The major findings in these projects were of the world wide significance and some of them are presented below.

Following Lenneberg's (1967) idea that the incidence of 'language learning blocks' increases after puberty, in her early research (1976a, 1976b, 1979, 1988), Vilke tried to find out whether, and to what degree, pre-puberty children learned EFL with greater ease than learners who had passed the critical period of 'maturation of the brain'. Her experimental study, in which she compared 60 beginners aged nine and 60 beginners aged 17, showed that older beginners performed better on the phonological, morphological, and syntactic post-tests at the perception level. However, post-tests at the production level showed striking phonological differences in favour of younger beginners: while older beginners' oral production was characterized by many L1 approximations, younger beginners' production showed native-like characteristics in pronunciation (e.g. when pronouncing alveolar t and d in words like *bedroom*, which older beginners replaced with Croatian dental t and d) and intonation. In terms of morphological aspects, articles – non-existent in their L1 – were found to present equal difficulties to both age groups, while a number of morphological relations tested (e.g. singular and plural of demonstratives) seemed to be too abstract for pre-puberty children. Interesting findings were obtained at the lexical level as well: younger beginners remembered easily those words that referred to concepts which were already part of their experience and mental repertoire (e.g. *bedroom*), but had great difficulty in mastering words like *drawing room*, which they could not fully conceptualize (most of the participants lived in small flats).

Investigating attitudes towards and motivation for EFL learning on 70 children aged 6–7, Vilke found that children's initial attitudes reflected their parents', but that they were soon replaced by attitudes that young learners formed on the basis of their language learning experiences and relationship with their EFL teacher. Interesting observations were made regarding parents' attitudes too. Many had neutral and some even entertained negative attitudes towards their children's learning of EFL at the start of the study. As a result of the children's enthusiasm about their English classes, however, the parents' attitudes turned positive by the end of the study. In terms of motivational orientations, children were found to want to master English in order to be able to communicate with foreigners, to travel abroad, and to understand films and music in English. Intensity of motivation was, to a great extent, related to the EFL teacher and her approach to children as well as to teaching young learners. On the basis of her analyses of the same young learners' errors from a longitudinal perspective, Vilke found that, contrary to Dulay and Burt's (1973) findings, children who learn English not as a second language but as a foreign one exhibit more interference than developmental errors. She attributed this to the significant differences in language exposure in these two different contexts: when children learn a FL under limited exposure conditions, L1 interference is much stronger, and it changes the 'natural order' of acquisition. Vilke also observed that children with above-average IQ scores found language learning easy already at age six, while by age eight most children managed EFL learning well. Therefore, she suggested that age eight should be considered the optimal starting age in the Croatian context at the time.

The 1991–2001 experimental project

Another set of insights that the *Learning English from an Early Age: Analysis of Learner Language* project is based on stems from research done as part of the 1991–2001 national longitudinal experimental project on early learning of foreign languages which was coordinated by Mirjana Vilke and Yvonne Vrhovac. The project was part of the medium-term Council of Europe programme entitled *Language Learning for European Citizenship,* which included a network of projects from 20 European countries and Canada. Three generations of Croatian first graders (age 6/7) learning one of four FLs (English, French, German, and Italian) were followed during the eight years of their primary education. The sample included over 1000 young learners. The project's activities went in two directions: a group of applied linguists investigated relevant aspects of young learners' characteristics and language performance, while each of the FL teachers was encouraged to rely on their own style of teaching, to follow their intuitions, and to be guided by the needs of the group of children they were teaching. The only thing the teachers were specifically asked to do in their classes was to make their pupils feel relaxed and happy so that receptive learning (Curran, 1972) could take place. FL teaching was organized so that in Grades 1 and 2, the children had five lessons (45 minutes each) of their respective FL per week, four weekly lessons in Grades 3 and 4, and three in Grades 5 to 8. While during the first four grades classes were split into two groups so that there were between 12 and 15 learners in a group, from Grade 5 on, language learning proceeded in intact classes with up to 30 learners per class. In each project school there was a control group – a Grade 4 class (age 9/10) where learners had just started their FLL according to the national curriculum, which at the time stipulated the introduction of FL in Grade 4. The control groups had two lessons of FL per week in Grade 4, three lessons from Grade 5 on, and the teaching was done in large groups (intact classes). They were followed in the same way as the experimental classes.

The findings (e.g. Mihaljević Djigunović & Vilke, 2000; Vilke & Vrhovac, 1993, 1995; Vrhovac, 2001; Vrhovac et al., 1999) showed that teachers found the work with young learners very difficult but highly rewarding. It required them to invest a lot of physical energy as well as emotional engagement, which Vilke (1995: 6) termed TER (total emotional response). The children became so attached to their teachers that their relationship influenced the children's attitudes and motivation to a high degree. Classroom activities were limited in duration to ten minutes in order to keep the young learners on task, and it was when they experienced the process of FLL as a kind of game that they were most eager to contribute. Although practically all the children were highly motivated and had positive attitudes towards FLL, individual differences were found in terms of some personal traits: at the very beginning some children were extremely shy and had to be allowed not to join in until they felt ready, regardless of what may have pleased the teacher; while some children were able to use their imagination a lot, the imaginations of others had yet to be aroused. Content-related teaching and storytelling were found to be two highly productive ways of teaching during the first four years. Comparisons of experimental and control EFL learners showed that the experimental learners were overall better than the controls. As far as motivation and attitudes were concerned, while the control learners' motivation decreased with years of learning, the experimental learners in most cases maintained their levels of motivation, in some cases even increasing them, till the end of primary education. In terms of language achievement, at the end of Grade 8, the experimental learners were found to be better than the controls in pronunciation, orthography, vocabulary, and reading. Interestingly, the controls performed better at grammar tests that required explicit knowledge of the grammatical system. The experimental learners scored significantly better on the C-test, which was used as a measure of overall competence in English. Based on the findings of this longitudinal project, it was proposed that introducing a FL into the primary curriculum from Grade 1 could enable learners to develop positive attitudes towards and high motivation for FLL, as well as achieve desired levels of language competence if three conditions were met: early FLL should be organized in groups comprising not more than 15 learners, in the first years it should be intensive (optimally four–five classes weekly), and the teachers should be specifically trained to teach young learners.

Description of the Current Project

The project *Acquisition of English from an early age: Analysis of learner language* started in 2007 as a five-year research project sponsored by the Croatian Ministry of Science, Education and Sport. The research team included ten researchers who, with the help of a varying number of assistants, conceptualized and carried out research activities during the five years. Investigations were carried out according to a pre-set protocol for each year.

The current context

Like any FLL context, Croatia has its specific characteristics that may distinguish it from some other contexts. However, it has far more similarities with other European socio-educational contexts than differences. This can be seen from previous and already mentioned studies on early EFL learning carried out in Croatia whose findings confirm and extend insights obtained elsewhere. More recently, the transnational *Early Language Learning in Europe* (ELLiE) project (www.ellieresearch.eu), which involved Croatian young EFL learners as well, showed that the data collected in Croatia were comparable to six other European contexts (England, Italy, the Netherlands, Poland, Spain, and Sweden).

The ELLiE study (Enever, 2011) followed young beginners of English in six countries and young beginners of French and Spanish in the seventh (England). The findings showed that the primary FLL processes in Croatia share all the key characteristics with the corresponding processes in the other countries. Thus, for example, the primary curriculum is centralized and in Grades 1–4 all EFL learners have two 45-minute lessons per week like in the Polish context; coursebooks are commonly used in teaching EFL like in Italy, Poland and Spain; in terms of oracy development in the first foreign language the aimed target at the end of Grade 4 is level A1 of the *Common European Framework* (2001) like in England, Italy, Poland, and Spain; like in all the ELLiE countries (except England, of course), English is the foreign language of choice, etc.

As already pointed out above, data collected from the Croatian cohort in the ELLiE study are comparable to those in the other six countries. In her analysis of the Croatian data Mihaljević Djigunović (2012) found that taking a contextualized approach to researching ELL helps put both the processes and the outcomes of primary English into perspective. The context in this sense is not a limiting factor which obstructs possible generalizations of findings, but a necessary pre-requisite for understanding the ELL process which has become a universal phenomenon taking place in increasingly similar contexts of the globalized world we live in.

In order for the reader to obtain a closer look into and understanding of the key aspects of the socio-educational context in which the studies described in the following chapters took place, we will briefly describe its main characteristics.

For more than six decades now, the Croatian educational system has consisted of a primary education stage, which lasts eight years, followed by a three- or four-year secondary education stage, and a tertiary stage including college or university education with its undergraduate, graduate, and postgraduate levels. Primary education is compulsory and consists of a lower primary phase (Grades 1 to 4; ISCED level 1) and an upper primary phase (Grades 5 to 8; ISCED level 2). Early introduction of FLs into the curriculum dates back to the first half of the 20th century (Vilke, 2007). In the beginning, the starting age was 10–11, that is, Grade 4 or 5, depending on the availability of qualified teachers. Since 2003, FL has been a compulsory subject in the primary curriculum from Grade 1. Different FLs have been popular since then, but in recent years, English has become the most attractive, as it is in many other European contexts. At the moment, over 85% of learners take English as their first FL in Grade 1, about 10% take German, and the rest take French or Italian (Medved Krajnović & Letica, 2009). The role of English is underscored by a regulation that those learners who did not start with English in Grade 1 have to take it in Grade 4 as a compulsory subject. In case of those learners who did start with English in Grade 1, a second FL is offered later during primary education only as an optional subject but still many students do take it. All this means that no learner is supposed to leave primary school without having learned English, be it as a first or a second FL. Since Croatian educational authorities follow the recommendations of the Council of Europe and aim at two FLs for all, a second FL is offered during secondary education (ISCED level 3), as well. At the college and university levels FL can be a compulsory or an optional course, depending on the programme. Being a rather small country whose economy relies heavily on tourism, the learning of FLs features as a high priority on policy makers' lists, although this is not always reflected in the amount of state investment in FLL. Still, generally speaking, attitudes towards FLL are very positive, especially in the case of English.

In Grades 1 to 4 of primary school, learners have two English lessons per week. From Grade 5 to Grade 8, they have three English lessons per week. All primary schools in the country follow the guidelines stated in the national framework curriculum. In terms of foreign languages, it quotes CEFR level A1 as the desirable target to be achieved by the end of Grade 4, and CEFR level A2 as target for the end of Grade 8. In cases English is a second FL, the target for the end of Grade 8 is level A1+.

Exposure to English outside school is extensive. Primary EFL learners have ample opportunity to hear English in foreign films and TV series (foreign programmes shown on national television are not dubbed) and music, or use it in computer games or to communicate through social networks. Opportunities for personal contact with English-speaking people are also numerous, especially with foreign tourists visiting Croatia during the summer. In the ELLiE project's comparison of mean hours of weekly exposure to English, Croatian young learners came second only to Sweden and were found to be more exposed than young learners in the Netherlands, Poland, Spain and Italy (Muñoz & Lindgren, 2011).

Croatian primary classes are generally monolingual. The only exception are schools situated near the border, where there are learners whose L1 is not Croatian. A typical primary class has 28 pupils on average.

To teach English in primary school, teachers need a university degree. There are two pathways in obtaining such a degree. One is by getting a university degree in English Language and Literature (teaching stream), the other is by obtaining a university degree in early education with a minor in English. While in the former case, the teacher can work in any type of educational institution (from kindergarten to university), the latter qualifies an individual only for teaching English in primary school. Like in many other European contexts (Enever, 2011), due to a shortage of qualified staff, in some (usually village) schools English is taught by unqualified teachers. Preservice teacher education at the university level has existed for decades and has recently, with the advent of the so-called Bologna process, replaced the concurrent, often 4-year model, with the successive, often 3 + 2 year model. This was accompanied by a significant rise in the amount of course work devoted to developing ELT competencies. At the in-service level, EFL teachers are offered workshops and seminars organized by the national Agency for Teacher Education and Training and publishers of teaching materials: these are usually aimed at updating teachers' practical teaching skills. In recent years, a growing number of EFL teachers have started to enroll in PhD programmes in FL education or in linguistics as a result of their interest in researching language acquisition and teaching.

Aims

In spite of the fact that there have been numerous investigations of EFL learning at the primary level, conspicuously few offer a more comprehensive and documented picture of the processes involved. Such insightful studies are necessary to enrich our understanding of the process of acquiring English and of ways of teaching that might be conducive to effective and efficient acquisition. What existing research has offered to date are mostly studies providing insight into fragments of the processes involved in learning English, while the 'big picture', which could form a framework for designing a modern approach to learning and teaching English in the modern world of today, is still missing.

The overall aim of the project was to shed light on the processes of EFL development in primary school learners (age 6–14) when this development is happening in a regular (non-experimental) institutional context.

This aim was operationalized through the following set of research foci: the affective characteristics of primary learners of EFL; the phonetic characteristics of primary learners' oral production; the language development of primary EFL learners at the morphosyntactic level; lexical development at the primary level; EFL development from the dynamic systems perspective.

Sample

The project was carried out with a convenience sample of Croatian young learners of EFL, as well as their teachers, school principals, and parents or caretakers. The total sample comprised 208 primary school learners, nine school principals, 14 EFL teachers, and 208 parents or caretakers of the participating children.

The primary school learners' sample was balanced in terms of gender (49.8% males vs. 50.2% females). Participants were drawn from a total of eight schools situated across Croatia. These were two city schools, three town schools, and three village schools. The sample included 100 learners who began their EFL learning in Grade 1 (age 6/7) and 108 learners who started learning EFL in Grade 4 (age 9/10). Both groups were balanced regarding the gender of the participants: in group 1, 49.43% of the participants were boys and 50.57% were girls, while in group 2, 51.9% were boys and 48.1% were girls.

As will be seen in the chapters that follow, different studies focused on different parts of the sample depending on the aim of the study at hand. Thus, while in some investigations all participants took part, in others only a subsample was studied. The latter refers in particular to the subsample of 'focal learners' (N = 66) who were involved in those parts of the project that required more detailed and intensive investigation, such as those where individual oral interviews, or close observation of individual learners' language behaviour during classroom activities were used. The focal learners were selected in the following way: six learners from each of the classes studied were chosen such that in each case they comprised two high-ability, two average-ability, and two low-ability learners. In each of the subcategories, one learner was male and one was female.

Instruments and procedure

Instruments

Many of the instruments used in the studies described in this book were adopted from the ELLiE project. The reason for this was that these instruments had been used on Croatian young EFL learners during the recent ELLiE investigations and their suitability for the Croatian context had been tested. Information about these instruments can be found on the ELLiE webpage (www.ellieresearch.eu).

Some of the instruments were designed by Hungarian experts (Alderson *et al.*, 2000; Fekete *et al.*, 1999) and their appropriateness was verified in an earlier large-scale Croatian national project called *English in Croatia* (Mihaljević Djigunović & Bagarić, 2007): these included two picture elicitation tasks used to elicit oral production, and a writing task in which participants were required to write a composition based on specific guidelines regarding the length and content of the composition.

Finally, some tasks were designed by the research team of the present project. These concern two cartoons used in different years to elicit written production.

Detailed descriptions of all the instruments can be found in the appropriate chapters.

Procedure

The research team members discussed the instruments at length before applying them. The instruments that had not been used on Croatian primary school learners before were piloted first. Research activities were organized in such a way that one research team member was responsible for one project class during all the project years. This resulted in a close relationship between the researcher, the young learners and their EFL teachers, and the school principals. Thus, over the years, each researcher was treated as a welcome guest in the school, and the investigations proceeded very smoothly throughout the project. At the start of the project, written informed consent was obtained from each of the learners' parents or guardians. Care was taken that the participants' identities were kept confidential: a coding system was developed to keep record of all the collected data. Oral language production and audio recordings of individual interviews were transcribed either in Microsoft Word or CLAN format.

Let us continue now, from chapter to chapter, with the presentation of the in-depth analysis of the project findings. Each chapter covers different linguistic and foreign language learning phenomena and skills, and different theoretical perspective.

References

Alderson, C.J., Nagy, E. and Öveges, E. (2000) *English Language Education in Hungary, Part II: Examining Hungarian Learners' Achievements in English*. Budapest: The British Council.
Curran, Ch. (1972) *Counselling Learning*. New York: Grune and Straton.
Dulay, H. and Burt, M. (1973) Should we teach children syntax? *Language Learning* 23 (2), 245–258.
Enever, J. (ed.) (2011) *ELLiE: Early Language Learning in Europe*. London: The British Council.
Fekete, H., Major, E. and Nikolov, M. (eds) (1999) *English Language Education in Hungary. A Baseline Study*. Budapest: The British Council Hungary.
Lenneberg, E. (1967) *Biological Foundations of Language*. New York: John Wiley and Sons.
Medved Krajnović, M. and Letica, S. (2009) Učenaje stranih jezika u Hrvatskoj: politika, znanost i javnost [Foreign language learning in Croatia: politics, science and the public]. In J. Granić (ed.) *Language Policy and Language Reality* (pp. 598–607). Zagreb: HDPL.
Mihaljević Djigunović, J. (2012) *Early EFL Learning in Context – Evidence from a Country Case Study*. London: The British Council.
Mihaljević Djigunović, J. and Bagarić, V. (2007) English in Croatia – from needs to achievement. *Metodika* 8 (14), 38–50.
Mihaljević Djigunović, J. and Vilke, M. (2000) Eight years after: wishful thinking vs facts of life. In J. Moon and M. Nikolov (eds) *Research into Teaching English to Young Learners* (pp. 66–86). Pécs: University Press PECS.
Muñoz, C. and Lindgren E. (2011) Out-of-school factors – the home. In J. Enever (ed.) *ELLiE: Early Language Learning in Europe* (pp. 103–122). London: The British Council.
Vilke, M. (1976a) Implications of the age factor on the process of acquisition of an L2. *Studia Romanica et Anglica Zagrabiensia* 21, 87–104.
Vilke, M. (1976b) The age factor in the acquisition of foreign languages. *Rassegna Italiana di Linguistica Applicata* 2 (3), 179–190.
Vilke, M. (1979) English as a foreign language at the age of eight. *Studia Romanica et Anglica Zagrabiensia* 24, 297–336.
Vilke, M. (1988) Some psychological aspects of early second language acquisition. *Journal of Multilingual and Multicultural Development* 9 (1–2), 115–128.
Vilke, M. (1995) Children and foreign languages in Croatian primary schools – four years of a project. In M. Vilke and Y. Vrhovac (eds) *Children and Foreign Languages II* (pp. 1–16). Zagreb: University of Zagreb.
Vilke, M. (2007) English in Croatia – A glimpse into past, present and future. *Metodika* 8 (14), 17–24.
Vilke, M. and Vrhovac, Y. (eds) (1993) *Children and Foreign Languages I*. Zagreb: Faculty of Philosophy, University of Zagreb.
Vilke, M. and Vrhovac, Y. (eds) (1995) *Children and Foreign Languages II*. Zagreb: Faculty of Philosophy, University of Zagreb.
Vrhovac, Y. (ed.) (2001) *Children and Foreign Languages III*. Zagreb: Faculty of Philosophy, University of Zagreb.
Vrhovac, Y., Kruhan, M., Medved Krajnović, M., Mihaljević Djigunović, J., Narančić Kovač, S., Sironić-Bonefačić, N. and Vilke, M. (eds) (1999) *Strani jezik u osnovnoj školi* [Foreign language in primary school]. Zagreb: Naprijed.
www.ellieresearch.eu (accessed 19 December 2014).

2 Individual Differences Among Young EFL Learners: Age- or Proficiency-Related? A Look from The Affective Learner Factors Perspective

Jelena Mihaljević Djigunović

Introduction

Although the field of individual learner differences (IDs) is by now considered to be well established (e.g. Arabski & Wojtaszek, 2011; Dörnyei, 2005; Robinson, 2002), it would be fair to say that it comprises many subfields that are still largely under-researched. This is even more evident when early foreign language learning (FLL) is concerned. Perhaps it is not too surprising that systematic research on IDs is especially lacking in studies focusing on early FLL: for a long time, young FL learners have been considered to be so similar to one another that no one considered it necessary to investigate individual differences among them. It is only more recently that the need for such studies has been pointed out (e.g. MacIntyre *et al.*, 2002).

Affective Factors and Young Foreign Language Learners

As pointed out in Heinzmann (2013), young learners' affective dispositions are a very relevant research topic because they are less stable than the affective dispositions of more mature learners. Besides, they are also malleable, which opens up the potential for educational interventions (Edelenbos *et al.*, 2006). Existing studies suggest that young FL learners' affective dispositions are multifaceted, dynamic, and non-linear.

Research on young learners' attitudes and motivation has undergone a shift in approach and focus. At first they were treated as monolithic, linear, and stable constructs. It was assumed that young learners adopt the attitudes of their significant others, such as parents, friends, or teachers. When more situated approaches were applied, it became clear that young learners form their own attitudes very early, based on their own perceptions of the language-learning process, and that these attitudes change over time. The main initial insights from research based on this new perspective showed that classroom processes and the FL teacher were key factors in the formation of young learners' attitudes (Nikolov, 1999; Vilke, 1993). On the other hand, it was subsequently found that direct contact with native speakers contributed to positive attitudes towards FLL (Marschollek, 2002). Another major finding was that early FLL has a positive effect on young learners' attitudes towards future learning (Kennedy *et al.*, 2000).

As far as motivation is concerned, research on young learners to date has offered rather conflicting results. One set of studies (e.g. Cenoz, 2003; Chambers, 1999; Marschollek, 2002; Mihaljević Djigunović, 1993, 1995) pointed to high initial levels of motivation, which may remain quite stable under favourable teaching conditions. However, motivational changes were documented in other studies. Thus, some studies (e.g. Kim, 2009; Lee & Park, 2001; Nikolov, 1999) offered evidence that, over time, young language learners' attitudes become less positive, and that their motivation decreases. This is in line with findings showing that motivation declines in all school subjects: Haladyna and Thomas (1979), for example, found that attitudes may become significantly less positive between grades 1 and 2, and between grades 6 and 7. On the other hand, there are studies which suggest that young learners' attitudes and motivation may in fact be more stable than we assume; thus, in her study of young learners of English as a foreign language (EFL) in Switzerland, Heinzmann (2013) found very little fluctuation in her participants' motivation during the two years in which their motivation was studied. She concluded that, by age nine, children's attitudes may already be established and not very prone to change. Finally, some studies (e.g. Donato *et al.*, 2000) found that attitudes may become more positive with an increase in the length of FLL.

There has been hardly any research on young FL learners' self-concept, which is a rather recent topic in FLL in general. Currently emerging recent studies rely on what has been concluded from research with more mature learners. Self-concept is defined as a psychological construct which involves one's self-perceptions of competence and self-evaluations (Mercer, 2011). Marsh *et al.* (1988) suggests that self-concept should be viewed as a domain-specific phenomenon. Viewing it at a more general level would not allow us to capture the fluctuations that occur in a specific domain such as FLL. Insights into a learner's self-concept may be extremely revealing because, besides being relevant in its own right, self-concept has been shown to be among the best predictors of learner motivation. As with young learners' IDs in general, the lack of research seeking insight into their self-concept can perhaps be attributed to the general belief that all young learners have positive self-concept as FL learners. Harter (2006) stresses that young children cannot conceive of their ideal or possible selves as separate from their actual selves, and that this leads to them developing unrealistically positive self-descriptions. Damon and Hart (1988) point out that self-knowledge becomes more complex and multidimensional as children become more mature. Some experts believe that children are not aware of their perceptions of inner processes, or that they cannot report on them. However, Kolb (2007) points out that, contrary to popular belief, young learners possess a remarkable awareness of their language-learning processes and that, based on their language-learning experiences and personal knowledge, they can develop quite elaborate language-learning beliefs. One dimension of these beliefs concerns their self-perception as language learners. A positive and realistic self-concept has acknowledged benefits for language learning (e.g. Mercer, 2011; Mihaljević Djigunović & Lopriore, 2011). Mercer (2011) focuses on inter- and intra-learner variability in FL learners' self-concepts, as well as the context-sensitivity of the self-concept construct. Such aspects are becoming increasingly evident thanks to new approaches to the study of self-concept which consider it as a situated and dynamic phenomenon.

Young learners are now increasingly considered to be not simply objects of research but also valuable sources of information about the role of individual learner differences in FLL. Several researchers (e.g. Kolb, 2007; Mihaljević Djigunović & Lopriore, 2011; Wenden, 1999) have pointed out that young FL learners are able to engage in reflective activities and provide data that are important for the understanding of early language-learning processes. Thus, more recent studies include the perspective of young learners themselves, as well.

Aim and Research Methodology

In the present study our primary aim was to obtain insight into the relationship of young learners' IDs with their age and language proficiency. Our focus was on the following IDs: attitudes, motivation, and self-concept. We approached these important IDs not as stable learner characteristics but as dynamic processes. As a corollary, we hoped to gain insight into affective processes that characterize early EFL learning. Following ideas about motivational evolution (Dörnyei, 2005; Ushioda, 2001), for example, we included the temporal dimension as one frame of reference, thus adding a longitudinal perspective to our study. Also, based on indications from recent studies on affective aspects of early FLL (e.g. Mihaljević Djigunović & Lopriore, 2011), and hoping to take a more situated approach, we decided to look into how young learners' attitudes, motivation, and self-concepts interact with contextual variables. Context was defined in this study as a binary value: the school context vs. the out-of-school context.

Our aim was operationalized by means of the following research questions:

Is there a relationship between young EFL learners' attitudes, motivation, and self-concepts and the age at which EFL learning begins?

Is there a relationship between young EFL learners' attitudes, motivation, and self-concepts and language proficiency?

What trajectories do young learners' affective dispositions follow between years 2 and 4?

Relying on insight from previous research (e.g. Lopriore, 2009; Mihaljević Djigunović & Lopriore, 2011; Nikolov, 1999, 2002; Szpotowicz et al., 2009; Vilke, 1993), we decided to focus on participants' attitudes towards the EFL learning and teaching process, which we consider the most relevant types of attitudes. Motivation was determined on the basis of whether the participants liked learning English in general, whether they liked learning new English words in particular, and whether they considered English as their favourite subject. EFL self-concept was conceptualized in terms of the participants' self-perceptions of how good they were at learning English in comparison with their classmates.

In this study, English proficiency was not measured by means of tests. It was taken as a variable that increases by default with each year of learning.

A detailed description of the total sample of 208 participants can be found under the *Sample* heading of Chapter 1.

The instruments used in this study were adopted from the Early Language Learning in Europe (ELLiE) project (Enever, 2011; www.ellieresearch.eu). Since the ELLiE cohort had included Croatian young EFL learners, the instruments could be considered suitable for the Croatian socio-educational context. Also, thanks to the application of instruments previously validated in six other contexts (England, Italy, the Netherlands, Poland, Spain and Sweden), some generalizations of findings from the present study may be allowed across contexts.

Data on the participants' motivation for learning EFL, their attitudes about language learning and teaching, and their EFL learner self-concepts were elicited by means of smiley questionnaires, individual oral interviews with learners, parents' questionnaires, and classroom observation. Information on contextual variables was collected through interviews with school principals and EFL teachers, parents' questionnaires, and school and classroom observation.

Motivation for EFL learning was studied by analyzing the scores on two smiley items: *How do you like learning English this year?* and *How do you like learning new English words this year?* The smiley faces represented three scale points: dislike, neither like nor dislike, and like. This was combined with an oral interview question: *Which is your favourite school subject this year?* In cases when participants did not mention English, they were explicitly asked if they liked English. Scoring was done in terms of whether participants mentioned English as their favourite subject, described it as one of their favourite school subjects, or explicity reported they did not like English at all.

Information about attitudes towards language learning and teaching was gathered by means of four pictures, each showing a different primary classroom arrangement. The first picture depicted a traditional classroom, in which pupils were sitting in rows and facing the blackboard; the teacher was pointing at something written on the board, and everyone was listening to her attentively. In the second picture, pupils were doing group work, while the teacher was standing in the backround. The third picture showed young learners and their teacher sitting in a circle on a carpet and doing an activity with flashcards. The fourth picture showed a disorderly classroom in which pupils were playing, jumping around and throwing things, while the teacher looked as though she were at a loss as to what to do. The participants were asked to select the classroom in which they thought they would learn English best, and to explain their choice.

To elicit information about their EFL self-concept, the participants were asked in the oral interview to compare themselves to their classmates and say whether they were better, just as good as, or worse at English than the other pupils in their class. They were also asked to explain how they knew they were better than, the same as, or worse than their classmates.

Data on contextual aspects were gathered by means of a set of instruments. The data on school context variables were collected by means of interviews with school principals and EFL teachers, a teacher questionnaire, and school and classroom observation. These referred to the principals' and teachers' attitudes towards early FLL, how well the school was equipped for FL teaching, the EFL teachers' formal qualifications, the approaches they implemented in their teaching, and their use of English (vs L1) in class.

To get an insight into the out-of-school context participants lived in, we measured their socio-economic status (SES), type and amount of exposure to English, and out-of-school language behaviour. SES was measured by the levels of their parents' education, English books that the participants had access to in the home, and whether they had access to the internet. Data on the remaining variables were gathered through the parents' questionnaire.

Each participant was assigned to a language-learning ability category (high ability, average ability, and low ability) on the basis of their teachers' and the researchers' joint estimation. The participants' end-of-year grades in

English were used to compare the focal learners in terms of their success in EFL learning.

During the three years of the study, interviews with principals were made once, as was the case with parents' questionnaire, which they filled in during year 3. Interviews with teachers were carried out each year during one of the school visits, and each teacher filled in one questionnaire during the three years. Classroom observations were done three times per year: they involved collecting data on both the teaching processes and the focal learners' language behaviour during English classes. Smiley questionnaires were administered at the end of each school year, so that the participants had the experience of a whole year to rely on in their replies. Since it was confirmed in some studies (e.g. Lamb, 2003) that data elicited by means of questionnaires can contradict young learners' self-reports obtained by means of other measures, we triangulated the smiley questionnaire data with those obtained through end-of-year oral interviews with individual focal learners, as well as through observation of their language-learning behaviour during EFL classes.

The mixed methods approach we applied in this study produced both quantitative and qualitative data on which we based the answers to our research questions. In the following section, we first turn to the quantitative analyses.

Results and Discussion

Quantitative analyses

The data collected by means of smiley questionnaires and oral interviews regarding motivation for EFL learning, attitudes towards EFL learning and teaching, and the learners' EFL self-concept were statistically processed. Independent sample t-tests and chi-square tests were performed to look into the differences in the scores on the same items between the two groups each year. To get a more comprehensive picture, we also decided to look into within-group differences in scores on the same items from year to year, and thus performed paired sample t-tests and chi-square tests separately on group 1 (younger beginners) and group 2 (older beginners).

Motivation for EFL learning

We compared scores on three items: smiley item 1 (*How do you like learning English this year?*), smiley item 2 (*How do you like learning new English words this year?*), and interview item 1 (*Which is your favourite school subject?*).

Results for group 1

The paired-sample t-test showed significant differences regarding how much group 1 participants liked EFL learning between years 2 and 3 (t = 3.226, p < 0.002), and between years 3 and 4 (t = 3.932, p < 0.001). The differences between year 2 and year 4 were not significant. The younger beginners liked learning English significantly more in year 2 than in year 3, just as they liked it more in year 3 than in year 4. No significant differences were found regarding the learning of new English words. Looking at the number of participants who cited English as their favourite subject, we can see that two-thirds mentioned it as their favourite school subject or one of their favorites in year 2. In year 3 a major drop in the number of such participants was observed: only one-third listed it as a favourite subject. In year 4 approximately the same number of participants mentioning English as a favourite subject could be observed: slightly more than 20% stated that English was their favourite subject, and just over 15% listed it as one of their favourite subjects.

Results for group 2

The only difference in how much group 2 participants liked EFL learning that was found to be significant was between years 2 and 3 (t = 3.167, p = 0.002): the year 2 scores were higher than those in year 3. The same was true about how much they liked learning new English words: the only significant difference was that between the scores for years 2 and 3 (t = 2.970, p < 0.004), with the former being higher than the latter. While in year 2 no participant mentioned English as a favourite school subject, in year 3 slightly more than 30% of the participants did, but this number dropped to less than 5% in year 4.

Group comparison

T-test and chi-square analyses performed on year 2 data established significant differences between the two groups in terms of how much the groups liked learning English in general (t = 2.234, p = 0.026) but not in terms of how much the participants enjoyed learning new English words. As was found in some earlier studies (e.g. Szpotowicz et al., 2009), both groups liked learning new words because they equated FLL with mastering vocabulary and probably perceived it as easier than mastering grammatical structures. Group 1 participants liked learning English more than those in group 2. In year 3, group 1 participants not only liked learning English significantly more (t = 3.598, <0.001) but also enjoyed learning new English words significantly more (t = 3.860, p < 0.001) than group 2 participants. In year 4 there was no significant difference between the groups in how much they liked learning new English words, but it was again established that group 1 participants liked learning English significantly more (t = 5.801, p < 0.001) than group 2 participants.

Interesting differences were found in whether participants in the two groups listed English among their favourite subjects. In year 2 participants from group 1 significantly more often (t = 5.043, p < 0.001) included EFL among the favourite subjects or, when asked explicitly, reported that they liked the subject more than group 2 participants. The difference was not significant in year 3, however. In year 4, English again featured as a favourite subject significantly more prominently (t = 2.807, p = 0.008) with group 1 than with group 2 participants.

Discussion

Our findings showed that younger beginners were generally more motivated than older beginners during all three years. This is in keeping with the now widely-acknowledged aim of early FLL: the development of positive attitudes and motivation (Edelenbos *et al.*, 2006).

Both younger and older beginners, however, experienced motivational declines at some point during the three years. This corroborates results found elsewhere (e.g. Nikolov, 2002) which also document a steady decrease in motivation over the years. Our study also suggests that younger and older beginners did not follow the same trajectories in terms of motivational dynamics. It seems that younger beginners reached a critical point in year 3 of their EFL learning. It can be assumed that in year 3, young learners experienced difficulties in coping with the growing amount of language material, which may have affected their motivation. By year 4 some young learners learned how to cope with the difficulties effectively, which prevented further motivational decline. To understand motivational developments in older beginners, we have to keep in mind that in year 2 they entered a transition period: they started a new stage of primary education in grade 5, when several new school subjects were introduced in the curriculum, each taught by a different specialist teacher. Thus, English became one of several subjects they had to focus on, and possibly some new subjects became more attractive because of the novelty. While in year 3 they may have felt settled in their new educational situation, in year 4 the situation became challenging again: the EFL learning material got more complex and perhaps too demanding for some learners, and puberty set in, bringing with it many additional challenges to deal with.

Attitudes towards language learning and teaching

Attitudes to language learning and teaching were investigated only in years 3 and 4. We tried to obtain insights into these attitudes by means of the interview item asking learners to select the classroom arrangement in which they would learn English best (for details see section on instruments).

Results for group 1

In year 3 the majority of group 1 participants (61.1%) decided that they would learn English best in a traditional classroom. Around one quarter preferred the circle arrangement. The group work arrangement was selected by less than 15% of the participants. No one opted for the 'disorderly' classroom. In year 4 the traditional arrangement again featured as the most frequent option (66.7%). However, the second most frequent choice was now not the circle arrangement (12.8%) but the classroom where group work (17.9%) was going on. Looking into the directions of preference switches, we observed that fewest changes occurred among participants who originally opted for the traditional classroom: over 80% opted for the same arrangement in year 4, while 10% switched to the group work and 10% to the circle arrangement. Half of those who had selected the group work classroom in year 3 did so in year 4; around one-third changed for the traditional classroom and a little over 15% switched to the circle arrangement. Only 20% of those who opted for the circle arrangement in year 3 displayed no change in their preferences in year 4 (making it the least stable choice); as many as 50% switched to the traditional classroom and 20% to the group work classroom arrangement.

Results for group 2

The majority of the participants opted for the group work arrangement in both year 3 and year 4 (61.1% and 65%, respectively). The second choice both times was the traditional classroom, followed by the circle arrangement (around 10% each year). If we look at the changes from year 3 to year 4, we can see that half of those who selected the traditional classroom in year 3 switched to the group work arrangement the following year, while the other half decided to stick with the traditional classroom. The same was true about those who had selected the circle arrangement in year 3: half maintained the same attitudes and half opted for the group work arrangement in year 4. Regarding those who started with the group work arrangement in year 3, two-thirds remained stable, while one-third changed in favour of the traditional classroom arrangement.

Group comparison

In year 3, the greatest differences between the two groups were found in preferences for the group-work classroom arrangement: while only 14.6% of group 1 participants opted for that arrangement, the percentage in group 2 amounted to 61.1. The two groups differed considerably in their attitudes towards the traditional classroom, which was significantly more popular among group 1 participants (61%) than among their counterparts (27.8%). In year 4, approximately the same pattern was established between the two groups.

Discussion

As found in the ELLiE project (Mihaljević Djigunović & Lopriore, 2011), here also younger learners seemed to need structure, order, peace and quiet, as well as teacher control to learn English best. Many participants reported that they liked the traditional classroom best because everyone was quiet and attentive and the teacher was pointing at things on the blackboard, which enabled all pupils to hear, understand, and learn better. Some participants started to see the potential of group work in language learning already in year 3, and the number of such learners increased in year 4. We assume that the older learners were more aware of the potential that group work has in FLL, and had also developed strategies for effective participation. Group work activities with 11–13 year olds are most often organized with more explicit learning outcomes in mind than is usually the case with younger learners, which makes them more purposeful and motivating. That may have contributed to this type of classroom arrangement being a key preference. Also, older learners can be assumed to have developed a certain level of learner autonomy and hence needed less teacher-imposed structure in their learning. Interestingly, younger beginners were more decisive in selecting the best arrangement than the older ones, who in year 3 often could not decide between two different teaching formats.

The popularity of the traditional classroom arrangement probably also reflected the fact that it was the format that most participants were exposed to most of the time.

The learner's EFL self-concept

During the oral interviews, the participants were asked to compare themselves to their classmates and say whether they were better, the same, or worse at English than their peers. They were also asked to explain their claims.

Results for group 1

Paired samples t-test results showed that the group 1 participants' EFL self-concepts were significantly more positive in year 2 than in year 4 ($t = 2.238$, $p < 0.032$). The other pairs of differences were found to be non-significant. The mean kept decreasing during the three years.

Results for group 2

The only significant difference was established between the older participants' self-perception in year 2 and year 3 ($t = -2.449$, $p = 0.028$): the participants' self-concepts were significantly more positive in year 3.

Group comparison

In year 2 there were no significant differences in self-concept between the younger and older beginners. Both groups had a rather positive self-perception as EFL learners. Significant differences, however, were found in years 3 and 4. Interestingly, in year 3 older learners had significantly more positive self-concepts ($t = -2.97$, $p = 0.005$), while in year 4 it was the younger beginners who reported significantly more positive self-concepts ($t = 2.544$, $p = 0.014$).

Discussion

Our findings suggest that, in terms of self-perception, younger and older beginners follow different trajectories. There are several possible explanations for this. One is that younger learners overestimate their abilities at the start. As Pinter (2011: 33) points out, when asked to rate their abilities, young children often turn into 'learning optimists'. With greater experience in language learning and increased exposure to their EFL teacher's feedback on their own language performance and that of their peers, they become more realistic over time. Although we do not have data on how the older participants' self-concepts in other school subjects developed, we consider it likely that the less positive EFL self-concept in year 2 may be connected with the transition to the new phase of primary education which, as already pointed out, occurs in year 2 (i.e. grade 5 of primary school). Once settled in the new educational situation, older beginners might develop a more positive outlook. The younger beginners did not experience such transitional problems before grade 5 of primary school. Another possible explanation is that young learners' self-concepts generally turn less positive, just as attitudes about and motivation for learning do among learners in general.

Qualitative Analyses

Six case studies

To get a more in-depth look into affective processes, we selected three younger beginners (participants from group 1) and three older beginners (participants from group 2) and drew up their profiles. In order to make their profiles as comprehensive as possible, we included information on their contextual backgrounds, as well: this included information about both the school context and the out-of-school context. We hoped that such a contextualized approach would help us to interpret our findings in a more meaningful way.

ZLATA (younger beginner; female; average language-learning ability; a successful learner)

> ***Contextual background information.*** <u>School context</u>. Zlata attended a town school with a tradition in early foreign language learning. English was treated as one of the key subjects in the curriculum, and the school invested a lot in teaching resources (dictionaries, English books for children, IWB, etc.). Zlata had a qualified teacher of English who had been trained specifically to teach young learners. The teacher applied age-appropriate methodology, relied on communicative activities, and used English about 80% of the class time. In year 2 she mostly used the traditional classroom arrangement, while in years 3 and 4 she introduced group work very often . <u>Out-of-school context</u>. At home, Zlata regularly informed her parents about what they had done in her English classes, and she practised English regularly at home too. Her parents reported that she was motivated to learn English, did not find language learning difficult, enjoyed speaking English, and felt proud and confident of her knowledge. Zlata regularly listened to the CD accompanying the textbook used in

school, and watched cartoons in English. Her parents reported that she spent up to five hours per week watching programmes in English. She also played games on the internet. When she needed assistance with her English homework, she would ask her mum for help. Zlata's first encounters with foreigners took place in year 4; however, she did not use the opportunity to communicate with them because she did not feel confident enough. Both Zlata's parents had secondary education. They had learned English in school but did not use it at work. Their home library included picture books in English, and they had an internet connection.

In-class language behaviour. Observation data showed that in years 2 and 3 Zlata was very shy and quiet during English classes. She would never raise her hand to volunteer an answer. Although she was attentive all the time and participated in most classroom activities, she generally displayed average interest and often low involvement during classes. Zlata became less shy and quiet during her EFL classes only in year 4. In this final year she participated in activities more actively and generally displayed greater interest and involvement.

MOTIVATION. English was one of Zlata's two favourite subjects in year 2. In year 3, she did not list it among her favourite subjects, but when asked explicitly if she liked it, she replied positively – though she could not explain why she liked it. In year 4, Zlata did not consider English to be among the subjects she liked: she seemed to be very decisive about which subjects she preferred (*Croatian* and *science*), and could elaborate quite extensively on why she liked them. While in all three years she claimed she enjoyed all the activities done in her English classes, her preference for learning new words (year 2) was, with time, replaced by reading and singing (year 3). However, to be able to really enjoy singing, she stressed, she needed to see the lyrics while singing. In year 4, Zlata could not single out any specific aspect that she liked: she claimed she liked everything about her English classes.

ATTITUDES TOWARDS LANGUAGE LEARNING AND TEACHING. Zlata's attitudes towards different teaching methods were not constant. In year 3, she opted for the group arrangement classroom. However, she could not provide much explanation for her choice apart from saying that the pupils were sitting in groups. In year 4, Zlata decided that the traditional classroom was the best place for her to learn English because everyone was quiet and listening to the teacher.

SELF-CONCEPT. Comparing herself to her classmates, in year 2, Zlata thought that others in class were better than her. She reported, '*I am doing a bit* *worse than the others because I cannot pronounce some word's'*. She continued to have this self-perception in year 3, claiming that she was always the last one to finish a task. A major change could be observed in year 4, when she said she was as good as others because she was one of those in class who had an A in English.

DOMAGOJ (younger beginner; male; low language-learning ability; below average succes in English)

Contextual background information. *School context*. Domagoj attended a city school in a working-class area. The school staff had generally positive attitudes towards foreign languages as school subjects. Foreign language teachers had access to basic teaching technology (DVD players, video). Domagoj's teacher was a specialist English teacher who had not been specifically trained to teach young learners but enjoyed teaching them all the same. In her teaching she relied on songs and games, and took special care to balance different types of activities to maintain her learners' motivation and keep them on task. She believed the teacher should be an authoritative figure because *'children like to have a leader'*, but should be flexible and sincere, because *'if children like the teacher, they will come to like the language itself.'* Most of the time her classes were organized in the traditional teacher-fronted format. Her use of English was about 80% on average. *Out-of-school context*. According to his parents, Domagoj would often tell them about his English classes, he would practise English at home, and he enjoyed speaking English in the presence of his family. At home, Domagoj sometimes read picture books in English, and he used the internet to play games in English. He also watched films and cartoons in English on TV almost every day. He had a chance to use English with foreigners. In year 2 he reported: *'Once I met a foreigner and said, "thank you" in English, and it felt great'*. He had other opportunities in year 4, when he could say things in English and understood his interlocutor. He reported that he had felt great about this experience. Domagoj's mother (a single parent) had a university degree and used English at work. They had access to the internet at home.

In-class language behaviour. During his English classes, Domagoj generally showed average interest in what was being taught. However, he often behaved hyperactively and impatiently. His attention span was quite short, on many occasions he would lose his concentration, and his involvement ranged from low to average. He often disrupted the teaching process by asking questions in L1. This continued throughout the three years, though with less intensity at times.

MOTIVATION. English was definitely not among Domagoj's favourite subjects during the three years. Still, when asked specifically whether he liked English at all, he replied positively in year 3, stressing that it enabled everyone to speak a foreign languge. In year 4, his attitudes were less positive, and he said, '*(i)t is a different language; there is no calculation, just grammar*', confirming his constant preference for mathematics. Still, he reported liking everything about his English classes in year 2, pointing out that he liked it best when they learned new words, which made their knowledge increase. This perception changed in years 3 and 4. While in year 3 he said he liked learning new English words and activities which involved playing with dice, he also reported disliking writing because too much writing made his hand hurt. In year 4, the activities he liked best included playing board games, because it was fun and not boring. What he did not like was grammar, because '*(i)t is difficult to think about all that*'.

ATTITUDES TOWARDS LANGUAGE LEARNING AND TEACHING. Domagoj selected the traditional classroom arrangement in both years 3 and 4, stressing it was ok to study hard in class because pupils '*have some free time outside anyway*'. He said the traditional format was the best, because learners were quiet and did not talk during the class (year 3), and were not having fun like in the other three classrooms (year 4). Obviously, from Domagoj's point of view, one learns English best if peace and quiet, not fun, prevail in the language classroom.

SELF-CONCEPT. Domagoj's self-concept remained low during all three years. At first, he simply claimed that others knew more than he did, and in year 4 he attributed his being slower than the classmates to his not practising enough at home.

LIDIJA (younger beginner; female; average language-learning ability; a successful learner)

> ***Contextual background information***. <u>School context</u>. Lidija attended the same school as Domagoj and had the same English teacher. <u>Out-of-school context</u>. Lidija's parents reported that she would regularly tell them about her English classes and would ask for help with her homework when necessary. Lidija, her parents claimed, was keen on speaking English, took pride in her knowledge, and did not find learning English hard. Lidija's out-of-school exposure to English was quite extensive and included watching TV programmes in English, a lot of listening to music, using the internet, as well as contacts with foreigners during the summer. Lidija would sometimes read texts in the English encyclopedia they had at home. In year 4 she had a chance to speak English to a foreigner she met but, due to high language anxiety, she managed to say

very little. Lidija's mother had a university degree, while her father had secondary education. Although both had learned English at school, neither had to use it at work. They had an internet connection at home, as well as an English encyclopedia.

In-class language behaviour. During her English classes, Lidija generally displayed high interest in what was going on and seemed very motivated. Although she was generally very attentive, on occasion she would lose her concentration and would be off task for a while. Also, during years 2 and 3, Lidija did not participate in activities as much as others, and seemed more quiet than her peers. This changed in year 4, when she became increasingly more engaged and participative during her English classes.

MOTIVATION. Lidija changed her favourite subjects every year. English was not among them in years 2 and 3, though: when asked explicitly in year 3 about whether she liked English, Lidija said she liked it because she enjoyed talking, and her aunt and cousin lived in London. In year 4, English was one of her two favourite subjects and she liked it, she said, because they learned new things. What she liked best in year 2 was that they always did something new, or revised things. In year 3, she still stressed liking the new things they did, as well as using English more when they talked in class, but she complained that they wasted too much lesson time on discussions about pupils who had not done their homework. In year 4, she liked best *'learning new words, reading a lot, listening a lot'*; she said she liked everything except the fact that sometimes pupils, including herself, did not do their homework.

ATTITUDES TOWARDS LANGUAGE LEARNING AND TEACHING. Lidija's attitudes towards teaching methods kept changing, as well. In year 3, she opted for the circle arrangement because *'the teacher is helping and they are learning through playing games'*. In year 4, her classroom of choice was the one with the group arrangement, because *'group work is fun'*.

SELF-CONCEPT. Changes were also observed in Lidija's self-concept. In year 2, she thought she was slower than others in class. The following year she believed she was just as good as others: she observed that when they read a text, she was neither ahead nor behind in comparison to her classmates. In year 4, Lidija said, *'I am better than some, and worse than others. Two pupils know more words and they are better than me, and those who sometimes don't understand, they are worse'*.

ZVONIMIR (older beginner; male; high language-learning ability; a successful learner)

> ***Contextual background information.*** <u>School context</u>. Zvonimir attended a town school. The school did not have a long tradition in early FLL but introduced it in 2003, when it became a compulsory part of the primary curriculum. The principal's as well as the teaching staff's attitudes towards early FLL were very positive. The school was averagely equipped by Croatian standards: EFL teachers had access to video and CD players and there were two classrooms specifically reserved for teaching EFL. There were a number of children's books and some dictionaries in the school library. Zvonimir was taught by a specialist EFL teacher. She thought teaching young learners was very demanding but interesting. However, she preferred teaching older learners because she could deal with more elaborate language aspects. Her teaching included many elements of the communicative approach, and she used age-appropriate methodology. Her teaching was organized mostly in the traditional way with occasional group- and pair-work activities. She used English about 40% of the time. <u>Out-of-school context</u>. Zvonimir's parents reported that, although he liked to speak English and took pride in his knowledge, he did not talk about his English classes at home. From time to time he would ask his parents and brother for help, and they often helped before a test by checking his knowledge. He would sometimes read a storybook in English and consult a picture dictionary. Zvonimir reported speaking English to a foreign pupil in his class, and to foreign tourists during the summer. He reported feeling great about being able to explain things to foreigners in English. He was exposed to English extensively through the internet, watching TV programmes and films on DVD, and listening to music. Both Zvonimir's parents had secondary education. They had an internet connection at home.

> ***In-class language behaviour.*** Zvonimir was highly engaged and active during EFL classes in year 2, and seemed to be very eager to show his good knowledge of the language. This changed in year 3, when he behaved less confidently, but was still highly participative. In year 4, his originally high interest in classroom activities faded a little; however, he still seemed generally highly engaged during classroom activities and was on task most of the time.

MOTIVATION. English was not among Zvonimir's favourite subjects in year 2. Still, when asked whether he liked English, he said he did and stressed that he liked especially '*when we read new things and learn new words.*' In years 3 and 4, he explicitly stated he did not like English. But in year 3 he stressed he enjoyed listening to audio cassettes and doing tests because, he claimed, he was good at English; he disliked grammar and revisions when he did not understand the things being revised. In year 4, Zvonimir explained that he did not like foreign languages at all. His favourite activities in his English classes were listening to stories and then working in pairs or groups. He made a point about the usefulness of listening, saying, *'(y)ou learn better while listening'*. Interestingly, doing tests turned into Zvonimir's least liked activity in year 4. Zvonimir said, *'Nobody likes tests. You have to study hard'*.

ATTITUDES TOWARDS LANGUAGE LEARNING AND TEACHING. In year 3, Zvonimir could not decide between the group work arrangement (*'They all listen to the radio and write nicely'*.) and the traditional classroom (*'The teacher points to the board, all listen nicely'*.). In year 4, he made up his mind and opted for the group-work arrangement because, he said, in groups pupils could help each other and the teacher looked pleased.

SELF-CONCEPT. In year 2, Zvonimir could not decide whether he was as good at English as others or worse. This perception changed in year 3, when he reported being better than some learners in his class. In year 4, he said, *'I'm better than some pupils, but there are others who are better than me'*.

STJEPAN (older beginner; male; low language-learning ability; low success in English)

> ***Contextual background information.*** *School context*. Stjepan attended the same school as Zvonimir (see above) but was taught by a different EFL teacher, also a specialist language teacher. She believed in the benefits of early FLL, but preferred teaching older learners. She used a lot of additional materials to complement the main textbook materials and also applied age-appropriate teaching methodology. Her use of English in class varied depending on the topic and language aspect she was dealing with, but generally amounted to 80% of the class time. The classroom format she used most often was the traditional one, but at times she would organize group work activities. *Out-of-school context*. Stjepan would tell his parents about his English classes, but would not ask for help and was not too keen on learning English. Still, he liked to speak English in the presence of his parents and was proud of what he could say. His parents said that Stjepan did not find learning English hard. Stjepan was exposed to English mostly through watching programmes in English, listening to music, and playing games. He did not have access to the internet at home but sometimes went to a friend's place to use the internet. It was only in year 4 that Stjepan used English in real communication with foreigners: he reported feeling good about being able to say something in English in such situations. Both Stjepan's parents had secondary education. At home they did not have books in English but had a picture dictionary that Stjepan could use.

In-class language behaviour. Stjepan often showed a lack of interest in classroom activities and, while everyone was engaged in solving a task, he would often start talking to fellow pupils in a disruptive way. He functioned well only during lock-step activities, when everyone had to be focused because the teacher took full control. Over the three years his behaviour slowly became less disruptive and a bit more on task, but he was never fully attentive. In year 4, he became more participative.

MOTIVATION. Although English was not on Stjepan's list of favourite subjects in any of the years, he still liked it. What he liked best was doing workbook exercises and, in year 4, he liked the fact that he was able to volunteer answers. What he did not enjoy was reading the same text many times (year 2: *'Boring!'*) and having to speak a lot of English during one lesson (year 3: *'It is difficult to speak that much English!'*). Interestingly, in year 4 there was nothing that Stjepan disliked about his English classes.

ATTITUDES TOWARDS LANGUAGE LEARNING AND TEACHING. In year 3, Stjepan opted for the traditional classroom because, as he reported, it looked organized and fun. In year 4, the circle arrangement was his choice because it was not traditional, everyone was speaking, and *'no one is less important!'*

SELF-CONCEPT. In all the three years, Stjepan perceived himself as doing worse than his classmates. In year 3, he explained his observation by the better grades that the others had, while in year 4, he attributed this to the fact that it took him a while to figure out things in English.

MAJA (older beginner; female; average language-learning ability; successful learner)

Contextual background information. <u>School context</u>. Maja attended the same school and was taught by the same EFL teacher as Stjepan (see above). <u>Out-of-school context</u>. Maja had books in English at home, as well as an internet connection. According to her parents, she did not talk to them about her English classes or tell them what she was learning in English class. She did not study or practise English at home, nor did she ask for help. However, Maja's parents reported that she was very keen on learning English, took pride in being able to speak English, and did not find it hard to learn. Maja sometimes read English books. She claimed that she even read a short novel in English one summer. She had a profile on Facebook, and used the internet for messaging in English. Reporting on her communication with foreigners in year 3, she said that she felt a bit anxious because she was not able to speak English accurately; but she still described the experience as nice overall. In year 4, she claimed that speaking English to foreigners was quite difficult but that she was good at it. Both of Maja's parents had secondary education.

In-class language behaviour. At the beginning Maja was an extremely quiet pupil. She practically never raised her hand and seemed highly insecure when she was called on to speak in class. Over the three years, however, Maja was always concentrated and on task, fulfilling all tasks on time and successfully. It seemed that she needed a lot of encouragement from the teacher.

MOTIVATION. During the three years, Maja never included English among her favourite subjects. Still, when asked if she liked her English classes, she said she did. In year 4, she said, '*Yes, I like English, but I like geography more.*' Throughout the three years, Maja always mentioned that she liked learning new words. Besides that, she said she liked playing games in class and the fact that the teacher was not strict (year 2); she also liked new tenses and being able to speak better (year 4). Among the things she did not like were her classmates' behaviour (year 2: '*The pupils are sometimes restless in class*'), doing workbook tasks (year 3), and activities that were too simple and slightly boring (year 4).

ATTITUDES TOWARDS LANGUAGE LEARNING AND TEACHING. In year 3, Maja found it hard to decide which classroom type to select, so she chose two classrooms: the group arrangement one and the traditional one. She explained that these two were the types of classrooms in which she would learn English best because '*it's nice when someone is speaking and we are all quiet and listening*'. However, in year 4 Maja found it easy to make up her mind about the best context to learn English: the traditional classroom. She explained her choice as follows: '*This is normal teaching. We are listening to the radio and the teacher is explaining. In groups we would start talking*'.

SELF-CONCEPT. In year 2, Maja believed she was learning English as fast as her classmates. Her perception changed in year 3, when she thought she was better than her classmates. Having a B in English, like most classmates, made her switch back in year 4 to seeing herself only as good as others.

Discussion

Our six case studies offer a wealth of qualitative data. As we will see in the analyses below, they point to the idiosyncratic nature of early FLL by young learners.

Zlata's EFL learning took place under quite favourable conditions. Her school environment was conducive to learning, both in terms of material resources and teaching quality. Out of school, she enjoyed her parents' support and had extensive opportunities for exposure to English in the home. Although Zlata generally enjoyed all the activities in her EFL classes, her main source of motivation was initially discovering new things in the language (an intrinsic motive), while later, she enjoyed most activities (e.g. reading, singing) in which she could rely on something concrete, like texts and lyrics. This may have been so because, being an average-ability learner, Zlata found English more demanding in later years. Although in the beginning she was extremely shy and quiet during her EFL classes and thought she was doing worse than her peers, she was still a successful learner; on the other hand, in the final year she was more confident about her English, and it was only her preference for the traditional teacher-controlled classroom setting that documented her high need for structure in FLL. Interestingly, she became more confident when English was not one of her favourite subjects any more, though she liked her English classes. However, her confidence disappeared during her first encounter with a foreigner in which she could use her knowledge of English in real-life communication. Zlata's profile suggests interesting developments in and relationships between affective, contextual, and temporal aspects of early FLL. The development of her attitudes, motivation and self-concept went through phases which did not happen simultaneously. Zlata was successful at English both when her self-concept was negative and when it turned positive. It is likely that this was made possible thanks to favourable contextual factors and high motivation during the three years.

Domagoj learned English in a different but also favourable school context. Still, his motivation kept decreasing over the three years, and his self-concept was consistently low. Domagoj's impatience, hyperactivity, and difficulties in maintaining concentration, combined with low language learning ability and average interest, made EFL learning in school too demanding for him. However, he seemed to perform well out of school: that context offered him plenty of opportunities for language exposure, which he used readily and was happy about. He could use his knowledge to play computer games or follow cartoons or read picture books. It seems that Domagoj developed two different self-concepts: one referred to him as a learner; the other, as a user of English. The former was negative, while the latter was positive.

Lidija had the same school context as Domagoj, but her classroom language behaviour was different: she maintained high levels of interest during classes, and, although she had infrequent attention problems, they decreased over the years, while her engagement and participation in classroom activities increased. Her motivation for all classroom learning was high all the time. She developed some sort of learning and teaching meta-awareness, thanks to which she could appreciate the benefits and value of focused teaching, which made her dislike wasting class time on discussions unrelated to the lesson.

In contrast to Domagoj, Lidija believed that learning EFL in class should be fun. Her self-concept improved each year. Out of school, she enjoyed her parents' support and took advantage of her extensive exposure to English. However, in spite of her growing knowledge and confidence, she developed language anxiety and could not use her English in real-life communicative situations.

The school context in which **Zvonimir** learned English was a bit less favourable than those of the younger beginners discussed above, but was still quite good. His in-class language behaviour was characterized by high interest, engagement and participation, but they all lost intensity over the three years. This was probably the result of his decreasing motivation. His attitudes towards learning and teaching became more mature and sophisticated with time: he appreciated the value of oral and written input, as well as of interaction through group work. His self-concept turned more positive and realistic, and was based on comparison with his classmates. In spite of decreasing motivation, and probably thanks to his positive attitudes and high language learning ability, Zvonimir was a successful EFL learner throughout all three years.

Stjepan learned English in a school context which was similar to Zvonimir's, except that his EFL teacher used more English during classes. His in-class behaviour documented low interest during all but highly controlled activities, and he was often disruptive. During the three years, he slowly became more focused and on task, as well as more participative. Structured activities were his favourite at the beginning, but he would easily get bored if the teaching became too repetitive, or would be put off if it became too demanding. Interestingly, his motivation was highest in the final year. Stjepan developed a sensitivity for everyone's right to feel important, which influenced his attitudes towards language learning and teaching in the final year. His self-concept was consistently negative. At first he based this on comparison with his classmates, but in the final year he relied on self-observation. Stjepan enjoyed his parents' support in his EFL learning but did not ask them for help. His exposure to English was relatively high but not as high as that of the other case study participants: he did not have regular access to the internet in the home. When he once got an opportunity to speak to a foreigner in English, he was very happy to be able to communicate English.

Maja attended the same class as Stjepan. She was a successful learner who performed well in class, although she started out as a very quiet pupil. Maja needed constant encouragement from the teacher and appreciated that the teacher was not strict. Her motivation was intrinsic and high most of the time; it would briefly ebb only when she had to deal with overly simple or boring tasks. Her attitudes towards FL learning and teaching were first not completely defined, but by the end of the three years, she could see the advantages and disadvantages of different approaches. Maja's self-concept underwent changes, as well: her self-perception as an EFL learner went from positive to highly positive and back to positive. In contrast to her need for constant encouragement in class, out of school Maja was very independent in her EFL learning. At home, she did not share her classroom experiences with her family or ask them for help, but made extensive use of all the opportunities she had to learn and use English. She found communicating in English with foreigners a little anxiety-provoking but did not give up, and she felt good about her accomplishments.

As can be seen from the six case studies, contextual differences were not salient at the inter-participant level, although we did establish some regarding available school and home resources, as well as the teachers' and parents' characteristics relevant to early FLL. In addition, contextual features did not change much during the three years of the study. It seems that the most relevant contextual changes were related to general educational and curricular aspects. Taking into account such contextual aspects, it could be observed that changes such as the introduction of more complex materials in the syllabus were related to a decrease in motivation (e.g. in Zvonimir's case) or to an attitudinal change (e.g. in Maja's case). Another case in point was Stjepan's starting with a rather negative outlook in year 2, which may have been related to his transition to a new stage of primary education. This transition, which occurs from 4th to 5th grade, means not having the same elementary school teacher that pupils have had for four years, but getting a different teacher for each academic subject, none of whom knows them as well as their grade 1–4 teacher. Sometimes the transition also involves a breakup of their grade 1–4 class. These changes can have a strong impact on some pupils.

The fact that contextual differences were not great makes the differences found through the longitudinal tracking of our six participants extremely interesting and insightful. What emerges as a key finding is that individual learner differences, observed from the affective perspective, were idiosyncratic. Idiosyncracies could be observed at different levels. First, our participants' attitudes, motivation, and self-concepts followed different developmental trajectories during the three years, and both intra- and inter-learner variability could be observed. Thus, for example, while Zlata maintained high levels of motivation during all three years, Domagoj's motivation fluctuated. On the other hand, Zlata's attitudes towards EFL learning and teaching kept changing, while Domagoj's attitudes remained stable. While Stjepan's EFL self-concept remained negative throughout the three years, Zvonimir's self-perception changed each year. Secondly, the patterns that emerged when considering these processes together at any point were unique and particular to individual learners. Thus, while Zlata's high motivation for classroom activities was accompanied with a not-too-positive self-concept, Zvonimir's drop in motivation in year 3 happened alongside the development of a more positive self-concept in that particular year.

Another interesting phenomenon that emerged in this study was that our participants seemed to develop different self-concepts as EFL learners in school and as out-of-school EFL users. Thus, even those whose school self-concept was negative perceived themselves as successful communicators in real-life situations: cases in point are Stjepan and Maja. An illustrative example is also Zlata, who developed a positive school self-concept in year 4, which did not match her low self-perception as a language user in a real-life situation when she had a chance to communicate in English. It is also interesting that all participants were described by their parents as being confident about their English, regardless of whether the participants themselves reported having positive self-perceptions or not. This goes to show that, for a thorough understanding of young learners' affective processes, it is important to consider their language behaviour not only in class but also in the home and in real-life communication situations.

Our findings corroborate what has been pointed out by several authors (e.g. Jagatić, 1993; Pinter, 2006): in the early phases of EFL learning, our participants were still struggling with controlling their emotions and learning school behaviour rules. However, not all the problems they were dealing with had the same impact on their learning. Thus, Zlata's shyness or Lidija's strong need for constant encouragement did not seem to interfere with their progress in EFL learning, but hyperactivity and difficulty in staying focused during classes in Domagoj's case did.

One thing that our analyses made salient concerns the participants' distinguishing their English classes from English as a school subject. It was quite interesting, and surprising, to observe that, while their reactions to classroom activities were very positive and suggested high motivation for classroom learning of EFL, our participants created a rather different picture when reporting on their favourite school subject(s). Thus, liking classroom activities did not seem enough to make English a favourite subject. This suggests that their motivation for learning EFL in the school context was not monolithic, and that their attitudes and motivation were multifaceted.

Conclusions and Implications

In this study we decided to use a mixed-method approach in the belief that using only quantitative or qualitative methods would not lead us to a comprehensive enough picture of such a complex phenomenon as early FLL. While quantitative data allow for generalizations, at least to a certain extent, they cannot uncover what really happens in the young learner as a 'person-in-context' (Ushioda, 2009), whose affective processes emerge as the result of non-linear relationships between many factors that impact FLL. As can be seen from the above analyses, a contextual longitudinal case study approach to researching early EFL learning can complement the quantitative approach, resulting in deeper and richer insights into affective processes taking place in young FL learners.

The findings from our study suggest that there is a relationship between young EFL learners' affective processes, age, and language proficiency. Our quantitative results suggest that, in terms of age, younger beginners are more motivated than older beginners. This is especially salient at the level of whether they like learning English in general, but not as apparent at the level of learning new words, which has been established as a highly important source of motivation in early FLL. Age was observed to relate to differences in attitudes towards EFL learning and teaching as well. Younger beginners seem to prefer learning in more controlled and structured teaching contexts, while older beginners prefer classroom arrangements which allow free interaction between pupils. Also, younger learners seem to be more decisive when deciding on the best teaching format than older learners, who are more able to see both the advantages and the disadvantages of different formats. In terms of the relationship between age and learner self-concept, our findings suggest that differences between younger and older beginners appear later than is the case with motivation and attitudes. Interestingly, older beginners seem to first develop a more positive self-concept than younger beginners, but later the situation tends to reverse itself. This is connected with the broader educational context: older beginners enter the new stage of primary school earlier than younger beginners. As mentioned in Chapter 1, Grade 5 is the beginning of the upper primary phase, when new school subjects are introduced into the curriculum and each subject is taught by a different specialized teacher. Older beginners face this big transition in their second year of EFL learning, while younger beginners are already in their fifth year of learning EFL.

As far as the relationship with language proficiency is concerned, significant differences emerged only when proficiency is considered in interaction with age. Thus, in the younger group, increasing proficiency was accompanied with increasing motivation as measured by how much they liked learning EFL in general; their enjoyment of learning new words was high all the time, while considering English as a favourite subject decreased each year. In the older group, an increase in motivation, as reflected through their liking of learning English in general as well as their liking of learning new words, paralleled an increase in proficiency only in the beginning; however, from the favourite subject perspective, the parallel increase was not observed until year 3. As far as attitudes are concerned, in both groups increasing proficiency was related to more frequent selection of the group-work teaching format. Regarding the learners' self-concepts, the younger beginners' increasing proficiency was followed by increasingly higher self-concepts, while in older beginners, increasing proficiency was not accompanied by increasingly positive self-concept until year 3.

Our qualitative results document the evolution of attitudes, motivation, and self-concept at the individual learner level. They also point to the idiosyncratic nature of these affective processes. Young EFL learners' attitudinal, motivational, and self-concept evolution seems to follow different trajectories. The obtained insights show not only changes that differ from learner to learner in terms of the temporal framework, but also that there is inter-learner variability in terms of interactions among these affective learner factors themselves as well as with contextual factors.

As McKay (2006) points out, early FLL does not involve only the development of language knowledge. Primary years in FLL involve many affective processes that young FL learners go through and need to deal with. Because of this, early FLL is not a linear phenomenon but, as authors such as Cekaite (2007) have already suggested, is multilayered, cyclical, and dynamic. Thus, in young learners' FL development we may encounter many ups and downs, and ebbs and flows, some salient and shared by many learners, others barely discernible and particular to individual learners. All this has important implications for early EFL learning. To make sure that early language learning is, on the one hand, effective and, on the other, that it is experienced in a positive way, teachers need to be fully aware of the multifaceted nature of the affective processes their learners are going through. It is as important that both teachers and parents are also aware of the idiosyncracies that characterize the evolution of young learners' affective development.

References

Arabski, J. and Wojtaszek, A. (eds) (2011) *Individual Learner Differences in SLA*. Bristol: Multilingual Matters.

Cekaite, A. (2007) A child's development of interactional competence in a Swedish L2 classroom. *The Modern Language Journal* 91 (1), 45–62.

Cenoz, J. (2003) The influence of age on the acquisition of English: General proficiency, attitudes and code mixing. In M. García Mayo and M. García Lecumberri (eds) *Age and the Acquisition of English as a FL* (pp. 77–93). Clevedon: Multilingual Matters.

Chambers, G.N. (1999) *Motivating Language Learners*. Clevedon: Multilingual Matters.

Damon, W. and Hart, D. (1988) *Self-understanding in Childhood and Adolescence*. New York: Cambridge University Press.

Donato, R., Tucker, G.R., Wudthayagorn, J. and Igarashi, K. (2000) Converging evidence: Attitudes, achievements, and instruction in the later years of FLES. *Foreign Language Annals* 33(4), 377–393.

Dörnyei, Z. (2005) *The Psychology of the Language Learner. Individual Differences in Second Language Acquisition*. Mahwah, New Jersey: Lawrence Erlbaum Associates.

Edelenbos, P., Johnstone, R. and Kubanek, A. (2006) Languages for the Children of Europe. Published Research, Good Practice & Main Principles. Final Report of the EAC 89/04, lot 1 study. Brussels: European Commission.

Enever, J. (ed.) (2011) *ELLiE: Early Language Learning in Europe*. London: The British Council.

Haladyna, T.M. and Thomas, G.P. (1979) The attitudes of elementary school children toward school and subject matters. *Journal of Experimental Education* 48 (1), 18–23.

Harter, S. (2006) The self. In W. Damon, R.M. Lerner, N. Eisenberg (eds) *Handbook of Child Psychology. Vol. 3. Social, Emotional, and Personality Development* (pp. 505–570). New York: Wiley.

Heinzmann, S. (2013) *Young Language Learners' Motivation and Attitudes. Longitudinal, Comparative and Explanatory Perspectives*. London: Bloomsbury.
Jagatić, M. (1993) Are available teaching time and the number of pupils important factors. In M. Vilke and Y. Vrhovac (eds) *Children and Foreign Languages I* (pp. 45–71). Zagreb: Faculty of Philosophy, University of Zagreb.
Kim, I.-O. (2009) An analysis of primary school students' English learning motivation based on their grade levels and regions. *English Language Teaching* 21 (2), 259–282.
Kennedy, T.J., Nelson, J.K., Odell, M.R.L. and Austin, L.K. (2000) The FLES attitudinal inventory. *Foreign Language Annals* 33 (3), 278–289.
Kolb, A. (2007) How languages are learnt: Primary children's language learning beliefs. *Innovation in Language Learning* 2 (1), 227–241.
Lamb, M. (2003) Integrative motivation in a globalizing world. *System* 32 (1), 3–19.
Lee, H.-W. and Park, M.-R. (2001) A preliminary evaluation of the elementary school English program in Korea. *English Teaching* 56 (1), 53–79.
Lopriore, L. (2009) Development of young learners' perception of foreign language learning and teaching. Paper presented at American Association of Applied Linguistics Conference, Denver, March 2009.
MacIntyre, P., Baker, S., Clément, R. and Donovan, L.A. (2002) Sex and age effects on willingness to communicate, anxiety, perceived competence, and L2 motivation among junior high school French immersion students. *Language Learning* 52 (3), 537–564.
Marschollek, A. (2002) *Kognitive und affektive Flexibilität durch fremde Sprachen. Eine empirische Untersuchung in der Primarstufe.* [Cognitive and affective flexibility in foreign languages. Empirical study of first grade]. Münster: Lit.
Marsh, H.W., Byrne B.M. and Shalveson, R.J. (1988) A multifaceted academic self-concept: Its hierarchical structure and its relation to academic achievement. *Journal of Educational Psychology* 80 (3), 366–380.
McKay, P. (2006) *Assessing Young Language Learners*. Cambridge: Cambridge University Press.
Mercer, S. (2011) *Towards an Understanding of Language Learner Self-concept*. New York, Berlin: Springer.
Mihaljević Djigunović, J. (1993) Investigation of attitudes and motivation in early foreign language learning. In M. Vilke and Y. Vrhovac (eds) *Children and Foreign Languages I* (pp. 45–71). Zagreb: University of Zagreb, Faculty of Philosophy.
Mihaljevic Djigunovic, J. (1995) Attitudes of young foreign language learners: A follow-up study. In M. Vilke and Y. Vrhovac (eds) *Children and Foreign Languages II* (pp. 16–33). Zagreb: Faculty of Philosophy, University of Zagreb.
Mihaljević Djigunović, J. and Lopriore, L. (2011) The learner: Do individual differences matter? In J. Enever (ed.) *ELLiE: Early language learning in Europe* (pp. 29–45). London: The British Council.
Nikolov, M. (1999) 'Why do you learn English? Because the teacher is short': A study of Hungarian children's foreign language learning motivation. *Language Teaching Research* 3 (1), 33–65.
Nikolov, M. (2002) *Issues in English Language Education*. Bern: Peter Lang.
Pinter, A. (2006) *Teaching Young Language Learners*. Oxford: Oxford University Press.
Pinter, A. (2011) *Children Learning Second Languages*. Basingstoke: Palgrave Macmillan.
Robinson, P. (2002) *Individual Differences and Instructed Language Learning*. Amsterdam/Philadelphia: John Benjamins Publishing Company.
Szpotowicz, M., Mihaljevic Djigunovic, J. and Enever, J. (2009) Early language learning in Europe: a multinational, longitudinal study. In J. Enever, J. Moon and U. Raman (eds) *Young Learner English Language Policy and Implementation: International Perspectives* (pp. 141–147). Kent: IATEFL.
Ushioda, E. (2001) Language learning at university: Exploring the role of motivational thinking. In Z. Dörnyei and R. Schmidt (eds) *Motivation and Second Language Acquisition* (pp. 91–124). Honolulu, BI: University of Hawaii Press.

Ushioda, E. (2009) A person-in-context relational view of emergent motivation, self and identity. In Z. Dörnyei and E. Ushioda (eds) *Motivation, Language Identity and the L2 Self* (pp. 215–228). Bristol: Multilingual Matters.
Vilke, M. (1993) Early foreign language teaching in Croatian primary schools. In M. Vilke and Y. Vrhovac (eds) *Children and Foreign Languages I* (pp. 10–27). Zagreb: Faculty of Philosophy, University of Zagreb.
Wenden, A. (1999) An introduction to metacognitive knowledge and beliefs in language learning: Beyond the basics [Special Issue]. *System* 27 (4), 435–441.

3 Croatian Primary School Pupils and English Pronunciation in Light of the Emergence of English as a Lingua Franca

Višnja Josipović Smojver

Introduction

The present study was motivated by the emergence of new varieties of English resulting from the globalization of the English language. English nowadays has the status of a global language, which was explicitly acknowledged in influential works on International English dating back to the beginning of the 21st century, such as Crystal (2003, 2004), Görlach (2002), Graddol (2006), Kachru et al. (2006) or Kirkpatrick (2007). A more specific variety of International English, the one used by non-native speakers to communicate among themselves, is referred to as English as a lingua franca (henceforth: ELF) and represents one of the relatively new and currently topical varieties of English in recent linguistic literature. For Croats this is an extremely important topic, because, as Vilke (2007: 23) observes, 'The citizens of Europe belonging to small language communities as ours will have to be able to communicate in two languages widely spoken', and nowadays probably no one would try to challenge the status of English as the Croats' main language of international communication. In the last decade ELF has been studied and described at all levels of linguistic analysis, and its current status and perspectives in teaching have been discussed by the leading ELF theoreticians, including Jenkins (2002, 2009) and Seidlhofer (2001, 2010). Although extensive studies have been done on the grammar (e.g. Ranta, 2009), phraseology (Pitzl, 2009), pragmatics (Cogo, 2009), and subvarieties of ELF (Ehrenreich, 2009), pronunciation, the sociolinguistically most indicative and linguistically most challenging manifestation of ELF, seems to be attracting more linguists' attention than other aspects of ELF. As Levis (2005: 376) observes, 'pronunciation theory, research, and practice are in transition'. What this implies is that inner-circle pronunciation models and native instructors have been increasingly challenged. Rather than striving to approach native-like pronunciation, according to leading ELF theoreticians, one should focus on international intelligibility. Thus Jenkins, who has emerged as the leading English as an international language (henceforth: EIL) and ELF theoretician devotes a number of her works (2000, 2002, 2005, 2007) to the phonology of International English. In particular, in her famous proposal for EIL pronunciation teaching, Jenkins (2002) establishes her widely quoted notion of *lingua franca core*. She identifies the so-called core pronunciation features, which, judging by the results of a wide corpus of intelligibility and misunderstanding studies, turn out to 'be crucial as safeguards of mutual intelligibility' in EIL (Jenkins 2002: 96). This, for example, includes the preservation of the phonemic contrasts within the consonantal and vocalic systems with some minor provisos, which will be discussed later. On the other hand, there are a number of non-core pronunciation features which have always been insisted upon in English teaching, as indications of 'nice' (i.e. native-like) pronunciation, but turn out not to help intelligibility. Cases in point are vowel reduction, probably the safest shibboleth of native pronunciation, and non-rhotic pronunciation, a feature of Received Pronunciation, traditionally the most widely preferred type of English pronunciation at Croatian schools. These two features not only do not help international intelligibility, but they even hinder it!

Empirical Research

Aim

The aim of the present study is to look at the presence or absence of both categories of features, core and non-core, in the speech of a group of 26 primary-school learners of English who were observed during a period of four years (fifth to eighth grade, i.e. second to fifth year of learning English at school) within the framework of the research project *Early acquisition of English as a foreign language: analysis of learner interlanguage*. In particular, the observed pronunciation features include acceptable vs. unacceptable substitutions in the consonant and vocalic inventory; features related to the glottal state – tense vs. lax contrasts and pre-fortis clipping in vowels on the one hand and presence vs. absence of aspiration in consonants on the other; consistency in rhoticity or non-rhoticity; application vs. non-application of native-like allophonic alternations such as that between clear and dark /l/; morphophonological and postlexical phonological rules such as those concerning the pronunciation of the regular plural ending, flapping, and final tensing; and finally, the appropriateness of the use of prosody. The data obtained by means of auditory analysis by three independent evaluators are assessed, discussed, and used as a basis for conclusions about the relative importance of individual features in teaching English pronunciation in Croatian primary schools to future speakers of EIL.

Research questions

To provide some general background for the present study, before looking at the main research questions about the core and non-core ELF features in the participants' pronunciation of English, we examined the degree of their awareness of the status of English as a global language, the importance of learning and knowing English, and their experience in using English for international communication and feelings about that. This was done by analyzing the explicit statements about these issues in the participants' motivation interviews. In addition, by way of introduction to the main topic of the study, we also looked at the motivational interviews for two other pieces of information necessary to clear up certain points made in the analysis of pronunciation features. First, we looked for clear indications of personality traits which related to the distinction between the user and the learner type as defined in Josipović and Stanojević (2012) and is notably different from the language learner/user concept as presented by Cook (1991, 2002, 2008). It emerged during the interviews that our participants, who notably belong to the generation of 'digital natives', quite often explicitly expressed their dislike of anything having to do with writing and their preference for oral production. Therefore, we make a point in the conclusion about the need to look for any possible correlations with the explicit preference for oral communication and the quality of English pronunciation.

Core features

As for the main topic of the present study, we first looked for the violation of core features as defined by Jenkins (2002). As concerns the phonemic inventory of English, the only outstanding and immediatey obvious violation in this sense is the mispronunciation of the English phoneme /æ/ as /e/, resulting in the absence of contrast between the two items in the target phonemic system. This feature of Croatian learners does not surprise, as it obviously results from the absence of /æ/ in Croatian and it is commonly found not only in the interlanguge of primary school learners, but also in the English spoken by Croatian speakers in general, even those highly proficient and fluent in English (Josipović Smojver, 2010). Another type of substitution referred to explicitly by Jenkins (2002) as undesirable because it reduces intelligibility concerns any non-standard pronunciation of the /ɜː/ vowel as in *bird*, which 'regularly causes problems'. (Jenkins, 2002: 97). Thus we also registered any cases of violating this core feature. Next we looked at a group of features having to do with the glottal state. The first one was tense vs. lax contrast in vowels, popularly, though somewhat wrongly referred to as constrasts of vocalic length, and along with it another related feature of native English pronunciation classified as a core feature, pre-fortis clipping. Secondly, in connection with the glottal state for consonants, the core feature analysed in the speech of our subjects was aspiration. All three of them, tense-lax contrasts, aspiration, and pre-fortis clipping, are predicted to create problems for Croatian speakers of English, due to the fact that English and Croatian are typologically notably different with respect to glottal-state features. As explained by Bakran (1996) and, even more insightfully, within the framework of the dimensional theory of feature geometry by Iverson and Ahn (2007), English, like the majority of other Germanic languages is an aspiration language, and Croatian is a voicing language. Phonologically, this means that for English voiceless consonants the relevant underlying property is not voicing or its absence, but rather the specification for the feature 'spread glottis'. Under this view, voicing in English is a redundant feature, implemented for contrast enhancements at the phonetic level, whereas in Croatian, like in other Slavic languages, voicing is a relevant underlying property. To put it more simply, from the phonetic point of view, using Bakran's terms, '...Croatian stops are not described as aspirated or not. The difference in the VOT (voice onset time) in Croatian is not intentional. In English VOT can be consciously regulated, and this is how the difference between aspirated and unaspirated segments is realised' (Bakran, 1996: 266, translation by VJS). The implication that this has for the present study is that Croats are generally expected to lack these three glottal-state core features, which can potentially result in misunderstandings and unintelligibility. Thus we identify such cases of voiceless target consonants sounding to speakers of aspiration languages as voiced (as in the loss of contrast between *pit* and *bit*) or target tense vowels sounding like their lax counterparts, as in *ship* sounding like *sheep*. Next we looked at cases of extreme disfluency. Like for other violations of core features, we observed whether and how participants who exhibited this feature in the first year of observation made progress by the end of primary school. Another core pronunciation feature we observed was rhoticity along with related phenomena. At this point it should be noted that in EIL theory rhoticity is a desirable ELF feature, contributing to international intelligibility, irrespectively of whether the speaker's pronunciation is generally closer to the British or American type of English. In particular, for each subject we counted cases of rhotic and non-rhotic pronunciation of individual items, looked at which of the two prevails, how consistent the subjects were in this respect and whether any progress was made for it in the course of the four years of observation. The fact that non-rhoticity is not an ELF target, by no means implies that American pronunciation, which is prevalently and typically rhotic, is favoured over the British pronunciation standard. It is always features contributing to intelligibility that are given priority in defining the ELF pronunciation targets. Thus the opposite situation is found with the last core feature we were looking at in the present study, the preservation of intervocalic /t/, i.e. the absence of flapping, as in *pretty* /'prɪtɪ/. This time we are dealing with a typical feature of American pronunciation, and being a post-lexical phonological rule, it is typically present in the most fluent and competent speakers. This is a paradox which deserves some theoretical consideration, and therefore the point will be resumed in the discussion.

Non-core features

As for non-core features (i.e. those which can be tolerated in ELF communication and do not cause misunderstandings), the present paper focuses on the following: mispronunciation of the dental fricatives, /θ/ and /ð/; violation of velar merger in syllable rhymes; mispronunciation of the regular plural ending; improper monophthongisation or diphthongisation, such as /dont/ for *don't* or /houbi/ for *hobby*; inconsistency in the use of American vs. British pronunciation apart from those related to rhoticity and discussed under 'Core features'; allophonic variation such as [l] – [ɫ]; and final tensing.

Finally, it should be stressed that in ELF theory all of prosody, including intonation, accentual phenomena (with the exception of contrastive stress), weakening, and native-like stress-based rhythm, as well as all other connected-speech phenomena, belong to the non-core area. According to Jenkins (2002) they require 'receptive flexibility' on the part of the listener, rather than attention in EIL teaching. Moreover, Jenkins (2002: 99) explicitly dismisses intonation as a subject of EIL teaching, characterising it as 'unteachable' and 'even if teachable, likely to be incorrectly linked to native-speaker attitudes and grammar'. Therefore, such prosodic phenomena were not the direct concern of the present study.

Methodology

The participants were four groups of learners from three different Croatian primary schools. Two groups were city children, and two were from a medium-sized town. Two groups included six children and two had seven learners, which altogether made up the total number of 26 participants. Half of them were girls and half were boys (13 + 13). In order to get a fair representation of subjects in terms of learning ability, their teachers chose the learners for observation so as to include learners of poor, average and high assessed learning ability into each group. The subjects were observed throughout the period of four school years, from grade 5 (second year of learning English at school) to the end of primary school (grade 8). At the end of each year the subjects' production was recorded. Each recording included two parts: a motivational interview in their native Croatian and the completion of an oral task in English. The latter initially consisted of the description of some picture, e.g. a family at home, a room in a house, a park, and the like, which was then used as a prompt for a personalized conversation. For example, if the task was to describe a kitchen from the picture, this was followed by questions about the subject's kitchen, home and family. Due to some data loss, the total number of interviews analysed was not the ideally expected 104, but 97. Out of these 97, due to the poor performance of several participants, a few were useless for the analysis of particular features. In the first year of observation, the average duration of the interview was eight minutes, in the second year it was 12 minutes, in the third year 16 minutes, and in the final year 12.5 minutes. The overall average was somewhat over 12 minutes per interview. Altogether it is estimated that the overall duration of the subjects' speech used for the present analysis was somewhat less than 20 hours, about half of which (between nine and ten hours) accounts for the English part of the interview, which served directly for the analysis of the pronunciation features.

Each production was analysed by two independent raters.[1] For each subject participating in the research we compiled a folder including the analysis of the core and non-core features observed in each interview, as compiled independently by both raters. These individual folders were then organized into four larger group folders, so we ended up with four focal-group folders that could be compared among themselves. It goes without saying that no interview or recording was done without the necessary consent of the parties involved: participants, their parents, teachers, and headmasters. To keep the confidentiality of the information obtained about individual participants, their identities were coded.

Results and Analysis

Introduction

Before proceeding with the results pertaining to the main topic of the present study, by way of introduction, let us briefly present the results of the analysis of the subjects' motivation interviews, mainly those for grade five, where explicit questions were asked in order to elicit responses about their awareness of the global status of English and the importance of learning the language. For the two town groups, seven out of 14 participants (i.e. half of them) explicitly expressed awareness of the contemporary status of English, whereas in the only city group for which the fifth-grade motivational interview was available, four out of six participants showed the same type of awareness. Those who did not know exactly where in the world English is spoken and in what function, were at least aware of the importance of learning English for the sake of their future employment prospects, typically quoting their parents, who had told them so. In the sixth to eighth grades, there were no explicit questions about this, but very often they would say things to the same effect when asked about their experience with using English to talk to foreigners: *'Everyone in the world speaks English'*.[2] (T1/05-5). Quite commonly, children expressed a feeling of pride (either personal or national) for being able to use English for international communication, illustrated by the following responses to the question of how they felt: *'Let them see!* [the French and the Spanish to whom she had spoken in English - VJS] *We are only children and can speak this global language'*. (T1/05-5); or *'I was very satisfied and proud to show those Germans and Italians that we Croats have risen above the level of the Balkans!'* (C1/01-7); or *'I feel cool...I admire myself.'* (T2/07-7). It should be noted at this point that some of the fifth-grade children were aware only of some or a few of the Inner Circle of English-speaking countries. That is, they were completely unaware of English as a second or international language. In the two town groups there were four such cases (out of 14) and in the city group, there was one subject out of six. Generally speaking, there were a few cases of extreme ignorance about where English is spoken as a native language, as in *'... somewhere in Africa...'* (Interviewer: Where else? Where in Europe?) *'... well, I can't remember, I guess in Austria as well'* (T2/05-5). In any case, the overall results of the analysis of the responses about their experience using English for international communication showed that by the end of primary school all participants had had such experience, and most of them felt good about it. Those who explicitly said they had not (four out of 26), were obviously those who turned out to be less proficient and basically disfluent, so they naturally felt frustrated about it.

The motivational interviews also clearly suggested that some participants had all the personality traits of a typical 'user', as opposed to a 'learner' as defined in Josipović and Stanojević (2012). In order to show that this definition of 'user' does not coincide with that used by Cook (1991, 2002), let us sum up what is meant here by the term 'user'. It refers to participants whose proficiency in English is generally higher than that of their peers, but who do not believe much in formal classes within the educational system. They even sometimes disparage English classes, often being overcritical of the teacher as well as the classes. They are extremely exposed to out-of-school sources of learning English and believe these are the right sources to learn 'real' English needed in 'real life'. Being typical members of the 'digital native' generation, they often express a strong dislike of writing, which includes written exercises and tests in school. It is then not surprising that they sometimes did not have the highest grade in English, which one would expect judging by their performance and which they felt they deserved. The gist of what is meant by the 'user mentality' in this sense is expressed in this reaction of the fluent and proficient subject in one of the city groups when the picture description task was over: (to the interviewer): *'Well, I did not know all these words needed for this picture of yours, but I do know all the words I need in real life*'. Perhaps an even more illustrative quotation of the same subject is the following: '*In ten years' time I'm gonna have a job, make a lot of money and won't have to listen to boring teachers*'. (C2/04-7). Before proceeding to the analysis of the subjects' pronunciation features, let it be said that the overall results of the analysis of the motivational interviews showed that in 38 interviews out of the 85 which were usable for this purpose, there were clear indications of a typical 'user mentality' in this sense.

Core features in the pronunciation of the 26 learners

As explained in 2.1, the first and the most obvious violation of a core pronunciation feature observed in the 26 participants was the substitution of /æ/ by /e/. This is what Deterding (2010) identifies as one of the main pronunciation features of Singaporean English, referring to it as the merger of the DRESS and TRAP vowels. Our findings are as follows:

In the first city group, coded as C1, a total of 23 oral productions were analysed. In two cases, both in the first research year, (i.e. the fifth grade) substitution is consistently present throughout a single interview. In 14 interviews, there are no such problems: the participants consistently distinguish /æ/ from /e/. In seven interviews they are inconsistent about it: for example, within the same interview they say [ded] for *dad*, but [flæt] for *flat*. Sometimes this inconsistency, like the inconsistencies concerning other pronunciation features, can be accounted for by the influence of the interviewer, who uses the correct core feature in her question (e.g. 'Do you live in a house or a flat?'). It is not uncommon for participants to repeat the right form in the immediate response (*I live in a flat* – with [æ]) and proceed with the description of her/his flat violating the core feature and referring to their [flet]. However, there are many cases of inconsistency occurring independently of the interviewer's prompts, so inconsistency in the violation of core features must be taken as a fact. Table 3.1 shows the status of the vowel /æ/ in group C1.

Before looking at the next city group, a few points must be made about the correlation of these results with the apparent competence of speakers, particularly when it comes to pronunciation. It is interesting to note that the only speaker who, according to both judges, consistently distinguishes

Table 3.1 The status of /æ/ for group C1

violation of the identity of /æ/	number of interviews out of 23
(+) = consistent violation, æ→ e	2
(−) = no violation, æ = æ	14
(+/−) = inconsistent violation, æ = æ/e	7

between /æ/ and /e/, C1/02, turns out to be one of the two best pronouncers of English, alongside C2/06. This will also be confirmed by the presence of such 'advanced', native-like features like aspiration, velar merger and the allophonic alternation between the 'clear' and 'dark' /l/. Interestingly enough, one of the participants from this group (C1/04), stops violating this feature in the sixth grade, the same year in which his mark in English goes up from 4 to 5.[3] The subject who eventually turns out to be the best overall speaker in the group, C1/01, behaves inconsistently when preserving the identity of /æ/ in the fifth and sixth grades, but then reaches a turning point in the seventh grade interview, in which he consistently distinguishes between the two vowels at hand, and continues to do the same in the final eighth-grade interview.

Next we look at the second city group, coded as C2. In this group only 19 interviews were usable for this purpose. In 10 of them the speakers consistently substituted /æ/ with /e/, and in 9 the distinction between the two phonemes was consistently preserved. Thus there were no cases of inconsistency within an interview. By analogy with Table 3.1, Table 3.2 shows the status of /æ/ for group C2.

In the first town group, 25 interviews were available for the purpose of this analysis. In 13 of them (i.e. more than a half) /æ/ was regularly substituted by /e/; in eight of them the phonemic contrast was consistently maintained, and in four interviews the participants maintained the contrast inconsistently. Two interesting points can be made about these inconsistencies. First, all three participants who exhibited this inconsistency at earlier stages eventually made progress and started distinguishing between the two items throughout an interview. Thus T1/04 made progress in this respect in the eighth grade; T1/05 in the seventh, and T1/07 progressed from consistent violation of the contrast in the fifth grade, to inconsistency in the sixth and seven grades, to stabilisation of the contrast in the final eight-grade interview. Secondly, it generally seems that violations of the contrast are more likely to affect grammatical words, such as the auxilliary *have* and the conjunction *and*, typically pronounced as [hev] and [end], respectively, than lexical words such as *family*. This is perfectly illustrated by examples from learner T1/07-6, where the subject repeatedly and consistently keeps saying [æ] in *family* and [e] in *have*, *has* and *and*. This issue requires more investigation, but a possible explanation might have to do with the higher frequency of

Table 3.2 The status of /æ/ for group C2

violation of the identity of /æ/	number of interviews out of 19
(+) = consistent violation, æ→ e	10
(−) = no violation, æ = æ	9
(+/−) = inconsistent violation, æ = æ/e	∅

Table 3.3 The status of /æ/ in group T1

violation of the identity of /æ/	number of interviews out of 25
(+) = consistent violation, æ→ e	13
(−) = no violation, æ = æ	8
(+/−) = inconsistent violation, æ = æ/e	4

grammatical words, which as such tend to be introduced into the English mental lexicon of the learner at an earlier stage, when the phonemic system of the target language has not been stabilized (cf. Cergol, 2011). By contrast, lexical words might be pronounced more correctly because they have been learned more recently. Alternatively, it is possible that the vowels of grammatical words tend to be more frequently mispronounced for the same reason for which English can 'afford' to obscure them in weakening: their functional load is not as great as that of lexical words, so one can unconsciously 'afford' to mispronounce them more easily than lexical words. In any case, the results for the first group of speakers from a medium-sized town are presented graphically in Table 3.3.

In the second town group, 27 interviews were available for the analysis of the core feature at hand. In 13 interviews, consistent violation of the contrast was established, in six interviews the opposite result was obtained, that is, the subjects consistently maintained the æ/e distinction, and in 15 interviews the distinction was inconsistently maintained. With those subjects who showed progress in this respect in the course of the four years of observation, the pattern described for the subjects from previous groups is repeated: one subject, T2/01, started distinguishing between the two items in the last year of observation, that is, in the eighth grade, and with one subject it is again possible to observe a gradual progress from consistent /e/ in the fifth grade, to inconsistency in the sixth and seventh grades, to stabilization of the æ/e distinction in the final eight-grade interview. Admittedly, there were a few cases of 'regression' from an initial /æ/ in the fifth and sixth grades to inconsistencies in the two final years, which seem odd at first but can easily be explained. It turns out that this happens with participants of low competence and extreme disfluency, who in the first two years of observation practically did not say anything in English apart from repeating isolated words after the interviewer. These they sometimes repeated correctly and sometimes not. When in the two final years they reached a level of competence at which they could say things in English independently of the interviewer, they constantly violated the contrast and by the end of primary school never reached the point of stabilisation of the English vocalic system. A case in point from this group is T2/03. Table 3.4 shows the status of /æ/ for group T2.

Finally, the overall results for the status of the phoneme /æ/ in all four groups is shown in Table 3.5.

Table 3.4 The status of /æ/ in group T2

violation of the identity of /æ/	number of interviews out of 27
(+) = consistent violation, æ→ e	6
(–) = no violation, æ = æ	6
(+/–) = inconsistent violation, æ = æ/e	15

Table 3.5 Overall results: The status of /æ/ in all four groups as a whole

violation of the identity of /æ/	number of interviews out of 94
(+) = consistent violation, æ→ e	31
(–) = no violation, æ = æ	37
(+/–) = inconsistent violation, æ = æ/e	26

Another undesirable type of substitution constituting a core-feature violation affects the identity of the English central vowel /ɜ:/ as in *bird*, which, according to Jenkins (2002: 97) 'regularly causes problems' for international intelligibility. Interestingly, in the 91 interviews available for the analysis of this feature, only two cases of violation were found. This happened with two different speakers from the same town group, who during their descriptions repeatedly pronounced *three persons* as [tri: 'pe:rsons]. One of them did it in the fifth grade, and for the other one the violation of this core feature was identified only in the sixth grade, which was when she actually said a few words of English for the first time. In short, this kind of core-feature violation in the sample we observed turns out to be marginal. Even in the low-competence speakers in whose speech it was identified, it completely disappears after the sixth grade.

Speaking of the instable quality of target English vowels, at this point it must be mentioned that the most variable one in terms of its phonetic quality turns out to be the BATH vowel. However, as most of its realisations identified in the speech of our participants do not represent a phonemic substitution, i.e. violation of a core feature, this issue will be resumed in the discussion.

As for the core features pertaining to the glottal state, we first turn to aspiration. According to Jenkins (2002), studies of international intelligibility and misunderstandings show that failure to aspirate English fortis consonants in the right context (foot-initially) can lead to the misperception of yet another feature, voicing, especially when communication takes place between speakers of aspiration languages on the one hand and those of voicing languages on the other. A point to be made in this connection is that aspiration obviously takes place in the speech of the best pronouncers of English, such as the already mentioned C1/02 and C2/06. The results for the feature at hand are shown in Table 3.6.

Table 3.6 Presence vs. absence of aspiration in interviews

GROUP	aspiration	no aspiration	number of interviews
C1	4	19	23
C2	2	16	18
T1	2	19	21
T2	1	26	27
OVERALL	9	80	89

In addition to aspiration, yet another English pronunciation feature is related to the glottal state and is considered a core feature, namely, pre-fortis clipping. It is hardly surprising that not a single case of clear pre-fortis clipping was identified in the total of 97 interviews analysed. As explained in 2.1, this is expected in view of the typological difference between English, an aspiration language, and Croatian, a voicing language. Notably, even to a linguistically educated native speaker of Croatian it looks odd that this feature should be included among the core features, but referring to large corpora of misunderstanding studies, Jenkins (2002: 99) explicitly includes this feature among the core features, seeing that the failure to clip vowels before fortis consonants can potentially lead to the misperception of consonantal voicing, resulting in phonemic substitution.

Another core feature related to the glottal state is the tense-lax (or popularly, long vs. short) distinction in vowels, which we turn to next. In group C1, out of 23 interviews we found a violation of this core feature in only one of them. This is when one participant in the fifth grade says [ʃi:p] for *'ship'*. In group C2 this feature is violated twice, both times in [slɪpɪŋ] for *sleepin'*. In T1 the same type of absence of the tense vs. lax contrast in vowels is found in five out of 24 interviews, whereas in T2 it happens in three out of 26 interviews. Apart from the above-mentioned lexical items *ship* and *sleep*, examples of violating the tense-lax contrast in vowels occur in words such as *kid, beach, teeth,* and *big*, pronounced as [ki:d], [bɪtʃ], [tɪt], and [bi:g], respectively. It is interesting to note that two participants overcome this difficulty and start distinguishing tense from lax vowels in the sixth grade, one shows progress in this respect in the seventh grade, and five of them only start making the distinction in the eighth grade. Admittedly, a few of them seem to exhibit regression, exhibiting a loss of the tense-lax contrast, but a closer inspection of their records shows that once again these are subjects who in the initial years spoke very little, using a rather limited vocabulary, so the chances of mispronunciation were smaller. Cases in point are T2/03, for whom the violation of the core feature under consideration was spotted in the seventh grade, or T1/07, for whom it was identified only in the eighth grade. The results for individual groups, as well as for overall results concerning the violation of the tense–lax contrast in vowels are given in Table 3.7.

Table 3.7 Violation of the tense-lax core contrast in vowels

GROUP	violation of the contrast	no violation	number of interviews
C1	1	22	23
C2	2	17	19
T1	5	19	24
T2	3	23	26
OVERALL	11	81	92

Another important core feature is fluency. What counts as a violation of this feature in ELF is extreme disfluency (cf. Jenkins, 2005). Although the criteria for establishing whether and to what degree a subject is disfluent are rather arbitrary, the three raters involved in the present study had no hesitation about which participants were extremely disfluent, which ones could be rated as 'moderately disfluent' and which ones as 'slightly disfluent'. In other words, the extremely disfluent subjects which we set out to identify simply could not complete the description and conversation tasks in a satisfactory fashion. Thus it does not come as a surprise that the raters were unanimous about it. There was only one subject, T1/02, who turned out to be definitely and extremely disfluent throughout the four years of observation, that is, she made no progress in the four years of learning. Curiously enough, the reasons for her disfluency in English seem to be psychological – she apparently suffers from language anxiety, as described by Mihaljević Djigunović (2002). All the remaining four participants (one from group C1, one from T1, two from T2 and none from group C1) who initially exhibited extreme disfluency did make some progress by the end of the fourth year. Thus C2/01, who has the lowest marks in English in his group (ranging from 1 to a 3), reaches a stage in the eighth grade which the evaluators rated as 'moderate' disfluency. Another subject, who initially exhibited extreme disfluency and eventually reaches moderate disfluency, explains in his motivational interview that he has been doing better since he started taking private English lessons outside school. Perhaps the most interesting case is T2/02, who for unclear reasons shows sudden progress in the seventh grade and by grade 8 notably becomes completely fluent! Obvious progress in the course of the four years is also found for subject T2/03-5. Individual cases of what we categorized as moderate or slight disfluency do not count as violation of a core feature, so they are of no concern at this point.

Two more features observed in the category of core features are rhoticity and flapping. We first turn to rhoticity. As already explained, rhoticity is a desirable ELF feature, because in international communication it contributes to intelligibility. The status of our participants in this respect is rather complex, as they generally turn out to be inconsistent. This is probably due to the wealth of sources of exposure which today's 'digital natives' have at their disposal. It should be noted that this inconsistency in sounding more or less American-like or British-like is found in other features as well, such as the vocalic quality in lexical sets BATH (æ/ɑː) and WASH (ɑː/ɒ), or in lexical items (e.g. *apartment/flat*). As the oscillation between American and British types of pronunciation will be discussed separately under non-core features, we shall now focus on the presence or absence of rhoticity as such.

In group C1 we find consistent rhoticity in 11 out of 23 interviews, in eight interviews the particpants are inconsistent in this respect within the same interview, and in four cases the subjects are consistently rhotic. It is important to note that the interviewer in the fifth grade was different than that for the remaining three years of observation, which necessarily influenced the results, as the former was rhotic and the latter was non-rhotic, and at this early stage of observation the role of the interviewer, who extensively provided prompts, was notably greater. On the other hand, it should be taken into consideration that towards the end of primary school, American (i.e. mostly rhotic) varieties prevail in the models which these 'digital native' children are increasingly exposed to through the internet. Thus for the inconsistent ones it is impossible to draw any safe conclusions about the development of the subjects' pronunciation in either direction. An interesting example of the lexical conditioning of rhoticity is C1/04-6. Here the otherwise consistently non-rhotic subject exceptionally becomes rhotic in the situation where he retrieves the American word *apartment* rather than the British one, *flat*, from his mental lexicon. Obviously, rhoticity here comes as part of the lexical information for that particular item. In group C2, out of the 17 interviews available for this analysis, in six of them we find consistent rhoticity, in ten inconsistency, and in only one interview was the subject consistently non-rhotic.

As for the two town groups, the results for rhoticity are similar. In T1, in 15 interviews out of 19 there is consistent rhoticity, in three interviews the participants are inconsistent, and in only one was the subject non-rhotic. However, this last piece of information about the non-rhotic subject should be taken with caution, as it refers to T1/02-6, the case of the extremely disfluent subject mentioned above, who in this particular interview only repeated a few words after the non-rhotic interviewer. For group T2, 24 interviews were usable for the present purpose. Out of these, 15 represent consistent rhoticity, six inconsistency, and three consistent non-rhoticity throughout the interview. An interesting case in this group is that of T2/06, who could be an interesting subject for a separate case study. In the first two years of observation she is consistently rhotic, even when repeating after the non-rhotic interviewer. However, in the seventh grade she becomes inconsistent, inserting occasional non-rhotic items, while in the eighth grade she is fully non-rhotic! What is even more interesting in her speech is that in her inconsistent seventh-grade stage there appears to be a clear pattern: she is rhotic in lexical words like *park* and *garden*, but repeatedly and consistently

Table 3.8 Rhoticity

Group	rhotic	Inconsistent	non-rhotic	interviews
C1	11	8	4	23
C2	6	10	1	17
T1	15	3	1	19
T2	15	6	3	24
OVERALL	47	27	9	83

Table 3.9 Flapping

GROUP	flapping	no flapping	interviews
C1	2	21	23
C2	5	13	18
T1	8	15	23
T2	4	23	27
OVERALL	19	72	91

non-rhotic in comparatives like *smaller* and *bigger*. This might again have to do with the sources from which she learned those items. Comparatives as grammatical structures are drilled at school, where the standard British English model of pronunciation, including non-rhoticity, still seem to be favoured in Croatia. This may be the reason why she associates these particular forms with non-rhoticity, in much the same way in which the otherwise non-rhotic C1/04-6 exceptionally became rhotic in *apartment*. Table 3.8 shows the results for rhoticity.

The last core feature we shall be looking at is the preservation of intervocalic /t/, i.e. the absence of lenition, which in most cases is manifested as flapping. It is a native-like feature, picked up from American-type pronunciation models, and, according to Jenkins (2005), it represents an undesirable feature in the context of ELF. It will therefore be registered as a violation of a core feature. However, this is not to say that we are implying any negative value judgements about the existence of this native-like feature in the speech of those who exhibit it. After all, these participants as a rule turn out to be the most fluent and most proficient speakers. They apply flapping in items like *potatoes, computer, go to school, pretty, spaghetti, daughter, water,* and the like. Table 3.9 shows the presence vs. absence of flapping.

Non-core features

We shall start the analysis of non-core ELF features in the speech of our 26 participants with a consonantal mispronunciation which represents an exception to the rule that in ELF phonemic substitutions are not tolerable.

This is a common non-native feature of mispronouncing the dental fricatives, /θ/ and /ð/, either as their homorganic stops [t] and [d], as in *thing* or *teeth* and *the* or *with,* respectively, or as fricatives, like [friː] for *three* or [baːs] for *bath*. Violation or non-violation of this non-core feature for the four groups of participants, as well as for all 88 interviews, are shown in Table 3.10.

The next feature we looked at seems not to have received explicit attention in ELF literature, but in the speech of our participants, it stands out as one of the most common points of difference from standard native-like pronunciation. This is the absence of the application of the historical rule of velar merger in the rhyme of the syllable, most notably in the *–ing* ending.

In group C1, in 13 out of 22 interviews the subjects regularly pronounce the final /g/ in words like *something* and *doing*; in seven interviews this is inconsistent, whereas in two of them the participants regularly apply the rule of velar merger, pronouncing the items under consideration with a final /ŋ/. Notably, this happens in the speech of one of the best pronouncers referred to in 3.2, C1/02. In group C2, the [g] is pronounced in eight interviews out of 18, inconsistently in five of these cases, while, somewhat surprisingly, the merger rule is applied consistently in five interviews out of the 18.

As for the two town groups, the situation is as follows: In T1, the number of interviews available for the analysis was 23. In 13 of them [g] was found in the context under consideration; in five interviews the subjects were inconsistent, and in five interviews the velar was consistently merged to the nasal, resulting in [ŋ]. In T2, the merger rule was consistently violated in 12 out of 23 interviews, there was inconsistency in two cases, and the merger rule was consistently applied in nine cases.

In connection with this feature it should be noted that there is no clear pattern as for the progress that participants made in the course of the four years of observation. On the one hand, in the speech of the generally most proficient subject, C2/03, who spent some time in the US, the turning point – transition from inconsistency to consistent application of the rule – occurs in the seventh grade, somewhat indicatively, after the summer he spent in the US. On the other hand, there are speakers who show regression in this sense and start consistently violating the rule in later years, like C2/05, from the same group as C2/03. This subject was found to be

Table 3.10 Phonemic substitution of dental fricatives

GROUP	substitution	no substitution	interviews
C1	10	12	22
C2	9	8	17
T1	12	11	23
T2	17	9	26
OVERALL	48	40	88

inconsistent in the application of the velar merger rule in the first two years of observation and in the last two years consistently violated the rule. A possible explanation for this could once again be the fact that in the first two years, due to the nature of the description tasks, speakers could 'get by' with repeating items after the interviewer, avoiding the *–ing* constructions, which accounted for the majority of contexts for the merger. In the last two years, the tasks were more demanding and the participants were expected to speak more freely, using a number of grammatical constructions involving the *–ing* ending, which they must have mastered by that time. In any case, it is safer not to make any sweeping generalisations about the development of this feature in the sample of subjects that we observed. In other words, it may be that they all tend to apply the rule variably, perhaps once again more commonly in lexical than in grammatical words for the reasons referred to above in connection with the preservation of phonemic contrasts. However, in the interviews in which they speak more, the chances of exhibiting variability are greater. In any case, Table 3.11 shows the situation in individual groups as well as for the entire sample with respect to the feature at hand.

Another non-native feature noticed in the pronunciation of our participants is the mispronunciation of the regular plural ending. Although it receives no explicit attention in ELF literature, here it is treated as a non-core feature, because, although it represents the violation of a phonemic identity, in the context in which it occurs, it is hard to imagine how it would hinder international intelligibility. Thus, in a sense it may be argued that as such it is marginal as an ELF feature. Still, being one of the most characteristic phonological rules of native English and commonly subject to violation in non-native speech, it probably deserves to be mentioned and illustrated at this point. Here are a few examples of the violation of this rule, which commonly occur throughout the four years of observation: T1/07-5 *things*[θɪŋgs]; C2/04-6 - *evenings* [iːvnɪŋgs], *friends* [frends]; T1/07-5 - *chairs* [tʃeəs]; T2/02-8 – *needs* [niːds]. Let us also mention at this point that, like all non-native speakers, our subjects occasionally exhibit a typical learners' phenomenon that is present in child language as well: they regularize irregular plurals, ending up once again with non-native-like forms like [ʃelfs] for 'shelves' (T1/01-7) or [piːpls] for *people* (T1/07-5).

Table 3.11 Velar merger rule

GROUP	–ŋg	–ŋg/ŋ	–ŋ	interviews
C1	13	7	2	22
C2	8	5	5	18
T1	13	5	5	23
T2	12	2	9	23
OVERALL	46	19	21	86

Next we look at cases of monophthongization and diphthongization. Like the mispronunciation of plural endings, such phenomena in principle lead to phonemic substitutions, but again occur in contexts where they are unlikely to cause misunderstanding. We shall now look at the occurrence of monophthongisation or diphthongisation in each of the four groups. Monophthongization being more common among our participants, we shall analyse it in more detail. It should be noted that the monophthongization of the GOAT vowel, which is the most common type of monophthongization found here, is a feature shared by various outer circle varieties of English, as established by Deterding (2010). In group C1 it happens in only one interview out of 23: C1/05-7 repeatedly says [doːnt] for *don't*, but in *home* and *no* pronounces the diphthong. This once again suggests that the difference between grammatical and lexical words might play a role in non-native pronunciation. In group C2 we find six interviews where speakers repeatedly monophthongize the same diphthong of the target language, mostly in the same context (*don't*) referred to above, but also once in *most* (C2/04-6) and once in *home* (C2/01-6).

In the two town groups one finds a similar situation. In group T1 there are four interviews out of 23 which exemplify the phenomenon at hand. The items affected, apart from the already mentioned *don't,* are *no* and *know*. An interesting situation occurs in connection with the latter two. While T1/02-6 repeatedly monophthongizes the English diphthong in '*no*' and preserves the diphthongal quality in '*know*', T1/07-8 does the opposite. While this could be purely idiosyncratic, there is always a possibility of a pattern behind such variation, but unfortunately, any generalisation to this effect would require a much greater corpus than the one we have for the present purpose. As for group T2, there are three interviews out of 23 in which we find monophthongisation. In two of them it involves again *don't* and *no*, and in one there is a new example, [boːt] for *boat* (T2/07-5). Table 3.12 shows the monophthongization results both for each group and for the whole sample.

The opposite feature, diphthongization, occurs only twice in the entire sample: in [drou] for *draw* in C2/01-5 and in [houbi] for *hobby* in T2/02-6.

Next a few words are due about the obvious and constant oscillation between the British and American pronunciation types. The inconsistency

Table 3.12 Monophthongization of diphthongs

GROUP	monophththongization	no monophthongization	interviews
C1	1	22	23
C2	6	11	17
T1	4	19	23
T2	3	23	26
OVERALL	14	75	89

in rhoticity (in 27 out of 83 interviews) that was shown in 3.2 is not the only aspect of this. Several other pronunciation features typically associated with the one or the other variety also co-occur within individual interviews. This can be best explained by giving examples from the speech of a few typically 'mixed' subjects. One of the two best pronouncers among our participants, C2/06, exhibits all the native-like pronunciation features, both core and non-core, observed in the present study, some of them already in the first year of observation. Thus already in the fifth grade she applies rules of connected speech assimilation, as in *not raining*, where she applies regressive place assimilation at the word boundary, ending up in the postalveolar [t̚]. She also exhibits other kinds of allophonic alternations, regularly and notably aspirates fortis consonants in the right contexts, applies the rule of velar merger, and has a definitely native-like quality of the lax vowel in the lexical set BIG. However, it is impossible to decide whether her pronunciation is more British or American. On the one hand, she is consistently non-rhotic, which is a typical feature of British standard pronunciation. In addition, as opposed to the majority of other participants, she pronounces the HOME diphthong with a central starting point, [əʊ], rather than [oʊ], which again phonetically brings her closer to British English. On the other hand, in items like *walk* and *not* her vowels definitely sound American: [wɑːk] and [nɑːt], rather than [wɔːk] and [nɒt]. Even more interesting seems to be the opposite example of participant C1/03. Generally, it is definitely American English that he speaks, especially after his visit to the US. However, in one particular item, *hot dog* he sounds British [hɒt dɒg], rather than [hɒːt dɔːg/dɑːg]. This again might have to do with the time and circumstances of the storage of the item into the English mental lexicon, as explained by Cergol (2011).

What has been said above about the extensive oscillation between the American and British type of pronunciation, however, does not imply that there are no subjects who can be neatly classified into one of the two categories. A case in point is T1/06, who is regularly exposed to Canadian English, i.e. the American type of pronunciation through his constant communication with a Canadian friend. In the sixth grade he explicitly shows his awareness of the differences between the two general types of native-English pronunciation. What makes him interesting in the present context is that he is the only subject who has the strong secondary accent, typical of the American pronunciation type in items like *library*, clearly sounding [ˈlaɪˌbrɛri].

Other non-core features which need to be mentioned here include some native-like allophonic alternations and post-lexical rules that have not been analysed in detail earlier and without which the description of our participants' English pronunciation would not be complete. So, we next turn to the alternation between 'clear' and 'dark' /l/, starting with the results for the two city groups and proceeding with the two town groups. In group C1 the alternation is present in 8 out of 23 interviews. It is equally distributed throughout the four years of observation, but without a clear pattern as to when exactly it appears. Generally speaking, the subjects from this group tend to be consistent in either sense within a given interview, with the exception of C1/03-7, who, although otherwise lacking this alternation, in one instance repeats the word 'hall' immediately after the interviewer with the 'dark' variety of /l/. In group C2 the alternation is found in six out of 19 interviews, in three different speakers.

In group T1, the alternation under consideration was established with certainty in only two interviews out of 25: a 'dark' [ɫ] was heard in *wall* (T1/06-6), *football,* and *basketball* (T1/05-6), with both participants in the sixth grade. In group T2 no cases of 'dark' [ɫ] were found. Complete results for this non-core feature are given in Table 3.13.

Another allophonic variation found in the overall sample in seven out of 90 interviews, without any clear pattern as to the time or reason of occurrence, is the realization of /t/ and /d/ before /r/ by their native-like, retracted, i.e. post-alveolar allophones. Here is the list of items where this feature was found: *tree, entrance, attract, children, trying and drink*.

The last non-core feature we shall be looking at is that of final tensing. This is another native-like post-lexical feature, which was identified in a few cases with three participants, generally very good pronouncers. One of them, C1/02, clearly exhibited this feature already in the fifth grade, but unfortunately, after that, she dropped out of the study, so it was impossible to continue the observation of her pronunciation. The remaining two are C1/03, who also applies final tensing in the fifth grade in items like *baby* and *lady*, but in subsequent years it was impossible to find any analogous examples in his speech; and T1/05, who extensively tenses not only word-final vowels and those in word-final syllables (e.g. *family, kitchen, refrigerator*), but also applies tensing to larger prosodic domains (e.g. ..... *for me.*).

Finally, for reasons explained in 2.1, non-core features such as connected-speech phenomena, qualitative reduction of vowels, stress-based rhythm, and intonation were of no direct concern for this study. Therefore, these will be referred to at this point by one general remark: native-like intonation and rhythm were not found in the speech of any of our subjects, not even those who by all criteria turned out to be the best in English in general or English

Table 3.13 Alternation between 'clear' and 'dark' /l/

GROUP	l ~ ɫ	no alternation	interviews
C1	8	15	23
C2	6	13	19
T1	2	23	25
T2	0	27	27
OVERALL	16	78	94

pronunciation in particular. This only seems to confirm Jenkins' (2002) claim that they are 'unteachable' for ELF purposes anyway.

Other features

It should be noted that the pronunciation features observed and described in the present chapter do not and cannot cover all aspects of English pronunciation. The aim was just to establish and analyse a few of the most characteristic core and non-core features found in our subjects as seen in light of ELF theory. At this point, a few other, sporadically found features not covered by Jenkins' list will be mentioned. These are all typical pronunciation features found with English learners generally, or 'Croglish' speakers specifically (cf. Josipović Smojver, 2010).

One such type of mispronunciation includes occasionally wrong, but non-distinctive location of word stress. As such, this does not represent a potential source of misunderstanding in ELF, but significantly contributes to the general impression of a foreign accent. A case in point is the pronunciation of *computer* with initial stress, ['kɒmpjuter]. Sometimes a misleading pronunciation of a word can result from a combination of core and non-core features, as in the example T1/01-7, where instead of *bathroom,* the subject says [bedrum]. Here, interestingly, the violation of the core feature, /ɑ:/, /æ/ → /e/, combined with the violation of a non-core feature, (θ → d) results in a wrong, unintended lexical item. At this point it is interesting to note that this particular word, *bathroom,* definitely turns out to be subject to the greatest pronunciation variability in the present corpus. What follows is a randomly ordered list of 14 different pronunciations noted for *bathroom.* Notably, we are still dealing with 'types', as we could not go into subtle phonetic details, such as the exact degree of closeness, backness, and tenseness of the target /ʊ/ vowel.

'basrum
'bæsrum
'batrum
'bɑ:θrum
'bætrum
'bɑ:srum
'bɑ:trum
'baθrum
'bæθrum
'bæ:θrum
'betrum
'besrum
'beθrum
'bedrum

What varies here are two basic parameters: the degree of the first vowel opening, ranging along the scale e - æ - a/ɑ, and the pronunciation of the target dental fricative /θ/: [t, s, θ, d].[4] The fact that the target standard native-like phonetic quality of the vowel /ɑː/ (RP) or /æ/ (Gen. Am.) taught at school never seem to be reached is a separate issue, which goes beyond the scope of this chapter. The same applies to the already mentioned target lax vowel /ʊ/ of the second syllable. The subject who sets a record in terms of this variability is T1/06-8, who produces most of the items from the above list in a single interview!

Two more interesting items that deserve to be mentioned here are the words used for *scale* and *sea*. In C2/04-5 the subject says 'vague', pronounced as /veɪɡ/, instead of the target word, *scale*. In T1/07-6 the subject says that in the summer he goes to the 'mare' /meə/ instead of the 'sea'. These both have to do with what Kormos (2006: 148) describes as 'phonological and articulatory substitution as a problem-solving mechanism in L2 speech'. The subjects at hand, not being able to think of the right English words, obviously resort to the corresponding Croatian equivalents to *scale* and *sea*, namely *vaga* and *more*, and reshape them phonologically according to similarly-sounding words in English, thus solving the problem of the missing English words.

Another case of mispronunciation for the explanation of which one needs to resort to the phonology of Croatian is the hypercorrect [tiː wiː] for 'TV'. This results from the absence of /w/ in the Croatian phonemic system and the common situation of classroom correction of /v/ into /w/ (cf. Josipović Smojver, 2010). Cases in point are found in C1/05-6, C1/06-7, and C2/04-6.

Finally, mention should be made of yet another typical interlanguage pronunciation feature, final devoicing. It should be noted that Croatian, unlike German or Dutch, does not have final obstruent devoicing as a phonological rule, except in some substandard dialects, which do not seem to play a role here. However, voiceless obstruents in the final position being universally unmarked, it is no surprise that final devoicing happens in interlanguage generally, and particularly at lower levels of proficiency. A case in point is T2/03-7, who pronounces *bed* as [bet]. In terms of Optimality Theory, at this level of interlanguage the markedness constraint prohibiting a word-final voiced obstruent takes precedence over the conflicting faithfulness constraint prohibiting the devoicing (i.e. unfaithfulness) of the output consonant.

Discussion

Using the above results, in the discussion we shall address three issues by providing answers to the following three questions:

(1) Is there a difference among individual groups, especially as concerns the city – town differences?

(2) What is the status of those non-core pronunciation features which in ELF theory are regarded as undesirable, as they reduce international intelligibility, but which in reality, as native-like features, are generally felt to be indications of good and desirable pronunciation and as such are encouraged at school?
(3) Is there a stage in the observed four-year period which represents a turning-point for some or possibly all pronunciation features?

To answer the first question, we shall focus on the four main, most prominent core features which we observed and compare the four groups in this respect.

A few words are first in order about the criteria of comparison. Where there is a lot of variability within individual interviews with respect to the presence vs. absence of a given feature, that is, when subjects are inconsistent within the same interview, we compare only the number of cases where the desirable ELF core-feature is consistently exhibited. Whether we count manifestations or violations of a given feature depends on what is more commonly found. So, for example, for the pronunciation of the English phoneme /æ/, individual groups are compared with respect to the number of interviews with a consistently correct pronunciation of this phoneme. If we did the opposite, i.e. based our comparison on the inconsistencies and incorrect substitutions within individual interviews, the comparison would not be fair, because, as a rule, participants prone to this kind of error tend to be less proficient and speak less in the interviews (in a few extreme cases they do not speak at all!) and thus have less chance of doing the substitution under consideration. Likewise, for aspiration we also base our comparison on the frequency of the feature's manifestation in the right context, rather than its absence.

On the other hand, with core features like preservation of the tense-lax contrast in vowels, we considered it appropriate to compare the groups in terms of the violation, rather than the preservation, of the contrast, because this situation is considerably less common, and relevant items like *ship*, *beach*, *sleeping* and teeth rarely, if ever, occur more than once per interview, so for this core feature the likelihood of inconsistency or contrast violation is relatively low. Likewise, when comparing the groups with respect to the cases of extreme disfluency, we simply count those few cases (if any) for each group.

Taking all this into consideration, in Table 3.14 we present a comparison of the four groups for /æ/, indicating the rank of individual groups on a scale ranging from 1 to 4, obtained by working out the ratio between interviews with consistent /æ/ and the overall number of interviews available in that group. In Table 3.15 we provide analogous data for aspiration.

For the reasons explained above, in Table 3.16, in which the groups are compared in terms of violation of the tense-lax contrast, the rank is worked out using the opposite procedure: the higher the rate of violations, the lower the rank.

Table 3.14 Preservation of the identity of /æ/

GROUP	ratio	rank
C1	14/23 = 0.61	1
C2	9/19 = 0.47	2
T1	8/25 = 0.32	3
T2	5/26 = 0.19	4

Table 3.15 Aspiration

GROUP	ratio	rank
C1	4/23 = 0.18	1
C2	2/18 = 0.11	2
T1	2/21 = 0.09	3
T2	1/27 = 0.04	4

Table 3.16 Tense-lax contrast in vowels

GROUP	ratio	rank
C1	1/23 = 0.04	1
C2	2/19 = 0.11	2
T1	5/24 = 0.21	3
T2	3/26 = 0.12	4

As for extreme disfluency, we ranked the four groups in terms of the number of extremely disfluent subjects, distinguishing four types of situation within the category of extreme disfluency. That is, we took into consideration the degree of progress the participants made by the end of the fourth year of observation. Thus we gave one point for disfluency when the subject made great progress and was no longer disfluent in the final eighth-grade interview. By analogy, we gave two points for initially extreme disfluency which in the course of the four years became only slight disfluency, three points for initially extreme but finally moderate disfluency, and four points for the only case of a subject who made no progress at all. The results of the group ranking are given in Table 3.17.

It is obvious at first glance that the two city groups rank higher than the two town groups. The only partial exception to this generalization is that for extreme disfluency T2 shares second place with group C2. The city group C1 turns out to be the best group for all four features without exception. However, the interpretation of this situation requires caution. The sample we are dealing with is too small to make claims to the effect that Croatian

Table 3.17 Extreme disfluency

GROUP	extreme disfluency index	Rank
C1	0	1
C2	1 x 3 = 3	2
T1	1 x 3 + 1 x 4 = 7	3
T2	1 x 1 + 1 x 2 = 3	2

city pupils pronounce English better than those from towns, that is, that city schools or English teachers are better, or the opportunities to learn English are better in the city. The explanation can always be in the choice of better learners. Although their teachers got the same instructions concerning the criteria of learner choice, it was impossible to control this procedure. By the same token, we could not rely on school grades to check this choice, because they are never reliable enough in such studies for at least two reasons. First of all, some teachers are generally more strict than others, and some incline towards what is usually referred to as 'grade inflation' in the final year, to help their pupils enrol into secondary schools of their choice. After all, school grades are supposed to reflect general proficiency in English, and not just pronunciation, which is the focus of the present study. Taking all this into consideration, it can be observed that the present results provide some interesting hints for future research, which certainly has to be done on a greater and more varied sample if generalisations to this effect are being made.

Now we turn to the second issue, concerning the status of ELF core features such as flapping, final tensing, connected speech phenomena, allophonic variation, and the like. From the perspective of ELF, flapping, for example, represents a violation of the core feature of preserved intervocalic /t/. As such, although being a native-like feature, manifesting the universal tendency of natural languages to save up on articulatory gestures (referred to technically as the ergonomy of speech) and being as a rule associated with more proficient learners, in ELF theory it turns out to be treated as an undesirable feature that reduces international intelligibility. The issue that arises concerns the right attitude toward such features in language teaching. Although this is not often explicitly addressed in the literature, it is implied that no native-like feature that is natural and comes naturally to English learners should be discouraged in favour of some ELF feature. Thus, according to Jenkins (2007), features such as stress-based rhythm should be taught to students who choose to strive for native-like pronunciation. After all, it is definitely not the purpose of ELF theory to discourage students from native-like features, and extensive recent research, such as Kaldonek and Jakupčević (2011) and Kukolja (2011), shows that both pupils and teachers in Croatia definitively prefer as native-like English pronunciation as possible. The idea of ELF theory is simply that insisting on such features in teaching English to future speakers of EIL is seen

Table 3.18 Progress in the main four core features by the end of the primary school

core feature	æ	tense vs. lax V	aspiration	fluency
progress	7/25	8/25	4/25	4/5
grade	(7 and) 8	n.c.p.	n.c.p.	n/a: gradual

as a waste of time, which could be better used for teaching core features and exposing pupils to a wide range of varieties of native, as well as non-native English, which would develop their receptive flexibility.

As for the question concerning the subjects' progress in terms of pronunciation over the four-year period of observation, Table 3.18 shows their progress with respect to the four main core features observed in the present study. The reason why the number of subjects here is 25, rather than 26, is that one subject (unluckily an excellent pronouncer) dropped out after the first year of observation. Before the presentation and interpretation of the results, a few points must be made about the criteria for measuring progress. What counts as progress here includes any improvement with respect to preceding years, that is, from initial consistent violation of a core feature to inconsistent violation or no violation per interview, or from inconsistency to the stabilization of a core feature. As for fluency, here we observe only cases of extreme disfluency and look at whether it improves by any notable degree in the course of the four years. It must be stressed that fluency and disfluency are inherently gradual features, so for the four (out of the five initially extremely disfluent participants) who did make progress, we found it more appropriate to compare the situation at the beginning of the four-year period of observation with that at the end, without trying to identify the year representing a turning point. Thus it should be noted that for fluency $N = 5$, whereas for the other three core features $N = 25$. Except for the identity of /æ/, for which participants seem to reach a turning point and stabilize its phonemic identity in the seventh or, more commonly, in the eighth grade, for other core features there emerged no clear pattern, which is indicated by the abbreviation 'n.c.p.' This is all shown in Table 3.18.

Before proceeding with the conclusion, a final remark needs to be made about parameters for which it is generally known to play a role in the quality of pronunciation, but could not be dealt with in the present chapter, because of the limitations of scope as well as the insufficient size of the sample. One of them is gender. The initial number of male and female participants was the same, and the fact that one girl dropped out of the study would not significantly affect the balance, but in any case, the number of participants we had would not be sufficient for any safe generalisations in this sense, especially as there are no obvious differences for any particular feature between the boys and the girls. Secondly, it is only too obvious that in this generation of 'digital natives' very important factors influencing the subjects' general proficiency as well as the quality of pronunciation are the degree and the nature

Conclusion

The present research shows that our participants, primary school learners, qualify as future speakers of International English, in particular ELF. In the four-year period of observation of their English pronunciation it has emerged that they are still in the process of mastering what in ELF theory is referred to as the 'core' features of ELF pronunciation. The four core features that turned out to be the most relevant to Croatian learners are the preservation of the identity of the vowel /æ/, the application of the aspiration rule in the right contexts, the maintenance of the contrast between tense and lax vowels, most notably, /iː/ vs. /ɪ/, and a level of fluency which does not represent a major obstacle to communication.

We found that the subjects from the city were better in all four core features than those from the town, but generalizations to this effect must be made with caution, because of the relatively small size of the sample. An important point was made about the non-core features identified in the speech of primary-school pupils. These often turn out to be natural, native-like features such as flapping, final tensing, allophonic variation, or connected speech phenomena. As such, they do not by definition contribute to EIL intelligibility, but as they are still generally perceived as desirable features of 'good' pronunciation, their non-core status in ELF should not be misinterpreted to the effect that they should be discouraged and corrected in favour of the more intelligible, but unnatural ELF features. The idea is simply that priority in teaching English pronunciation to future ELF speakers should be given to core features, but without underrating those non-core features, which are still generally felt to be indications of 'good' pronunciation. However, it seems that many English teachers around the world no longer feel obliged to constantly make reference to native-like pronunciation norm and increasingly feel, as Kirkpatrick (2007: 189) nicely puts it, that 'English belongs to them as much as to anyone else'. Whether Croatian teachers are yet ready for this kind of attitude is still questionable, but Stanojević and Josipović (2011) point to some important developments in this direction among Croatian university students.

All of our participants made definite and notable progress with respect to the most important core features. However, except for the stabilization of the identity of /æ/, which happens most of the time in the eighth grade or, somewhat less commonly, in the seventh grade, it was impossible to establish a clear pattern as to the turning point in the progress.

Finally, as guidelines for further research, four parameters influencing the quality of the learners' pronunciation but going beyond the scope of this study were identified as interesting topics for further research: gender, starting age, preference for oral communication, and the degree and nature of out-of-school exposure to English in the 'digital native' generation of Croatian learners. It would also be interesting to obtain analogous data for younger primary-school learners and see whether pronunciation learning at earlier stages follows patterns comparable to those described above, but this was also beyond the scope of the present study and should be dealt with in future research.

Notes

(1) The author wishes to thank Mirjana Markovinović and Aleksandra Martinović, each of whom rated half of the interviews independently of the author.
(2) The English translations of the original Croatian responses are the author's.
(3) In Croatia, marks range from 1 (fail) to 5 (excellent).
(4) In some other items the dental fricative /θ/ is also commonly pronounced as [f], as in 'three' [fri:], but for this particular word such examples were not found.

References

Bakran, J. (1996) *Zvučna slika hrvatskoga govora. [The Acoustic Picture of Croatian Speech]* Zagreb: Ibis grafika.
Cergol, K. (2011) Jezična aktivacija i leksički pristup u stranom ili drugom i materinskom jeziku [Language activation and the Lexical Approach in L2 and L1]. PhD thesis, University of Zagreb.
Cogo, A. (2009) Accomodating difference in ELF conversations: A study of pragmatic strategies. In A. Mauranen and E. Ranta (eds) *English as a Lingua Franca: Studies and Findings* (pp. 254–273). Newcastle: Cambridge Scholars Publishing.
Cook, V.J. (1991) The poverty-of-the-stimulus argument and multi-competence. *Second Language Research* 7 (2), 103–117.
Cook, V. (2002) Background to the L2 User. In V.J. Cook (ed.) *Portraits of the L2 User* (pp. 1–28). Clevendon: Multilingual Matters.
Cook, V. (2008) *Second Language Learning and Language Teaching* (4th edn). London: Hodder Education.
Crystal, D. (2003) *English as a Global Language* (2nd edn). Cambridge: Cambridge University Press.
Crystal, D. (2004) *The Language Revolution*. Cambridge: Polity Press.
Deterding, D. (2010) Variation across Englishes: Phonology. In A. Kirkpatrick (ed.) *The Routledge Handbook of World Englishes* (pp. 385–399). London, New York: Routledge.
Ehrenreich, S. (2009) English as a Lingua Franca in multinational corporations – exploring business communities of practice. In A. Mauranen and E. Ranta (eds) *English as a Lingua Franca: Studies and Findings* (pp. 126–151). Newcastle: Cambridge Scholars Publishing.
Görlach, M. (2002) *Still More Englishes*. Amsterdam, Philadelphia: John Benjamins Publishing Company.
Graddol, D. (2006) English Next. www.britishcouncil.org/learning-research (accessed 18 November 2014).
Iverson, G.K. and Ahn, S.-C. (2007) English voicing in Dimensional Theory. *Language Sciences* 29 (2–3), 247–269.
Jenkins, J. (2000) *The Phonology of English as an International Language: New Models, New Norms, New Goals*. Oxford: Oxford University Press.

Jenkins, J. (2002) A sociolinguistically based, empirically researched pronunciation syllabus for English as an international language. *Applied Linguistics* 23 (1), 83–103.
Jenkins, J. (2005) Implementing an international approach to English pronunciation: The role of teacher attitudes and identity. *TESOL Quarterly* 39 (3), 535–543.
Jenkins, J. (2007) *English as a Lingua Franca: Attitude and Identity*. Oxford: Oxford University Press.
Jenkins, J. (2009) English as a lingua franca: interpretations and attitudes. *World Englishes* 28 (2), 200–207.
Josipović Smojver, V. (2010) Foreign accent and levels of analysis: interference between English and Croatian. In E. Waniek-Klimczak (ed.) *Issues in Accents of English 2: Variability and Norm* (pp. 23–35). Newcastle: Cambridge Scholars Publishing.
Josipović Smojver, V. and Stanojević, M.M. (2012) Stratification of English as a lingua franca: Identity constructions of learners and speakers. In E. Waniek-Klimczak and L. Shockey (eds) *Teaching and Researching English Accents in Native and Non-native Speakers* (pp. 193–207). New York, Berlin: Springer.
Kachru, B.B., Kachru Y. and Nelson, C.L. (2006) *The Handbook of World Englishes*. Malden, MA: Blackwell.
Kaldonek, A. and Jakupčević, E. (2011) Nastavnik stranog jezika u očima potreba studenata (analiza potreba studenata) [The foreign language teacher in the light of student needs]. Paper presented at the 25th International Symposium of the Croatian Applied Linguistics Society, Osijek, May 12–14, 2011.
Kirkpatrick, A. (2007) *World Englishes: Implications for International Communication and English Language Teaching*. Cambridge: Cambridge University Press.
Kormos, J. (2006) *Speech Production and Second Language Acquisition*. Mahwah, New Jersey, London: Lawrence Erlbaum Associates Publishers.
Kukolja, M. (2011) Kompetencije nastavnika stranoga jezika – usporedba stavova učenika i nastavnika. [Foreign language teacher competences – a comparison between the attitudes of learners and teachers]. Paper presented at the 25th International Symposium of the Croatian Applied Linguistics Society, Osijek, May 12–14, 2011.
Levis, J.M. (2005) Changing contexts and shifting paradigms in pronunciation teaching. *TESOL Quarterly* 39 (3), 369–337.
Mihaljević Djigunović J. (2002) *Strah od stranoga jezika. [Foreign language anxiety]* Zagreb: Naklada Ljevak.
Pitzl, M.-L. (2009) We should not wake up any dogs: Idiom and Metaphor in ELF. In A. Mauranen and E. Ranta (eds) *English as a Lingua franca: Studies and Findings* (pp. 298–322). Newcastle: Cambridge Scholars Publishing.
Ranta, E. (2009) Syntactic features in spoken ELF – learner language or spoken grammar? In A. Mauranen and E. Ranta (eds) *English as a Lingua Franca: Studies and Findings* (pp. 84–106). Newcastle: Cambridge Scholars Publishing.
Seidlhofer, B. (2001) Closing a conceptual gap: the case for a description of English as a Lingua Franca. *International Journal of Applied Linguistics* 11 (2), 133–158.
Seidlhofer, B. (2010) Lingua franca English: The European context. In A. Kirkpatrick (ed.) *The Routledge Handbook of World Englishes* (pp. 355–371). London, New York: Routledge.
Stanojević, M.M. and Josipović Smojver, V. (2011) Euro-English and Croatian national identity: are Croatian university students ready for English as a lingua franca? *Suvremena Lingvistika* 37 (71), 105–130.
Vilke, M. (2007) English in Croatia – a glimpse into past, present and future. *Metodika* 8 (14), 17–24.

4 Acquisition of Markers of Definiteness and Indefiniteness in Early EFL

Lovorka Zergollern-Miletić

Introduction

Native speakers of Croatian, like speakers of many other languages, are not aware of the existence of definiteness and indefiniteness in their language, which becomes especially obvious when they learn foreign languages in which these two categories are grammaticalized in the articles (Zergollern-Miletić, 2008). We believe that this view is in line with the notion of the importance of language awareness (Bagarić, 2003, 2005; Hawkins, 1994). Definiteness and indefiniteness are learned by native speakers of Croatian only as grammatical categories, and are often wrongly linked with adjectives. In his article 'Izražavanje neodređenosti/određenosti imenica u hrvatskom jeziku' [Expressing the indefiniteness/definiteness of nouns in Croatian], Pranjković (2000) points out that definiteness and indefiniteness are semantically linked with nouns, rather than adjectives. Nouns carry the meaning of definiteness/indefiniteness, and they determine the choice of the adjectival form.

The categories of indefiniteness and definiteness are semantic, syntactic and logical categories, connected with pragmatics and text linguistics. In his book *Definiteness* (1999), Christopher Lyons comes to the conclusion that most theories revolve around the concepts of *identifiability/familiarity*, *inclusiveness/exclusiveness* (i.e. whether the referent includes all the members of a set), *uniqueness* and *countability/uncountability*. These two categories are not explicitly expressed in all languages, and are grammaticalized in a limited number of languages. In English, definiteness and indefiniteness are expressed by, and grammaticalized in articles, personal and indefinite pronouns, demonstratives, quantifiers and possessives. Articles are considered to be prototypical markers of those two categories.

In modern English grammars articles are cited as *determiners*. In this way they are put in the same category with other grammatical elements that have the same position in the noun phrase (i.e. before the noun). Determiners are grammatical words which express definiteness and indefiniteness in different ways and to different extents. Their meanings may sometimes overlap (e.g. articles may in certain contexts be interchangeable with demonstratives or quantifiers).

For learners of English whose mother tongues do not possess articles (such as Croatian), the acquisition of articles represents a major problem. The numerous researchers who have addressed this problem include Grannis (1972), Huebner (1983), Master (1990), Tarone and Parrish (1989), Trenkić (2000, 2002, 2007, 2008), Humphrey (2007), and Zergollern-Miletić (2008, 2009, 2010a, 2010b), to name a few. Kałuza (1963) was among the first who pointed out the problem of teaching the English article to speakers of Slavic languages in general. It has been suggested by a number of researchers that the early stage in learning English is strongly marked by the omission of articles, and later followed by substitution, usually in favour of the definite article (Trenkić, 2002). Some authors (e.g. Trenkić, 2002) suggest that using 'the' is a 'safe or safer bet' than using the indefinite article.

Our expectations in the research we are about to present were that in the early stages of learning English as a foreign language (EFL) Croatian young EFL learners' production would show a general omission of articles. These expectations were further strengthened by the problems demonstrated and described by Croatian university majors in English, by teachers of English and by translators (Zergollern-Miletić, 2008, 2010a, 2010b).

The Study

Aim

In the study we are about to present we looked into the acquisition of the English markers of definiteness and indefiniteness by primary school pupils who started learning English in the fourth grade, the age of onset being approximately 10 years.

Methodology

Sample

The participants included pupils from four Croatian primary schools. There were 24 participants drawn from four classes: two from a large city, and two a medium-size town. Based on their EFL performance during the four years 2 participants were categorized as high-proficiency, 18 as average-proficiency and 2 as low-proficiency learners.

Instruments

Oral production

Oral language production in EFL was elicited over a period of four years (grades 5, 6, 7 and 8) by means of several elicitation tasks which differed slightly in each grade in order to be age- and proficiency-appropriate.

Grade 5

Five tasks were used to elicit oral production in Grade 5. First the participants were asked 12 questions about some personal data (name, age, siblings), hobbies, pets, favourite food and the TV programmes they liked to watch. In the second task, the fifth graders had to describe a picture of a house and the activities that the people in the house were engaged in. The nouns that the pupils needed for the description were as follows: *house, window, woman, man, child, cat,* and *cupboard*. The description of the house was followed by a dialogue (the third task) between the interviewer and the pupil about the pupil's house/flat and his or her family. This was followed by a description of a picture of a park and a garden (the fourth task). The nouns that were supposed to be used are as follows: *park, tree(s), children, pram, bench, boat, football, swing, garden, man (men), woman, flowers, dog, boy, hedge, house, window(s), grass,* and *book.* Finally, the fifth task included a dialogue in which the pupils were asked whether there was a park near their home, and what they did in their free time.

Grade 6

Two oral elicitation tasks, each of which included one subtask, were administered. The first required the young learners to describe a picture of a dining room and a living room. The nouns that the pupils could choose to describe the picture were as follows: *dining-room, living-room, bookshelf, chair, cupboard, TV, wall, painting, woman, man, hand, table, children, book, mother, father, son, daughter, armchair, plant,* and *homework*. Once the descriptions were completed, the participants were asked about their own home and family. The second task was also a picture description task: the participants were asked to describe a picture where people were enjoying their free time. The possible vocabulary for the description consisted of the words: *park, parasol, waiter, café, steps, book, drinks, man, people, chair, door, holidays, sports, children,* and *beach*. This was followed by a dialogue revolving around the participants' free time and holidays.

Grade 7

The same type of tasks and subtasks were used in Grade 7. First, the participants were asked to describe a picture of the facilities within a family house, and the activities performed by the family. The pupils were encouraged to describe everything in detail. To accomplish that task they needed approximately 40 nouns. After the description, the young learners were engaged in a conversation thematically linked to the picture.

Grade 8

In the final year, the participants were supposed to give a detailed description of a picture of a kitchen and the activities going on there. A conversation about the pupils' kitchens and their families' eating and cooking habits followed the description. Again, to accomplish this task the pupils needed to use approximately 40 nouns.

Written production

Written production was elicited during three years when the pupils were in Grades 6–8.

Grade 6

In Grade 6 the learners were asked to write a short composition entitled **'My best friend'**. They were instructed to answer the following questions in their composition:

What is your friend's name?
How old is your friend?
Where does your friend live?
Has your friend got brothers and sisters?
Has your friend got any pets? Which?
What does your friend look like?
Do you see your friend very often?
What do you do with your friend when you are together?
Why is he/she your best friend?
What else can you say about your best friend?

Grade 7

In Grade 7 the participants were required to describe a cartoon. The cartoon was about two girls who enter a candy shop. They talk to the shop-assistant and, when he turns his back, one of the girls steals some candy. The girls go home, and eventually go to sleep. The girl who stole the candy has bad dreams. Feeling guilty, the following day she goes to the shop and pays for the candy she stole.

Grade 8

Another cartoon was used in Grade 8. It was about a man named John who was jogging one morning. Another man bumped into him. John exchanged a few words with him. John went home and realized that he did not have his wallet on him. He started thinking that the man who had bumped into him had taken his wallet. John took a shower. Having done that, he got dressed, during which he found his wallet in a garment he hadn't been wearing during the jogging session. The end is open – we don't know what John did after he had found the wallet, so the pupils had to come up with their own ending to the story.

Procedure

The participants' language production was elicited during all four years: from Grade 5 to Grade 8. Towards the end of each grade, the participants were engaged in oral elicitation tasks, and their oral performance was audio-recorded. Starting from Grade 6, their written production was elicited by means of guided compositions. While the oral tasks were done on an individual basis, the written tasks were administered in groups.

Results and Discussion

Oral production

Oral production in Grade 5

Personal pronouns – Pupils did not seem to have any problems using them. There were a few occurrences of low-proficiency pupils using *it* for a person.

Pupils tended not to use **indefinite pronouns**.

The **quantifiers** *some* and *any* were found in a limited number of cases, and were used correctly. No other quantifiers were used.

The **demonstrative** *this* was used. It is interesting to note that the demonstrative *that* never occurred in the interviews in any grade. Our assumption is that, since the picture was near to the participants, they did not consider the demonstrative *that* appropriate, or they simply had not mastered the use of the demonstrative *that*. What can also be noticed in the interviews is that most young learners, when referring to a group of people, used *this* instead of *these*. This might be a matter of incorrect pronunciation, or the pupils hadn't mastered the use of *these*.

The pupils tended to use **possessives** with nouns denoting parts of the body and those denoting family members, which is typical of English, but not typical of Croatian. In this respect we can talk about native-like production. Nevertheless, there were two occurrences of average-proficiency pupils using the non-existent form *she's*.

Use of **articles**: As we have already mentioned above, our expectations were that, at this early stage of learning EFL, oral production would show a general omission of articles. Surprisingly enough, the results indicate that the omission of the articles with countable singular nouns was around 15%, which cannot be considered as problematic. The omission occurred mainly in the production of low-proficiency pupils. What can also be noted is the correct use of indefinite countable nouns in the plural, or their use with the quantifier *some* (e.g. *Some boys are playing football*). The indefinite article was incorrectly used on three occasions (*playing a football, make a dinner,* and *in front of a shower*) and the definite article on five occasions (*finish the college, this is the sink, play the football, on the vacation,* and *there are the kids*).

Oral production in Grade 6
   Personal pronouns – The pupils did not have any problems using them.
   Only one **indefinite pronoun** was found, and it was used once (*someone*).
   The **quantifiers** *some* and *any* were found in a limited number of cases, and were used correctly. No other quantifiers were used.
   The **demonstrative** *this* was used. On three occasions, *this* was again used instead of *these*.
   Possessives were used correctly, except for one occasion where *she's* was used instead of *her*.

   Use of **articles**: The results indicate that the omission of articles with countable singular nouns occurred with about the same frequency as in Grade 6. The indefinite article was used by a low- proficiency pupil on two occasions with countable nouns in the plural (*a drinks, a games*), and once by a high-proficiency pupil with an uncountable noun (*a homework*). In the latter case we can assume that the pupil mapped the meaning of the Croatian noun for homework (which is a countable singular noun *zadaća*) onto the English noun. We might conclude that pupils at this stage do not generally link the meaning of a particular English noun with the meaning of articles. Nevertheless, there seems to exist a certain awareness of the tight connection between English nouns and articles: two pupils even used the indefinite article with Croatian nouns in singular (a *polica* = shelf, a *fotelja* = armchair).

Oral production in Grade 7
   Personal pronouns – The pupils generally did not have any problems using them. Nevertheless, one lower proficiency pupil used *it* instead of *he* on two occasions, one average- proficiency pupil confused *he* and *she* on two occasions, and one average pupil used *she* to denote a house. In the latter example we can talk about the interference from Croatian, where the word for 'house' (*kuća*) is a feminine noun.
   Indefinite pronouns were used on three occasions: *somebody* was used twice, and *something* once.
   The **quantifier** *some* occurred in the oral production of most pupils, with uncountable as well as with countable nouns. One pupil used the quantifier *both*.
   The **demonstrative** *this* was used correctly.
   Possessives were used correctly, except for one occasion where *mine* was used instead of *my*.

   Use of **articles**: The results indicate that the omission of the articles with countable singular nouns occurred less frequently (13%). The use of the indefinite article with countable nouns in the plural occurred on three occasions (one lower-proficiency pupil and one average-proficiency pupil). The definite article was used instead of the indefinite (substitution) on two occasions where a countable noun was mentioned for the first time:

There is <u>the</u> carpet in this room.
There is <u>the</u> table.

The definite article was also used by an average-proficiency pupil with abstract nouns:

I concentrate on the learning, not on the playing.

Oral production in Grade 8

Personal pronouns – The pupils generally did not have any problems using them. One average-proficiency pupil used *she* instead of *he* on one occasion.

No **indefinite pronouns** were used.

Very few **quantifiers** occurred in the oral production of eighth-graders. *Any* occurred in the oral production of one pupil. *Many* was used twice correctly, and once incorrectly (*many fruit*). *Much* was used once incorrectly (*much people*).

The **demonstrative** *this* was used four times correctly, and once incorrectly (*this clothes*).

Possessives were used correctly.

Use of **articles**: The frequency of the omission of the articles with countable singular nouns was about 12%. The use of the indefinite article with countable nouns in the plural occurred on one occasion (one lower-proficiency pupil). There was also an occurrence of the indefinite article with an abstract noun (*a work* – by an average-proficiency pupil). One average-proficiency pupil said she 'ate in *a* dining room at home'. This may support our assumption that at this age pupils still do not understand the meaning of English articles, that is, that the articles may express countability, uniqueness and familiarity.

We must point out here that two pupils said almost nothing in their interviews. Their oral production was very weak.

Among the 8th grade pupils there were two occurrences of the definite article with nouns that were being mentioned for the first time:

There is <u>the</u> man on the sofa.
There is <u>the</u> child near the bed.

Just as with similar examples in the Grade 7 pupils' production, we may assume that the pupils used the definite article considering the objects or persons they indicated as being familiar.

One high-proficiency learner, who used more nouns and noun phrases than other learners, had problems with the phrase *on holiday*, in which he inserted the indefinite article before the noun. The other high-proficiency participant used the noun *homework* in one context with the indefinite article, and in another context with the definite article, which might support our claim (Zergollern-Miletić, 2008) that abstract nouns and phrases present the most difficult problem in the acquisition of the English articles by native speakers of Croatian.

Conclusions on the use of markers of definiteness and indefiniteness by Croatian young learners in their oral production in EFL

Our analysis of the participants' oral production suggests that young Croatian EFL learners are aware of the fact that English singular nouns should be preceded by determiners. Some pupils in our sample even put English articles in front of Croatian nouns that they used when they did not know the English equivalents.

We can make a general conclusion that there were no considerable developmental differences in the use of markers of definiteness and indefiniteness across the grades. The young learners tended not to use indefinite pronouns, and the use of quantifiers was very limited. They tended to use only the demonstrative *this*, while the plural *these* was problematic. The use of possessives seemed to come naturally and rather accurately in their discourse. As to the use of the articles, there were fewer problems than expected. Omission did not flood the discourse. Nevertheless, we might conclude that by the end of Grade 8 the pupils had not mastered the use of the English articles.

Written production
Written production in Grade 6

The texts that the participants produced contained 70 words on average, out of which approximately 15 were nouns. The nouns that were used most are as follows:

friend, years, hair, eyes, brother(s), sister(s), pet(s), dog, cat.

The pupils also used place names, and nouns denoting pets other than cats and dogs.

Here is a sample text composed by a high-proficiency pupil:

My best friend's name is Julian. He is twelve. He lives in Pula, Croatia. He's got one brother. He's got one parrot. He's got brown hair and brown eyes. He is as tall as me. I usually see him once–twice per week. We usually play yu-gi-oh cards, board games or video games. He's my best friend because I know him since I was two and I like hanging around with him. He's an exelent student and a nice person, too.

The following are the results of our 24 participants:

Personal pronouns were used correctly.
No **indefinite pronoun** was used in any of the pupils' texts.

The **quantifier** *any* was correctly used in three texts.
No **demonstrative** was used.
Possessives were used correctly.

The results for **articles** are as follows:

There was a higher rate of article omission when compared to those in the oral task (20% in the written task as compared to 15% in the oral task), but it occurred mostly in the texts of the low-proficiency pupils, and in some average pupils' texts.

Among the low-proficiency pupils one pupil tended not to use any article before countable singular nouns, and used the indefinite article before plural nouns.

Another problem encountered by two pupils (both with low proficiency) was the uncountable noun *hair*, before which they used the indefinite article.

The definite article in front of the adjective *same* was omitted by two low-proficiency and two average-proficiency pupils. Only three more pupils used the adjective *same* in their texts, and all of them did it using the definite article.

Written production in Grade 7
The average number of words the learners used was 90, and the nouns they could use to describe the cartoon are as follows:

Sue, Anna, girl(s), shop/store/candy shop, bag, candy, purse/bag, friend, shop-assistant/sales person, nightmare/bad dream(s), police/policeman/cop, jail, money, tears, face, and *day.*

Some of the nouns were repeated several times.
Here is a sample text by an average-proficiency pupil:

One day Sue and Anna ... came to the candyshop. Anna has told to the seller that she want some candys from the shelf behind seller. He has turned around and in that moment Sue was putting candys in her bag. When they came out Sue has asked Anna if she want her candy but Anna said: "no, thanks." It is dark. Sue can't sleep because she has got bad dreams. She is dreaming that she will end in the jail because she has stoled candys.

Next day in the morning Sue went to the candyshop and gave money to the seller with tears on her face.

Personal pronouns were used correctly.
No **indefinite pronoun** was used in any of the pupils' texts.
The **quantifiers** *some* and *any* were used with the nouns *candy* and *money*, and were used correctly.

Only one pupil used a **demonstrative.** He used *this* (instead of *these*) with the noun *candies*. No other demonstratives were used in any of the texts.

Only the **possessive** *her* was used, and it was used correctly.

As for their use of **articles**, low-proficiency pupils had problems ranging from omission to substitution. Nevertheless, although their texts were in part incomprehensible, they showed at least some awareness that English countable nouns should be preceded by determiners.

All the pupils introduced the story by saying, 'Sue and Anna went to *the* shop.' We assume that they used the definite article because the shop is familiar to them, and they did not take their reader into consideration.

All the high-proficiency and average-proficiency pupils used the definite article with the noun *shop assistant* (or another noun denoting the person selling in that particular shop). The low-proficiency pupils omitted the article. We may assume again that the pupils who used the definite article might have expressed their own familiarity with the person. Nevertheless, we are more inclined to believe that they were pointing out the *uniqueness* of that person.

When the context required the repetition of the noun *candy/candies*, 60% of them used the definite article, showing that the referent was known. We may conclude that most pupils understood the notion of *familiarity*.

Of the ten pupils who used the noun *policeman* (the high- and average-proficiency pupils), three average pupils used it without an article, and the rest with the definite article. We can assume that the latter decision was made because the policeman was the only one that came to the little girl in her dream, so they expressed uniqueness. Another possibility may be that they used *the* instead of *that*, as if they were pointing at the policeman (the deictic function of the definite article). The third possibility may be that they used *the* as 'a safe bet' (Trenkić, 2002).

Written production in Grade 8
Here is a sample text by an average-proficiency learner:

> *That morning John went jogging in the park. One guy from the different direction accidently crushed with him. John thought he wanted to stole his wallet and he yelled at him in the middle of the park. When he came home he calmed down and took a shower. When he was done with showering he went to change his clothes. In his jacket he found his wallet. He was thinking for a little bit and admitted that he was wrong about the guy from the park. The next morning he bought a chocolate and went to apologize to the poor guy.*
>
> *I would probably just think that he accidently hit me while he was running and I wouldn't do such a panic.*

This was another demanding task, in which the learners had to use rather broad vocabulary and various grammatical structures. The average number of words used was 90, and the nouns used are as follows:

morning, John, park, man/guy, wallet, home, shower, clothes, apology, jacket, and *pocket.*

Here is the analysis of the use of the markers of definiteness and indefiniteness:

Personal pronouns were used correctly.
Indefinite pronouns were not used at all.
The quantifiers *some* and *a little* were used by a limited number of pupils, and they were used correctly.
Only two pupils used the **demonstrative *that*** (*that morning*), and they used it correctly.
Possessives were used correctly.
The omission of **articles** occurred in nine cases, which is very low.
One average pupil used *an* in his text when *a* was correct. Another average pupil used the definite article before the proper noun *John.*

Conclusions on the use of markers of definiteness and indefiniteness by young Croatian learners in their written production in EFL

We expected the written tasks to be more demanding than the oral tasks, and that the participants would face considerable difficulties in the production of the markers of definiteness and indefiniteness, primarily articles. However, the results were similar to those obtained on the oral task. The low-proficiency pupils experienced considerable language problems, but their use of the markers of definiteness and indefiniteness seems to have improved over the years. In Grade 8 the results on the written task were slightly better than those on the oral task, especially when articles are concerned. A possible reason for this might be that the written task required the use of nouns that were familiar to the pupils. In addition, it was not necessary to use any abstract nouns or phrases.

General Conclusion

Our study has brought us to the conclusion that there are no considerable differences across the grades or between the two tasks. The overall results may be described as follows:

Personal pronouns were used mainly correctly.
Indefinite pronouns were used in a very limited number of cases. We would like to suggest three explanations for this:

(1) The pupils had not mastered their use in English.

(2) They simply did not feel any need to use indefinite pronouns in their discourse (both oral and written).
(3) They did not use indefinite pronouns in their mother tongue either, since indefinite pronouns belong to a more sophisticated type of discourse.

Quantifiers were used by a limited number of pupils, in most cases correctly. We suggest that for this low occurrence of quantifiers the same explanations might be provided as for the low occurrence of indefinite pronouns.

As for **demonstratives,** both in oral and written production the pupils mainly used *this*. The reason for this may be that they were describing pictures that were close to them. In both oral and written production, it was noticed that the pupils did not use *these* for the plural. The demonstrative *that* was only used twice – by two learners in written production.

Possessives were mainly used correctly.

In terms of **articles**, there were fewer problems than expected. The pupils did not omit articles in many cases. They seemed to understand that English nouns should be preceded by determiners, so some of them even used English articles with Croatian nouns when they could not remember the right English ones. Nevertheless, some pupils made the mistake of putting the indefinite article before plural nouns, thus showing that they did not understand the meaning and function of the English indefinite article. In our analysis we have noticed that the notions of *familiarity, countability,* and *uniqueness* have been internalized to a certain extent, but we believe that the pupils had not entirely mastered the use of English articles. Very few abstract nouns and phrases were used by our respondents, and the use of articles was problematic in those cases (*the football, a homework, on a holiday*), which is in line with our previous findings (Zergollern-Miletić, 2008, 2009, 2010a, 2010b) with very advanced learners of English (university English majors), who also had problems with the use of articles with abstract nouns and phrases.

The results of our study do not show any considerable problems in the use of the means of expressing the categories of definiteness and indefiniteness by Croatian young learners of EFL. Nevertheless, we have to bear in mind the fact that indefinite pronouns were used by our participants on very few occasions, and so were quantifiers. Some mistakes concerning possessives and personal pronouns also occurred, mainly caused by the interference from their first language, Croatian. The demonstrative *this* tended to be used when *these* was correct, and the participants did not seem to have fully mastered the use of articles, although their results were better than expected.

In their last year of primary school (Grade 8), our pupils reached the end of the sensitive period for language acquisition (Ellis, 1985, 1997; Medved Krajnović, 2010). Leaving that period learners will continue to be exposed to constant input of new linguistic information (concerning both grammar and vocabulary) and unlike during the sensitive period, they will need explanation, which is not always adequately provided by teachers. Apart from giving explanations, teachers should not neglect the pupils' cognitive abilities, nor their level of acquisition of their mother tongue. They should also be aware of the fact that there are various extrinsic and intrinsic factors that may either encourage or hinder the acquisition of a foreign language, out of which language anxiety is not the least important (Mihaljević Djigunović, 2002, 2006).

In order to gain deeper insight into the process of acquisition of the English markers of definiteness by Croatian EFL learners and to devise strategies for enhancing it, we believe that extensive research at the higher levels of education should also be conducted. It might also be useful in future research to ask learners to explain why they use a particular marker of definiteness or indefiniteness.

References

Bagarić, V. (2003) Što je jezična svjesnost? [What Is Language Awareness]. *Strani jezici* 32 (4), 233–242.
Bagarić, V. (2005) Svjesnost i učenje (stranog) jezika. [Language awareness and foreign language learning]. *Strani jezici* 34 (1), 7–20.
Ellis, R. (1985) *Understanding Second Language Acquisition*. Oxford: Oxford University Press.
Ellis, R. (1997) *Second language Acquisition*. Oxford: Oxford University Press.
Grannis, O.C. (1972) The Definite Article Conspiracy in English. *Language Learning* 22 (2), 275–289.
Hawkins, E.W. (1994) *Awareness of Language*. Cambridge: Cambridge University Press.
Huebner, T. (1983) *A Longitudinal Analysis of the Acquisition of English*. Ann Arbor: Karoma Publishers Inc.
Humphrey, S.J. (2007) Acquisition of the English article system: Some preliminary findings. *Nagoya University of Foreign Studies Journal of School of Foreign languages* 32 (2), 301–325.
Kałuza, H. (1963) Teaching the English article to speakers of Slavic. *Language Learning* 13 (2), 113–24.
Lyons, C. (1999) *Definiteness*. Cambridge: Cambridge University Press.
Master, P. (1990) Teaching the English Articles as a Binary System. *TESOL Quarterly* 24 (2), 461–478.
Medved Krajnović, M. (2010) *Od jednojezičnosti do višejezičnosti [From monolingualism to plurilingualism]*. Zagreb: Laykam international.
Mihaljević Djigunović, J. (2002) *Strah od stranoga jezika [Foreign language anxiety]*. Zagreb: Naklada Ljevak.
Mihaljević Djigunović, J. (2006) Beyond Language Anxiety. *Studia Romnica et Anglica Zagrabiensia* 49, 201–212.
Pranjković, I. (2000) *Izražavanje neodređenosti/određenosti imenica u hrvatskom jeziku [Expressing the indefiniteness/definiteness of nouns in Croatian]*. Proceedings of the conference *Riječki filološki dani* (pp. 343–349). Rijeka.
Tarone, E. and Parrish, B. (1989) Task- related variation in interlanguage: The case of articles. *Language Learning* 38 (1), 21–44.

Trenkić, D. (2000) The acquisition of English articles by Serbian speakers. PhD thesis, University of Cambridge.
Trenkić, D. (2002) Form–meaning connections in the acquisition of English articles. In S. Foster-Cohen, T. Ruthenberg and M.-L. Poschen (eds) *EUROSLA Yearbook* (Vol. 2, pp. 115–133). Amsterdam/Philadelphia: John Benjamins Publishing Company.
Trenkić, D. (2007) Variability in second language article production: Beyond the representational deficit vs. processing constraints debate. *Second Language Research* 23 (3), 289–327.
Trenkić, D. (2008) The representation of English articles in second language grammars: Determiners or adjectives? *Bilingualism: language and Cognition* 11 (1), 1–18.
Zergollern-Miletić, L. (2008) Određenost i neodređenost u engleskom i hrvatskom jeziku. [Definiteness and indefiniteness in English and Croatian]. PhD thesis, University of Zagreb.
Zergollern-Miletić, L. (2009) The categories of definiteness and indefiniteness as a problem in translating from Croatian into English and vice versa. In M. Cichonska (ed.) *Kategorie gramatyczne i semantyczne a pragmayczne w językach słowiańskich [Grammatical, semantic and pragmatic categories in slavonic languages]* (pp. 70–80). Katowice: Instytyt Filologii Słowiańskiej, Uniwersytet Śląski.
Zergollern-Miletić, L. (2010a) Percepcija odnosa engleskoga člana i diskursa [Perception of the relationship between the English article and discourse]. In V. Karabalić, M. AleksaVarga and L. Pon (eds) *Discourse and Dialogue: Theories, Research Methods and Application* (pp. 371–381). Osijek: Croatian Applied Linguistics Society.
Zergollern- Miletić, L. (2010b) English Articles Revisited. In R. Lugossy, M. Lehmann and J. Horváth (eds) *Empirical Studies in Applied Linguistics 2010* (pp. 165–173). Pécs: Lingua Franca Csoport.

5 Present Tense Development in 11- to 13-Year-Old EFL Learners

Marta Medved Krajnović and
Irena Kocijan Pevec

Introduction

One of the basic aims in the early stages of teaching English as a foreign language (EFL) is the acquisition of constructions which express present, or more precisely, the acquisition of the English Present Simple (PS) and Present Continuous (PC) tenses. Learners are introduced to these structures quite early, and they practice them a lot, but even at the advanced levels of EFL learning, many learners encounter difficulties with PS and PC and make functional and formal errors in spoken production. What are the causes of these errors, and is it possible to explain them by means of a cognitive-grammar and usage-based approach, as well as some second language acquisition (SLA) postulates? This is what we will try to explore on the pages to come.

Cognitive Approaches to Language and Language Ability

Cognitive linguistics looks at language as a complex symbolic system which reflects the human conceptual system. We code and express our thoughts by using linguistic symbols which have definite form and meaning. Symbolic grammatical units or constructions represent linguistic expressions of conceptual units (Croft, 2007; Croft & Cruse, 2004; Fillmore & Kay, 1993; Goldberg, 1995; Lakoff, 1987; Langacker, 1987). The process of conceptualization can be performed in different ways and is determined by various cognitive processes, as well as by a speaker's communicative intention. Repeated single uses of certain linguistic symbols give rise to conventional constructions which consequently form a symbolic linguistic system. Tomasello

(2003: 6) calls these repeated single uses *patterns of use*. Patterns of use become *grammatical constructions* through the process of *grammaticalisation* (Croft & Cruse, 2004; Langacker, 1987; Radden & Dirven, 2007; Tomasello, 2003).

In addition to the assumptions that linguistic structures emerge from language use and that all grammatical constructions or linguistic units are symbolic in nature, cognitive approaches to language regard language and language ability as belonging to general cognitive abilities. Language processing thus takes place in the central cognitive system and not in an autonomous language processing module, as it is proposed in formal linguistic theories.

The basic general cognitive abilities activated during language processing are *perception, attention, memory,* and *categorisation*. These abilities are evident in numerous cognitive processes and operations, and grouped in various ways by different authors (Croft & Cruse, 2004; Evans & Green, 2006; Langacker, 1987, 2008; Radden & Dirven, 2007). For the research presented in this chapter, **categorization** is the most relevant of the above-mentioned cognitive abilities.

Cognitive linguists base linguistic categorization on a psychological prototype theory whose main assumption is that conceptual categories are the result of perception and the subjective process of conceptualisation (Lakoff, 1987). This view of categorization supposes that not all the members of a category have the same status, and that there is often a member, called a *prototype*, which is the best representative of a category, while all other members have more or less common distinctive features (Croft & Cruse, 2004; Lakoff, 1987; Radden & Dirven, 2007; Taylor 2004). Many conceptual categories are also laid down in language as linguistic categories (Radden & Dirven, 2007: 3). Cognitive approaches to the linguistic system stress that categories also exist in phonology, morphology, syntax, etc., as well as in the lexicon, where they are the most obvious because of the overlapping of conceptual and linguistic categories. This chapter will later discuss prototypicality, which can be noticed in perfective and imperfective processes in the English language. It will be postulated that prototypicality influences the success in the acquisition of the English present constructions acquired by EFL learners.

Linguistic system in cognitive grammar

In his theory of cognitive grammar, Langacker (1987, 1991, 2008) offers a cognitive view of the grammatical subsystem, that is to say, grammatical units. His minute analysis of conceptual and grammatical phenomena shows that grammatical meanings can be expressed by various grammatical units (e.g. countable-uncountable nouns, perfective-imperfective aspect, passive-active voice) which are at the same time grounded in the external world phenomena perceived by people in different ways and therefore are coded in language differently. Cognitive linguists claim that all linguistic units that possess either content meaning or schematic meaning code the external reality through the following concepts: TIME, SPACE, FORCE-DYNAMICS (Langacker, 1987). In his model, Langacker divides the linguistic system into two broad basic categories of linguistic units called *nominal and relational predications*. Nominal predications refer to 'things', whose symbolic structures are categorized as nouns. Relational predications consist of *temporal* and *atemporal relations*. Atemporal relations refer to adjectives, adverbs, and prepositions, while temporal relations refer to processes and are coded by verbs (Langacker, 1987: 214).

Conceptualisation of time according to cognitive grammar

The basic feature of the TIME domain is movement, which entails dynamics in changing the scene observed by the viewer-speaker. Langacker calls these dynamics a **process** (Langacker, 1987: 244–265) and defines it as a series of relations whose evolution in conceived time is scanned sequentially (Langacker, 1991: 194). The processes are grammatically expressed by verbs, and they can be divided into two basic categories: perfective and imperfective. Real or prototypical processes are perfective because they involve a change in time, while imperfective processes consist of states which are identical, i.e. there are no changes in time (e.g. *have, believe, love, surround*). The differences in meaning entail grammatical differences, too. However, it is very important to mention that Langacker stresses that the 'perfective'–'imperfective' dichotomy does not imply two distinct and closed categories but, on the contrary, a flexible categorization with more or less prototypical processes.

According to Langacker (1987) all perfective processes are bounded in time, which means that they carry information about the beginning and end of an activity. Apart from boundedness, it is important to mention a characteristic which refers to an inherent end or final point of a process and which is called **telicity**. Sometimes a bounded process can be either telic or atelic. For example, the perfective process in the sentence *She cooked lunch.* is both bounded and telic, which means that cooking has a conclusive end-point, while the sentence *She cuddled her son.* provides an example of a bounded but atelic process, since the verb *cuddle* lacks a conclusive end-point. Another important characteristic of perfective processes is replicability, which implies that it is possible to repeat or replicate a completed activity. According to Langacker, imperfective processes are unbounded and non-replicable because of the absence of change in the time frame. The irreplicability criterion provides imperfective processes with a holistic (i.e. homogeneous) character, which means that the component states are identical, and the situation is viewed as constant, with no changes occurring during the time segment. The temporal profile of imperfectives can be expanded or contracted, which ensures its coincidence with the time of speaking. That is why imperfective processes are referred to in the English simple present and cannot be referred to in progressive constructions; in fact, Langacker claims (1991: 206) that only real, prototypical perfective processes can be referred to in a progressive construction. However, there are many ambivalent verbs whose perfective or imperfective meaning is construed according to the situation, or 'grounding process'. Thus, simple and progressive constructions are used to make various aspectual construals possible.

Cognitive linguists see **aspect** as a grammatical form used by a speaker to express his specific view of the temporal structure of a situation (Radden & Dirven, 2007: 176–177). The speaker's view is closely associated with a cognitive operation of perception, and it can be depicted metaphorically as a viewing frame, which can be restricted or maximal. If we perceive and conceptualize a situation externally and in its entirety, the viewing frame is maximal, and events are bounded and expressed by a non-progressive grammatical construction (e.g. *Mary found a job.*), formally a simple verb. On the other hand, the restricted viewing frame is characteristic of a situation seen internally, in progression, with implied boundaries (e.g. *John is looking for a job.*). Such unbounded events are expressed in the progressive aspect. The progressive grammatical construction used in English consists of the auxiliary verb *to be* and the inflectional marker *-ing*.

Tense

The analysis of perfective and imperfective processes and temporal relations shows that in cognitive grammar traditional grammatical notions such as verb, tense, and aspect are regarded as related phenomena and their main connection is the construal of meaning. A starting point for the construal of meaning is the pragmatic grounding of an utterance, which means that the description of a scene will be defined by the circumstances of the speech act (time, place, participants). The fundamental function of tenses is to ground a situation in time from the speaker's viewpoint. The moment of speaking serves as the deictic centre and allows the speaker to refer to three time spheres: the present time sphere, the past time sphere (as the time lying behind the speaker) and the future time sphere (as the time lying ahead of the speaker). These three time spheres are described as deictic times and are expressed in English by simple tenses (Radden & Dirven, 2007: 201, 204).

According to Langacker (2001: 259–260), the essence of the present is immediacy to the speech event. Therefore, the real present tense in English is present simple (PS), while the progressive construction, traditionally called present continuous (PC), is an aspectual construction because its grammatical marker, the morpheme *-ing*, cannot conceptualize a profiled process in relation to the moment of speaking. It merely carries the information about the inner structure of the process, and it is actually an auxiliary verb which grounds a situation in time. The only tense in English which possesses a grammatical marker (zero or *-s/es* morpheme) grounding a situation in the speech time is PS. However, the problem with PS is that there are only a limited number of verbs expressing an event which coincides with the moment of speaking (e.g. *order, promise, pronounce*), while, with most other verbs, the progressive construction is necessary to express that meaning. Therefore, many authors regard English PS as a problematic tense, but Radden and Dirven (2007: 208–211) offer a convincing explanation of both PS and PC constructions.

To conclude, although there are a number of uses of English PS in which a speech act coincides with the evolution of the event, there is an array of perfective verbs which have to undergo the process of imperfectivization through a progressive construction in order to express an event coincident with the speech act. These cognitive explanations of the progressive and simple present will be the starting point in the analysis of the use of the above-mentioned constructions in the speech production of Croatian 11- to 13-year-old EFL learners.

It is also interesting to mention that in the Croatian language tense and aspect cannot be separated, which can be seen even in a traditional grammatical analysis (Silić & Pranjković, 2007). Like other Slavic languages, Croatian is a highly inflected language, so both tense and aspect are morphologically marked. In most verbs, perfective aspect is marked by special prefixes or suffixes, although there are a certain number of verbs which possess both perfective and imperfective meaning. The present construction, which expresses events coincident with the moment of speaking, has present morphological markers and can be formed with imperfective verbs only. This construction is called 'absolute present'. The present construction using perfective verbs expresses meanings which can be referred to as 'relative present' (Silić & Pranjković, 2007), such as repetitive present activity, timeless present, future activity, or historical present (used to report about past events). However, the morphological markers of Croatian present constructions are the same for both imperfective and perfective verbs.

Cognitive approaches to second language acquisition

Cognitivists believe that, since language acquisition and use is determined by psychological, neurobiological, and social processes, an interdisciplinary approach is needed in order to research both first and second language acquisition (Ellis, 2008). However, the most prominent theory of language acquisition developed by cognitivists themselves is *usage theory,* or *emergentism,* which claims that language develops through spontaneous use (Barlow & Kemmer, 2000; Ellis, 2003, 2008; Tomasello, 2003, 2007). Although the differences between the first and second language processes are significant, cognitivists still believe they have much in common and can be compared (Ellis, 2003, 2008; MacWhinney, 2005, 2008), since in both cases language learners have the same goal: they have to learn how to extract language patterns from the language they are exposed to and how to make use of these patterns in order to express themselves and communicate. Language learners do this by employing their general, non-language-specific learning mechanisms.

Cognitivists believe that all language constructions can be described as consisting of language function, language form, and conceptual structure. In other words, language constructions are linguistic units in which function-to-form mapping occurs, and the role of the language learner is to appropriately connect certain functions to certain linguistic forms (Goldberg, 1995, 2003, 2006; Taylor, 1998, 2002; Tomasello, 1992, 2003). This is done by employing different psychological processes: noticing, attention focusing, associative learning of strings, generalization, categorization based on prototypes, implicit and explicit learning, automatization. These processes are in the focus of cognitivists' research, and it can be said that some hypotheses about how they connect with different characteristics of language input in the process of language development have been confirmed (Dabrowska, 2004; Dabrowska & Lieven, 2005; Diesel & Tomasello, 2000, 2005; Slobin, 1985); however, more quality research is needed, especially in second language acquisition contexts.

The features of language input that influence the development of constructions are the frequency of use of certain constructions, their functional and formal complexity, and the level at which competent speakers of a language adapt their speech to the language learner/user.

Frequently using certain constructions positively influences their acquisition and can be measured in two ways: by token frequency and type frequency. **Token frequency** relates to the number of instances of use of a certain linguistic unit (phonological, morphological, lexical) in language input. For example, English irregular verbs in the simple past tense have different token frequencies: the verb form *went* has high frequency, while the verb form *knelt* is used much less often, which means that both first and second language learners will acquire *went* faster and more easily than *knelt*.

Type frequency refers to the number of occurrences of a certain pattern in language input. A pattern represents a combination of linguistic units at different levels (phonological, morphological, syntactic, and lexical). An example can be taken from the morphological level: the pattern of simple past construction in English. The combination of the stem + suffix −(e)d (*watch–watched, live–lived*) is a much more common type than the change of the middle vowel (*know–knew; blow–blew*), which allows children and second language learners to perceive the first type more clearly and acquire it faster. When a combination of high-frequency types and high frequency-tokens is present in language input, the acquisition of a certain construction and the process of its generalisation is made easier (Goldberg & Casenhiser, 2008; Lieven & Tomasello, 2008). Furthermore, frequent repetition of a construction lowers the effort of its processing, which also contributes to easier acquisition (Goldberg & Casenhiser, 2008). These findings come from first language acquisition research, but high type and token frequency, as well as the nature of language input, play a significant role in second language acquisition, too (Bybee, 2008; Ellis, 2003, 2008).

As already stated, cognitivists believe that, while acquiring constructions in their first language, children use their general language learning mechanisms. In the early stages of acquisition, children start recognizing patterns in the input and memorizing smaller linguistic units, the so-called chunks. They also develop the ability to predict what unit will follow in a certain sequence. The knowledge of these sequences in adult native speakers is present at all levels and makes automatized language production possible. In the early stages of learning, children memorize the most frequent patterns, which allows for certain automaticity in speech already at the age of 2–3. However, at that stage children still lack the ability to creatively use speech characterized by abstract grammatical patterns. It seems that this creative aspect develops in children after the age of four, when they start creating syntagmatic categories (e.g. sentence word order in English) by analysing input and then abstracting regularities from it. In first language acquisition, children usually organize these schematic constructions around a prototypical member of a category and similar processes have also been documented in second language acquisition

However, second language learners/users rarely master the second/foreign language to the native speaker level. Therefore, cognitivists believe that an interdisciplinary approach and longitudinal research taking into account the level of learner cognitive development, the role of the first and previously learned second languages (Ringbom, 2007), the nature of input, and other factors is a necessary prerequisite for better and deeper insight into the specific nature of second language acquisition (Ellis & Robinson, 2008). Cognitively-oriented second language researchers also often take into account corpus linguistics analyses (Biber *et al.*, 1998; Biber *et al.*, 1999; Hoey, 2005; McEnery & Wilson, 1996; Sinclair, 1991, 2004) since the analysis of second language learners' speech production – i.e. of language users' interlanguage – is very important for the formulation and testing of hypotheses about second language development.

Interlanguage and Crosslinguistic Influence

Interlanguage is a complex linguistic system that learners create in their attempt to produce utterances in the target language (Selinker, 1972, 1992). It is a dynamic system that changes with the level of learner proficiency, and errors, developmental stages, and variability are some of its inherent features (Eubank *et al.*, 1995). In our research we concentrated on the interlanguage of Croatian learners of English.

Nowadays, a somewhat traditional term connected with interlanguage is that of language transfer, which primarily denotes the influence of the first language's features on the production of the second language. Language transfer has been studied extensively, and different linguistic theories (structuralism, UG, cognitivism) have offered different explanations for it. Furthermore, over the years, different terms for the same phenomenon have been suggested and used, such as *crosslinguistic influence, linguistic interference, the role of the mother tongue, native language influence, language mixing* (Odlin, 2003). However, in the last decade, and especially because of the development of research into multilingualism, the term *crosslinguistic influence* (proposed already in 1983 by Kellerman & Sharwood Smith) established itself as the most prominent one. Its advantage is that it not only allows for the first language to influence other languages being acquired but also stresses the presence of the influence of other second languages on the one currently being acquired, and a possible influence of the second language on the first (Kellerman & Sharwood Smith, 1986; Odlin, 2008). Crosslinguistic influence is present in all language subsystems, during the processes of both language comprehension and production. In crosslinguistic influence research, which is considerably varied and extensive (Jarvis, 2000; Klein & Perdue, 1993; Pienemann, 1999), cognitively-oriented researchers stress the role of conceptual transfer, saying that the way we conceptualize can significantly influence the process of second language acquisition. Therefore, Pavlenko (Jarvis & Pavlenko, 2008) differentiates between linguistic and conceptual transfer. Linguistic transfer is studied at the phonological, morphosyntactic, semantic, pragmatic and discursive levels, while conceptual transfer is most frequent in the following domains: OBJECTS, EMOTIONS, TIME, SPACE, GENDER, NUMBER, MOVEMENT.

In this chapter we will concentrate on morphosyntactic transfer and the TIME domain.

Morphosyntactic transfer

Morphosyntactic transfer is not as observable as phonological and lexical transfer is, and its effects have often been attributed to other interlanguage processes, such as simplification or overcorrection. However, research shows that interlanguage identifications between bound and free morphemes in the first language and corresponding structures in the second language are very frequent (Collins, 2002; Jarvis & Odlin, 2000; Jarvis & Pavlenko, 2008; Selinker & Lakshamanan, 1992). Morphological transfer can be observed with noun endings and tenses, but also with prepositions. Research on the morphosyntactic influence of the second language on the first is also on the increase (Pavlenko & Jarvis, 2002).

Despite research findings, the influence of the first language verb tense and aspect on the second language acquisition process was neglected for a rather long time (Bardovi-Harlig, 2000). However, Collins' (2002) research on how speakers of French as L1 acquire Present Perfect Simple, and how speakers of English L1 acquire Passé Composé, two formally similar, but semantically different verbal tenses, showed that there is morphosyntactic transfer during tense and aspect acquisition. Collins' research was confirmed by Polunenko's research (2004) on how Russian L1 speakers acquire English as L2. Russian speakers tended to use English past tenses with the verbs whose Russian equivalents were telic, and English progressive tenses with those whose Russian equivalents were atelic.

Conceptual transfer in the time domain

Time is a concept inherent to human cognition, but its perception can be expressed by different linguistic means, which may create difficulties during the second language acquisition process.

According to Pavlenko (in Jarvis & Pavlenko, 2008; Odlin, 2008), there are three main types of difference that can be sources of difficulties. The first type includes differences in the grammatical (tense and aspect) and lexical (adverbs, temporal metaphors) means used in conceptualizing time. The second type is when one language (e.g. English) has grammatically marked time, while the other (e.g. Chinese) has only lexically marked time. The third type of difference that can cause difficulties in second language acquisition is in the way a scene (time, event, context, communicative intention) is grammaticalized. For example, Slavic verbs have morphologically marked aspect, while English verbs do not. Conceptual transfer then occurs when second language users do not mark temporality according to the rules of the language they are acquiring, but according to the rules of their first language. This was confirmed by Pavlenko & Driagina's study (2006), in which native speakers of English acquiring Russian often used atelic instead of telic Russian verbs in order to describe punctual events.

Since Croatian L1 speakers learning EFL have similar difficulties when trying to master English tenses, in this paper we will concentrate on the analysis of morphosyntactic and conceptual transfer in the time domain as a source of variability in Croatian learners' interlanguage.

The Study

Aims

There were two main aims of our study.

The first research aim was to gain insight into the process of mastering linguistic means of expressing present in EFL by 11- to 13-year-old learners. Our initial hypothesis was that greater length of learning (and presupposed higher frequency of use) would positively influence the process.

The second research aim was to gain insight into the individual lexical and morphosyntactic development of our learners' interlanguage, focusing on developmental stages in expressing the present, the relationship between lexical and morphosyntactic development, and instances of morphological and/or conceptual transfer from learner L1 (Croatian). Our initial hypothesis was that there would be a gradual developmental increase in the correctness of the use of PS and PC, that lexical and morphosyntactic development would be interconnected, and that we would find examples of morphosyntactic and conceptual transfer in all three years of research.

Participants and corpus

Our corpus is part of a larger corpus collected within the research project *Acquisition of English from an Early Age: Analysis of Learner Language* (for details see Chapter 1).

For the purposes of our research, we selected 12 pupils from two classes in two project schools. In each grade (5–7), we selected six learners (three girls and three boys) with different levels of language proficiency. One participant (a girl) withdrew from the study after year one, that is, at the end of Grade 5 (G5), and one (a boy) after year two, that is, at the end of Grade 6 (G6). All the participants started learning English in Grade 4 (G4) and were at proficiency level A1 according to CEFR (2001). Towards the end of the study, that is, at the end of Grade 7 (G7), some of them were approaching level A2.

Instruments and procedure

In order to elicit learners' oral production, a semi-structured interview based on a pictures description task was used. The interviewer had a list of questions directly related to a set of pictures and some personal questions related to the themes in the pictures (home, family life, holidays, free time). All the participants were asked the same questions, but the interviewer was allowed to ask some additional questions in order for the interview to run more smoothly. The chosen picture descriptions were supposed to elicit the use of present continuous, while the personal questions were designed to elicit the use of the present simple. The interviews were done individually and lasted from 10 to 15 minutes. Each interview was recorded and transcribed using the CHAT (*Codes for Human Analysis of Transcripts*) conventions and coded for further analysis using CLAN (*Computerized Language Analysis*), both of which today are standard tools for analysing children's and second language learners' speech. In the analysis of our results, we used the programs FREQ (Frequency) and MLU (Mean Length of Utterance). FREQ calculates the frequency of particular words and the type-token ratio, while MLU calculates the total number of morphemes and utterances, and the mean length of the number of morphemes per utterance, which is an indicator of syntactic development.

The interviews were conducted at the end of G5, G6, and G7, which means after the second, third, and fourth year of institutionalized English language learning, so we could compare the participants' lexical and morphosyntactic development over three consecutive years.

Method of data analysis

Both quantitative and qualitative data analyses were performed.

Lexical diversity and the mean length of utterance were calculated with the use of the CLAN programs FREQ and MLU, and the ratio between the number of correct instances and the number of attempted instances of both simple and progressive present tense use was calculated and expressed in percentages. Qualitative analysis was done along the principles of error analysis.

In order to gain insight into each learner's individual development, learner profiles consisting of the following quantitative data were constructed: total number of utterances, total number of morphemes, MLU, type-token ratio (lexical diversity)[1] and the ratio between correct and attempted instances[2] of English present tense use.

These parameters allowed us to show how learner utterances became longer and more complex, how the lexis became more complex and varied, and what the increase in the correct use of English present tenses was, i.e. they helped us gain insight into both the lexical and the grammatical development of the participants in this study. Based on these data, individual learner profiles were made.

In order to get a better picture of the development of present tenses use for all 12 learners in the sample, instances of incorrect use of the present simple and present continuous were analysed. First we calculated the frequency of erroneous uses in G5, G6, and G7; then we made a distinction between formal and functional errors, and discussed possible sources of errors.

Results and Discussion

Individual learner profiles

In the tables below, individual learner data are presented. The first column shows the grade, the second column shows the total number of utterances[3] per interview, the third column presents the total number of morphemes, the fourth column lists the mean length of utterance, i.e. the average number of morphemes per utterance, and the fifth column presents the type/token ratio. Columns six and seven present the ratios of correct instances to attempted instances for PS and PC use.

School 1

As data in Table 5.1 show, Ana shows constant progress. The number of utterances in G5 is higher than the number of utterances in G6 and G7, which could be explained by the general tendency on the part of learners to use greater numbers of shorter utterances in the beginning stages of learning. The MLU and type/token ratio data show constant improvement, and there is absolute correctness in the use of PS. A slightly lower correctness can be seen in the use of PC in G6, which can be explained in two ways. First of all, the overall number of utterances in G6 is the highest, so the possibility of errors occurring is also higher. Secondly, this could be an example of the U-shaped curve of learner interlanguage development, where, in the process of grammatical development, there is a temporary backsliding in the level of correctness due to the restructuring of grammatical knowledge (Kellerman, 1987).

With Iva (see Table 5.2) we can also observe a decrease in the number of utterances and an increase in the number of morphemes as competence progresses, meaning that a higher number of shorter utterances is replaced by a lower number of longer utterances. What falls outside predictions is that the type-token ratio is better in G5 and G6 than in G7; however, as already explained, this is probably due to a particular question in the interview that asked the learners to describe the house in the picture ('Can you tell me everything you see in the bathroom/bedroom/living-room?'), which resulted in Iva using *This is a ...* construction a lot, which lowered lexical diversity values. All other data (MLU, correctness in the use of present constructions) show that this is a learner with a very good command of English.

Table 5.1 Ana

Grade	No. of utterances	No. of morphemes	MLU	Type/token ratio	Present simple	Present continuous
5	101	245	2.426	0.472	24/24	10/11
6	87	315	3.621	0.425	34/34	12/15
7	89	435	4.888	0.314	55/55	6/6

Table 5.2 Iva

Grade	No. of utterances	No. of morphemes	MLU	Type/token ratio	Present simple	Present continuous
5	129	341	2.643	0.384	20/21	8/9
6	102	318	3.118	0.397	22/22	12/12
7	86	369	4.393	0.241	46/46	5/6

Table 5.3 Marko

Grade	No. of utterances	No. of morphemes	MLU	Type/token ratio	Present simple	Present continuous
5	133	589	4.429	0.272	63/64	13/18
6	135	746	5.526	0.381	65/65	16/16
7	166	1024	6.271	0.268	112/112	2/2

All the data in Table 5.3 indicate that here is a case of a communicatively very proficient English language learner, in terms of both the amount of language produced and grammatical correctness. The only data showing slightly lower values is the type/token ratio, and this is due to Marko's frequent repetition of the constructions *There is/are ..., This is a ...,* and *I/you can – infinitive ...* while describing pictures or activities. An interesting point to observe is that this high level of communicative proficiency can be related to the learner's overall communicativeness, because when asked, 'Do you have any hobbies?', his answer was, 'Yes, I like to talk. That's my favourite hobby. Just talking'.

Ivan's English language proficiency is also very high, which can be seen from all the data in Table 5.4, and primarily from the MLU values and the correctness in the use of PS and PC. In terms of the tenses there was only one functional mistake in G6, when PS was used instead of PC. We could say that this is a learner who already in G5 had a high level of proficiency in English, which continuously increased.

Petar (see Table 5.5) was not tested in grade seven, but all the data from G5 and G6 indicate a learner who had difficulty speaking English, his results being even worse in G6 with a lower number of utterances and morphemes, a lower value for MLU, and incorrect use of present tenses. The number of correct instances of PS use was lower in G5 than in G6, while in G6 there were only three instances of correct PC use. These are probably examples of memorized chunks, because the learner used *They're eating.,* and then with the same verb but a different subject he omitted the auxiliary verb: **This people eating.* It also has to be pointed out that the type/token ratio data are

Table 5.4 Ivan

Grade	No. of utterances	No. of morphemes	MLU	Type/token ratio	Present simple	Present continuous
5	123	599	4.870	0.356	63/63	17/17
6	92	492	5.348	0.382	37/37	16/17
7	216	1141	5.282	0.305	67/67	5/5

Table 5.5 Petar

Grade	No. of utterances	No. of morphemes	MLU	Type/token ratio	Present simple	Present continuous
5	149	371	2.490	0.367	18/22	0/11
6	85	252	2.965	0.476	8/15	3/10

Table 5.6 Lovorka

Grade	No. of utterances	No. of morphemes	MLU	Type/token ratio	Present simple	Present continuous
5	114	398	3.491	0.389	43/44	5/7

not valid because the learner often used Croatian phrases in his English constructions.

Lovorka (Table 5.6) was interviewed only in G5, so we cannot comment on her interlanguage development.

School 2

In some aspects of his performance, Igor (see Table 5.7) shows progress over the three years, while some values remain constant. Improvement can be observed in the MLU, which indicates more complex syntax, while the number of utterances is highest in G6, when the learner talked a bit more about his personal experiences than in other two interviews. In G6 there were also a significant amount of functional errors in the use of PC in the sense that the learner used imperfective instead of perfective constructions. It seems he was relying heavily on memorized chunks which can be observed in the type/token ratio, which remains constant over the years, but shows lower lexical diversity when compared with the other learners.

As can be seen in Table 5.8, there are several interesting aspects in the data for Anita in G6. That is when the lowest number of utterances, the lowest MLU value, and many errors in the use of present tenses were recorded, but also the highest lexical diversity. This is probably because in

Table 5.7 Igor

Grade	No. of utterances	No. of morphemes	MLU	Type/token ratio	Present simple	Present continuous
5	75	366	4.880	0.373	25/26	9/13
6	81	473	5.840	0.368	23/24	15/25
7	71	419	5.901	0.360	31/31	5/7

Table 5.8 Anita

Grade	No. of utterances	No. of morphemes	MLU	Type/token ratio	Present simple	Present continuous
5	59	209	3.542	0.474	7/16	1/8
6	54	169	3.130	0.521	5/16	5/10
7	84	410	4.881	0.361	49/52	1/2

Table 5.9 Zoran

Grade	No. of utterances	No. of morphemes	MLU	Type/token ratio	Present simple	Present continuous
5	63	176	2.794	0.483	8/9	8/8
6	54	213	3.944	0.314	16/16	14/14
7	72	276	3.833	0.417	26/27	5/5

the G6 interview there was a high omission of functional words (e.g. auxiliaries, pronouns) that are normally used extensively in everyday speech and thus make lexical diversity values lower. A significant improvement can be seen in G7, when there was an increase in the number of utterances, in the MLU, and in the correctness of present tense use.

The speech production data for Zoran (see Table 5.9) indicate that he does not produce many utterances, and the ones he produces are rather short during all three years. However, the correctness of the use of the observed structures is almost 100% in all three grades, which is an indicator of good competence, although the small number of longer utterances and low level of lexical diversity indicate frequent repetition of certain morphosyntactic constructions. All in all, we could say that here we have a case of a learner who does not say much, but does it in a grammatically correct way, which makes his communication successful.

The data in Table 5.10 show complete correctness in the use of PC and PC over all three years and a significant improvement in the MLU from G5 to G7. The number of utterances varies slightly, being highest in G6, when Silvija described the pictures in great detail. It might be surprising that the

Table 5.10 Silvija

Grade	No. of utterances	No. of morphemes	MLU	Type/token ratio	Present simple	Present continuous
5	49	179	3.653	0.536	17/17	7/7
6	68	394	5.794	0.368	36/36	15/15
7	62	367	5.919	0.381	33/33	8/8

Table 5.11 Mario

Grade	No. of utterances	No. of morphemes	MLU	Type/token ratio	Present simple	Present continuous
5	90	269	2.989	0.470	12/15	14/15
6	66	266	4.030	0.458	18/18	12/13
7	72	347	4.819	0.386	25/27	3/3

type/token ratio was highest in G5, but a more detailed analysis of the interview shows that this learner, while describing the pictures, went into great detail just naming the objects in the picture and thus increased the lexical diversity values. We could say that here we have a learner who expresses himself in a precise and complex way, which indicates a good level of linguistic and communicative competence.

Mario (see Table 5.11) shows continuous improvement in MLU and high levels of correctness in the use of both present tenses. In the case of PS use in G5 there was one formal error, while the two other errors and both errors in G7 were functional, meaning that PS was used instead of PC. The type/token ratio shows good lexical diversity, and a decrease in its value in G7 is related to the aforementioned problem with one interview question. Altogether, Learner 11 showed a good level of English language oral production within this task.

Sandra (see Table 5.12) was not interviewed in G5, and her results in G6 and G7 illustrate those of a competent speaker of EFL. The very high type/token ratio shows a good command of English vocabulary, while the MLU indicates syntactic complexity. The level of correctness is also high, and some of the errors, e.g. the omission of the auxiliary, can be explained by the fact that while describing the pictures the learner just continued her train of thought and omitted both the subject and the auxiliary. In one utterance the learner used PC instead of PS, probably due to conceptual transfer.

The individual learner profiles tell us a lot about the lexical and grammatical component of the learners' speech. Most of the participants progressed during the three years in all observed categories: the MLU continuously increased, as well as the accuracy of the use of PS and PC, which were all indicators of the increase in the learners' grammatical competence. As for lexical diversity, i.e. the type/token ratio, there were certain

Table 5.12 Sandra

Grade	No. of utterances	No. of morphemes	MLU	Type/token ratio	Present simple	Present continuous
6	69	235	3.406	0.479	15/16	11/16
7	64	299	4.672	0.405	22/23	7/7

inconsistencies which could be explained in several ways. First of all, the technique of a semi-structured interview allowed for higher variation in the use of linguistic means of expression which were repeated more or less often. Secondly, some learners often repeated memorized phrases in order to gain more time to plan their answers, while some used simple, precise, and varied answers, so there was not much repetition. Nevertheless, in 17 out of 32 measurement instances the type/token ratio was between 0.350 and 0.400, which is a very good result. Also, we could observe that lexical diversity, i.e. lexical competence, correlated with grammatical competence because type/token values over 0.400 are present in the learners who had high levels of correctness in their use of the investigated grammatical structures. It was also observed that all the participants from School 1 had significantly higher numbers of utterances than the participants from School 2, while the other data were similar. This is probably due to the nature of the interviewer in School 1, who asked more subquestions.

Entire Sample Results

Quantitative analysis of the use of present tense

After quantitative data indicating lexical and grammatical complexity is presented, an analysis of all the utterances containing English present tenses will be made in order to determine the ratio of their correct and incorrect usage and its change over time. We were interested in whether the level of correctness increases as a result of longer use and, presumably, better entrenchment.

The data will be presented graphically for both schools over three years, separately for PS and PC. One figure (Figures 5.1 and 5.3 for PS and PC, respectively) will present the percentage of correct and incorrect uses for each year, while the other (Figures 5.2 and 5.4 for PS and PC, respectively) will display the number of incorrect and attempted uses. After interpreting the figures, we will qualitatively analyse the examples we took our data from.

What we can see from both schools' figures is that the learners have mastered the use of PS. There is a high percentage of its correct use during all three years (94% and 93% in G5 and G6, increasing to 98% in G7).

The frequency of use of PS can be explained by the structure of the interview, which elicited descriptions of everyday activities and habits, as well as descriptions of pictures with the construction *There is/are*... The small number of errors could be explained by the fact that PS was used mostly in the first person singular, which has simple morphology (no suffix). However, in cases of the use of the third person singular, where the *–s/-es* ending is necessary, not many mistakes were observed. It also has to be pointed out that the highest number of attempted uses was in G7, when there was also the lowest number of mistakes, which also indicates progress.

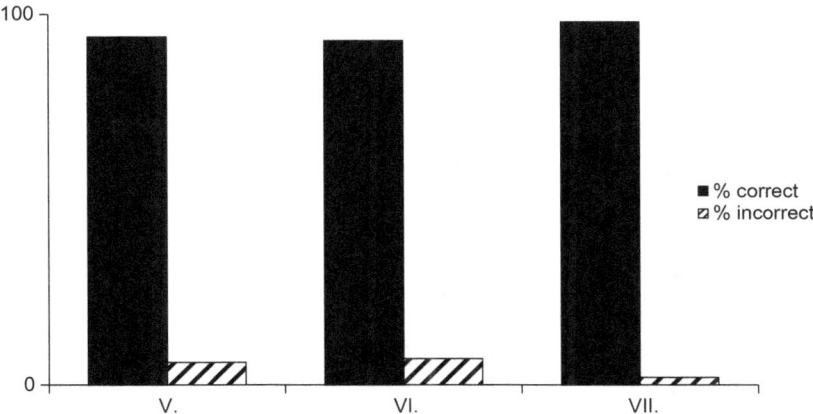

Figure 5.1 Present Simple: Percentage of correct and incorrect use over three years

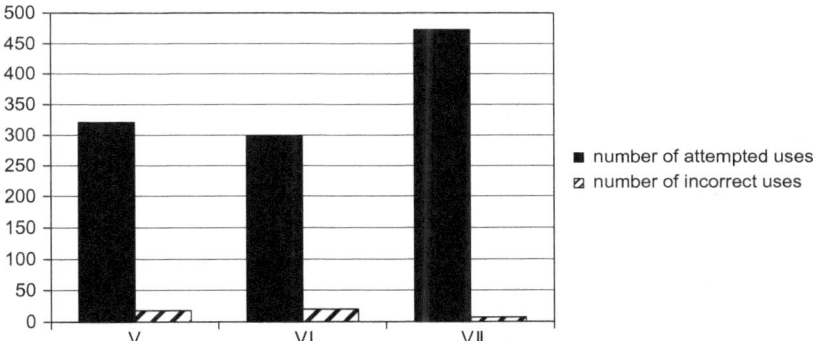

Figure 5.2 Present Simple: Number of attempted and incorrect uses over three years

Figures presenting the use of PC also show progress. The largest number of PC occurrences was in G6 (139 instances of attempted use), while the smallest was in G7 due to the structure of the interview.

Qualitative analysis of the use of present tense

This qualitative analysis of the use of PS and PC will be based on error analysis. The errors will be classified into several groups: errors in form for PS, errors in form for PC, and errors in function (the use of PS instead of PC and vice versa).

Errors in Form

The verb *to be* appears in English in two basic functions: as a lexical verb primarily expressing existence, and as an auxiliary verb in progressive tenses

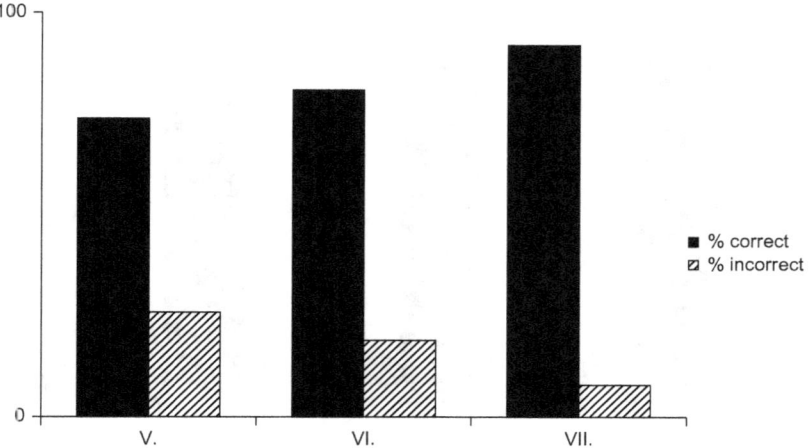

Figure 5.3 Present Continuous: Percentage of correct and incorrect use over three years

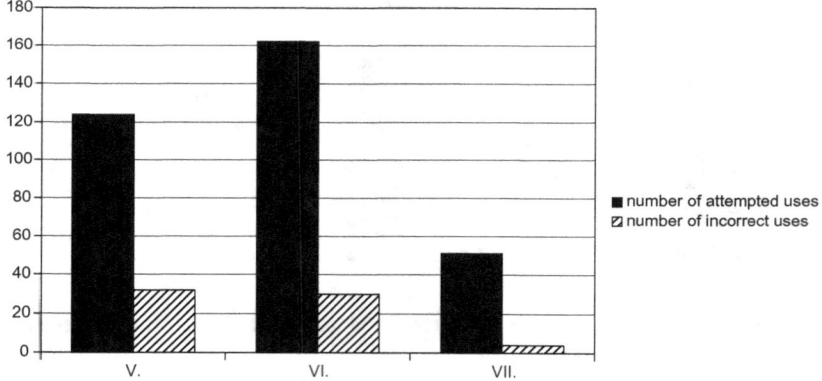

Figure 5.4 Present Continuous: Number of attempted and incorrect uses over three years

and in the passive. Here we are interested in the verb *to be* both as a lexical verb in PS and as an auxiliary in PC.

Based on our corpus analysis, we can conclude that our research participants successfully acquired the English verb *to be* in its predicative function as a copula, which can be explained by both conceptual and formal transfer because in this function it coincides with the function of the verb *to be* in the participants' first language (Kalogjera, 1970). The participants successfully acquired all three forms (*am, are, is*) in both positive and negative form, and in the first and third person singular and plural. Because of the nature of our corpus, we did not obtain data of its use in the second person singular and

Present Tense Development in 11- to 13-Year-Old EFL Learners   99

Table 5.13 Present Simple: Errors in form

GRADE 5	GRADE 6	GRADE 7
*There is two big…	*There's many boo… shelves with books.	*My mum don't like it.
*My hobbies is badminton and cello.	*In my house lives six people.	*In the cupboard there are some medicine.
*There are central park…	*When she come home, she …	*There is c carpets in the …
*There is my friends.		*There is toys and, …
*There is three people.		*There's some umbrellas in the can for the umbrellas.
*There is two tree.		*… and there's two windows.
*Er, wash, wash baby.		*There are my stuff.
*And one eat.		*I haven't a window…
*One wash, wash her baby.		*I haven't a lamp…
*One wash her face.		

plural. The participants also used two types of contractions: *It's not very small.; It isn't very big.*

The most frequent type of error while using the verb *to be* as a copula happened in the phrase *There is/are …*, mostly when the singular form of the verb was used with a plural noun: **There is a carpets.; *There's two windows.* This was probably due to the transfer of training where learners experience *There is …* structure more often than *There are …*. However, we also found two examples of the use of the verb in plural with the noun in singular: **There are medicine.; *There are my stuff.*

According to cognitive grammar, both of these nouns are unbounded, which indicates that they are non-countable and should agree with the verb in singular, but at the same time they are heterogeneous because they indicate a group of separate items which then learners interpret as a grammatical plural and accordingly use a plural verb form. Moreover, these nouns appear in plural form in the learners' first language.

While using lexical verbs in the present simple form (see Table 5.13), our participants made only a few errors, probably due to the fact that the morphology of English PS is very easy. The majority of participants mastered the use of the suffix –*s*/-*es*, too; however, with weaker learners we found examples of errors even in the third year of research, that is, in G7. In G5, the most frequent omission of the suffix –*s*/*es* was with the verb *wash*, which was probably due to phonological reasons (since the verb already ends with a fricative sound, not –*s* but the less frequent –*es* ending had to be added).

In G6 we found only two examples of formal errors: **When she come home …; *In my house lives six people.*

The error in the first example might be the result of redundancy, since the subject *she* already carries the information about the 3rd person singular, so the learner might unconsciously believe that another indicator of the same, i.e. the suffix –s is not necessary. Also, it might be that this was an example of an occasional mistake, since other data for this particular learner showed the correct use of the 3rd person singular form.

The second example shows the opposite case – the use of the morphological marker for singular with the noun in plural. We might speculate several explanations for this:

- hypercorrection – out of 'fear' not to omit a 'difficult' construction emphasized a lot during the process of teaching, the learner started exaggerating in its use;
- the second reason might be that this structure is actually frequent in input, and therefore becomes well entrenched;
- the third possible reason might have to do with the word order which in this case was wrong (CVS instead of more neutral SVC), the learner instinctively knew it, and actually aligned the verb with the compliment which took the subject position;
- it could also be that we are talking about first language transfer, because the learner used L1 word order, and in the learner's L1 the verb would in this case be in the 3rd person singular form.

When using the negative form in the first person singular and plural and in the third person plural, the learners did not make errors. However, in the third person singular, even better learners made mistakes with the negative construction such as in **My mum don't like it*.

This can perhaps be interpreted as an error due to the entrenchment of *I don't like it*, a phrase that learners use a lot, or a result of the redundancy of the morphological marker in terms of communicative efficiency.

Furthermore, we observed the developmental error in the use of the negative PS form of the verb *to have*. Due to learning new structures, specifically the structure *haven't got*, instead of constructing the negative form with the auxiliary *do,* some learners started using the negation *haven't* without *got:*

e.g. **I haven't a window.*

It has to be stressed that a larger number errors of this kind have been observed with the learners whose other parameters of the linguistic competence were lower too.

In PC, the verb *to be* is in the function of the primary auxiliary which expresses temporality, i.e. the present, while the present participle of the lexical verb expresses the continuous aspect. Despite the formal differences between the learners' L1 Croatian and L2 English, the majority of the participants have acquired the English PC, which is in line with the previous research (e.g. Dulay & Burt, 1974) into the acquisition of English as a first or

Table 5.14 Present Continuous: Errors in Form

GRADE 5	GRADE 6	GRADE 7
*Playing with ball.	*They're watch.	*In other pictures somebody sleep.
*Talking and playing.	*He reading.	*He read newspaper, newpapers.
*Sittin, playing with some people.	*He walking.	*He watch some…
*Girls, boys playing a football.	*Playing something.	*Boy are brushing his teeth.
*We going around the school.	*Play.	*The girl are, is taking bath.
*People are? They? Playing with her, er, him.	*This people eating.	
*A man's play football.	*This man watching tv.	
*Boys with ball, football.	*This man sleep.	
*'Mama' cooking.	*This man sleeping.	
*Dad have a shower.	*This man read and this man, these people's talking.	
*Son write the homework.		
*Ne, draw a homework.		
*Cat eat.		
*(They) talk.		
*The man play with his dog.		
*'Mama', mum, er, write a book.		
*Play football.		
*And here play with dog.		
*Pa this is one man who watch (2) watch this family.		

second language which shows that the *–ing* construction is one of the first to be mastered. However, less proficient learners from our sample experienced difficulties with this form even in G7, as can be seen from Table 5.14.

The most common type of error was auxiliary omission, while the first example of erroneous concordance between the subject and the verb was recorded in G6. However, we might speculate here that we are talking about a mistake, not a systematic error as a result of utterance encoding – the participant started the utterance with a singular subject (*this man*) and then decided in mid sentence to continue with a plural subject (*these people*).

The examples *Boy are brushing his teeth.* and *The girl are, is taking bath.* came from the same subject in G7. Since in the second example we have self-correction, we could talk about the variability in this learner's interlanguage.

In addition to these errors related to the auxiliary *to be*, we also observed formal errors related to the main, lexical verb, especially frequent in G5 with weaker learners. They tend to use the basic form of the verb, without *–ing* or an auxiliary, which could be misinterpreted as the use of PS instead of PC, but the surrounding linguistic context implies that the learner actually wanted to use the continuous form, but had not yet fully/systematically acquired it. Therefore, we can refer to this as a developmental error here.

Functional Errors

The participants made very few mistakes when they used PS instead of PC (see Table 5.15). In the entire corpus, in G5 this happened only nine out of 131 times when the participants' utterances required the use of PC. In G6 it happened five out of 175 times; in G7 four out of 59 times. All these utterances were used in the picture description task and were prompted by the interviewer's question that contained PC, but still in some cases the answer was in PS, probably due to the stronger entrenchment of that construction.

Qualitative analysis of the use of PS and PC shows that functional errors mostly happen in 'free speech', meaning when the learners are describing their own experience and use PC instead of PS (see Table 5.16). This use can certainly be explained by conceptual transfer caused by differences in how perfective and imperfective processes are expressed in English and Croatian. In Croatian, telic or atelic aspect is expressed lexically, with the main verb, while in English this aspect is grammaticalized and expressed by the auxiliary *to be*.

So Croatian learners perceive English PC as a construction which expresses an action/process that has not reached its final point, an unbounded

Table 5.15 Examples of use of Present Simple instead of Present Continuous

GRADE 5	GRADE 6	GRADE 7
*Er, wash, wash baby.	*Mum wri, writes something.	*He sleeps.
*And one eat.	*Mum brings lunch.	*He reads something.
*One wash, wash her baby.	*She slee, he sleep.	*She reads on floor.
*One wash her face.	*He read.	*… and one guy, he reads newspapers.
*She cooks.	*This man brings the eat, food on the table.	
*She washes her face.		
*They play football.		
*They talk.		
*This boy take a bath.		

Table 5.16 Examples of use of Present Continuous instead of Present Simple

Grade 5	Grade 6	Grade 7
*She's learning. (the question was: 'What does she do?')	*I'm watching TV. (the question was: 'What do you usually do?'	No examples.
*We're playing there.	*She is working.	
*We, we're running () down the street.		
*I'm playing football.	*Sometimes I'm eating in the living room. (self-correction: I eat.)	
*I'm like, er, I'm skating.	*I'm chatt, I chat. (self-correction)	
*I usually walk by, too, when I'm going to my day activities like…	*She's going late from the work.	
*… and then talking to my friends.	*In summer I'm swimming.	
*I'm going outside my building.	*I'm listening to music.	
*She is not opening her soul to us.	*But I'm writing there homework.	
*She's reading all the time.	*I am, I'm on internet, I'm looking for some pictures.	
*I'm climbing on trees and something like this.	*I'm playing with my BG.	
	*I'm eating lunch and dinner.	
	*I'm playing with my parents sometimes.	
	*My mum is cooking and delivering…	
	*We are there talking or …	
	*If are, we are having a problem, we, we're talking about friends.	
	*I sitting.	
	I playing comp, computer.	
	*I watching tv.	

process where the course of action is important. Therefore they produce most of the errors with verbs that they do not perceive as prototypically imperfective or perfective and in order to stress the imperfective aspect in the former, and avoid the perfective aspect of the latter, they use PC for the situation that they consider atelic and unbounded.

Examples:

*I'm climbing on trees and something like this.
*We, we're running down the street.
*I'm playing football.
*In summer, I'm swimming.
*I'm there writing homework.
*I usually walk by, too, when I'm going to my day activities like...

The last example is especially interesting because here, one of the learners used PS for a verb that he perceived as describing a perfective situation, and PC for a situation where the accent is on the action in progress (unbounded) where the end has not been reached.

We should also mention utterances where the participants would start with PC, prompted by the semantic component of the action that is continuous, but then self-corrected, and used PS. Here are two examples:

*'Sometimes I'm eating in the living room. I eat.' (self-correction)
*'I'm chatt..., I chat.' (self-correction)

On the other hand, while describing the picture, the participants were mostly correct in using PC, which could be explained by several factors. First, they might have been prompted to use PC by the examiner's questions (e.g. *What are the people in the picture doing?*). While this might be true for some participants, examples of the use of PS in picture description tasks show that the structure of the question was not a decisive factor. We got further proof that the structure of the question was not crucial in the examples of wrong use of PC when the input question was in PS (e.g. *'What do you usually do?'* – *'I'm watching TV.'*). So it seems that the use of one of the tenses was prompted more by the entrenchment of the construction, or by how the participant perceived the situation (situation construal) – either as telic or atelic. The entrenchment of PC is probably the result of the emphasis that is put on that construction during the teaching process in G5 and G6. We also have to point out that the greatest number of errors in the use of PC came from one learner, while the others used the form mostly correctly. Unfortunately, due to the structure of the interview in G7, we did not get frequent examples of PC use.

Conclusion

In this chapter we have tried to gain insight into the question of how primary school learners gradually learn to express present actions in English as the first foreign language. We took an interdisciplinary approach in analysing the learners' oral production: from the cognitive theory perspective, i.e. the processes of conceptualization, grammaticalization and emergentism, we tried to explain the use of the present tenses in English. From the second language acquisition perspective, we relied on the phenomenon of crosslinguistic influence and language transfer, and in order to describe the participants' overall communicative competence we relied on the CEFRL model.

In analysing learners' utterances we focused on the errors learners made while conceptualising the present in English. We believe that morphological and conceptual transfer in the TIME domain was the major source of errors in our data/sample. While learning English constructions that conceptualize, i.e. that express the present, primary school learners mostly made errors in using English PC with ambivalent, non-prototypical constructions whose telic or atelic meaning is constructed according to the situation. More concretely, when native speakers of Croatian want to conceptualize a process as imperfective and iterative, they use English PC instead of PS because they identify English PC with the imperfective aspect of verbs in Slavic languages.

In addition to conceptual transfer, we also noted developmental errors, but to a lesser extent. Such errors became less frequent with the number of years of EFL learning. A developmental pattern could also be observed in the sense that, during the first testing, we found many utterances containing holophrases, and learners heavily relied on lexical means in order to express themselves. In the next two years, the use of morphological means of expression increased, as well as the level of correctness, and the expressions became longer and more complex. With some learners we could also observe backsliding, i.e. the U-shaped curve of interlanguage development.

The individual learner data supported the hypothesis that the development of lexis and grammar are interconnected. Quantitative data about lexical diversity, MLU, and the correctness of the use of constructions expressing the present correlate in the majority of cases. In some learners we observed gradual progress in all the observed elements during the three years of study, while in the learners who already had high competence in English in G5, i.e. the first year of testing, there was no major progress, but the correlation exists.

The last level of analysis concerned the hypothesis that the frequency of use of a certain construction/expression affects its entrenchment and the level of correctness of its use. Our corpus is not large enough to confirm this hypothesis, but we did observe that the learners made fewer errors when using the most frequent constructions and did rely heavily on these constructions;

furthermore, the number of errors in production decreased from G5 to G7 thanks to longer exposure and practice of these constructions.

Finally, we could conclude that cognitive theories offer a good framework for the analysis of learner interlanguage during the process of second language acquisition. We believe that our findings based on this limited-scale sample provide insight into how the process of expressing present tense by learners of English as a foreign language develops, and can offer guidance for a future study that would have to be conducted on a larger sample.

Our study might also have implications for the process of teaching English present tense constructions, especially in cases where there is a difference in conceptualising perfective and imperfective processes between L1 and L2. If we know how the constructions are being mastered and which input may be optimal, we can develop teaching material that would support these processes.

Notes

(1) A side note has to be made that in order for the lexical diversity calculation to be valid, texts of similar length have to be compared. The interviews in our research were rather similar in length across the years and the participants, except for the G7 data when one question prompted extensive use of existential *This is / There is*... This affected the overall result in the sense that the overal number of tokens of this type increased, while the number of types was reduced which resulted in lower and less valid results for lexical diversity (especially for some participants).
(2) Instances of attempted use are utterances in which it was clear which structure (PS or PC) the learner wanted to use, regardless of whether its use was grammatically correct or not in that particular context.
(3) According to the cognitivist usage theory, an utterance is a complex linguistic unit which presents a coherent message intended for the interlocutor.

References

Bardovi-Harlig, K. (2000) *Tense and Aspect in Second Language Acquisition: Form, Meaning and Use*. Oxford: Blackwell.
Barlow, M. and Kemmer, S. (2000) *Usage-based Models of Language*. Stanford, CA: CSLI Publications.
Biber, D., Conrad, S. and Reppen, R. (1998) *Corpus Linguistics: Investigating Language Structure and Use*. New York: Cambridge University Press.
Biber, D., Johansson, S., Leech, G., Conrad, S., and Finigan, E. (1999) *Longman Grammar of Spoken and Written English*. Harlow, UK: Pearson Education.
Bybee, J. (2008) Usage-based grammar and second language acquisition. In P. Robinson and N.C. Ellis (eds) *Handbook of Cognitive Linguistics and Second Language Acquisition* (pp. 216–236). New York: Routledge.
Collins, L. (2002) The roles of L1 influence and lexical aspect in the acquisition of temporal morphology. *Language Learning* 52 (1), 43–94.
Croft, W. (2007) Construction grammar. In D. Geeraerts and H. Cuyckens (eds) *The Oxford Handbook of Cognitive Linguistics* (pp. 463–506). Oxford: Oxford University Press.
Croft, W. and Cruse, D.A. (2004) *Cognitive Linguistics*. Cambridge: Cambridge University Press.

Dabrowska, E. (2004) Rules or schemes? Evidence from Polish. *Language and Cognitive Processes* 19 (2), 225–271.
Dabrowska, E. and Lieven, E. (2005) Towards a lexically specific grammar of children's question constructions. *Cognitive Linguistics* 16 (3), 437–474.
Diesel, H. and Tomasello, M. (2000) The development of relative constructions in early child speech. *Cognitive Linguistics* 11 (1/2), 131–152.
Diesel, H. and Tomasello, M. (2005) A new look at the acquisition of relative clauses. *Language* 81 (4), 882–906.
Dulay, H. and Burt, M. (1973) Should we teach children syntax? *Language Learning* 23 (2), 245–258.
Ellis, N.C. (2003) Constructions, chunking, and connectionism: The emergence of second language structure. In C.J. Doughty and M.H. Long (eds) *The Handbook of Second Language Acquisition* (pp. 63–103). London: Blackwell Publishing.
Ellis, N.C. (2008) Usage-based and form-focused language acquisition: The associative learning of constructions, learned attentiona, and the limited L2 endstate. In P. Robinson and N.C. Ellis (eds) *The Handbook of Cognitive Linguistics and Second Language Acquisition* (pp. 372–405). New York: Routledge.
Ellis, N.C. and Robinson, P. (2008) Conclusion: Cognitive linguistics, second language acquisition and L2 instruction – issues for research. In P. Robinson and N.C. Ellis (eds) *The Handbook of Cognitive Linguistics and Second Language Acquisition* (pp. 489–545). New York: Routledge.
Eubank, L., Selinker, L. and Sharwood Smith, M. (1995) *The Current State of Interlanguage*. Amsterdam and Philadelphia: John Benjamins.
Evans, V. and Green, M. (2006) *Cognitive Linguistics: An Introduction*. Edinburgh: Edinburgh University Press.
Fillmore, C.J. and Kay, P. (1993) Construction grammar coursebook. Unpublished manuscript, Department of Linguistics, University of California, Berkeley.
Goldberg, A. (1995) *Constructions: A Construction Grammar Approach to Argument Structure*. Chicago: University of Chicago Press.
Goldberg, A. (2003) Constructions: a new theoretical approach to language. *Trends in Cognitive Science*, 7 (5), 219–224.
Goldberg, A.E. (2006) *Constructions at Work: The Nature of Generalization in Language*. Oxford: Oxford University Press.
Goldberg, A.E. and Casenhiser, D. (2008) Construction learning and second language acquisition. In P. Robinson and N.C. Ellis (eds) *The Handbook of Cognitive Linguistics and Second Language Acquisition* (pp. 197–216). New York: Routledge.
Hoey, M.P. (2005) *Lexical Priming: A New Theory of Words and Language*. London. Routledge.
Jarvis, S. (2000) Semantic and conceptual transfer. *Bilingualism: Language and Cognition* 3 (1), 9–21.
Jarvis, S. and Odlin, T. (2000) Morphological type, spatial reference and language transfer. *Studies in Second Language Acquisition* 22 (4), 535–556.
Jarvis, S. and Pavlenko, A. (2008) *Crosslinguistic Influence in Language and Cognition*. New York: Routledge.
Kalogjera, D. (1970) The Primary Auxiliaries BE, HAVE, DO, and Their Equivalents in Serbo-Croatian. *The Yugoslav Serbo-Croatian-English Contrastive Project. Reports.* 88–105. Zagreb: Zavod za lingvistiku Filozofskog fakulteta Sveučilišta Zagreb.
Kellerman, E. (1987) Aspects of transferability in second language acquisition. Unpublished PhD dissertation, University of Nijmegen.
Kellerman, E. and Sharwood-Smith, M. (1986) *Cross-Linguistic Influence in Second Language Acquisition*. New York: Pergamon Press.
Klein, W. and Perdue, C. (1993) Utterance structures. In C. Perdue (ed.) *Adult Language Acquisition: Cross-Linguistic Perspectives* (Vol. II) (pp. 3–40). Cambridge: Cambridge University Press.

Lakoff, G. (1987) *Women, Fire, and Dangerous Things*. Chicago: The University of Chicago Press.
Langacker, R.W. (1987) *Foundations of Cognitive Grammar (Vol. 1): Theoretical Prerequisites*. Stanford, CA: Stanford University Press.
Langacker, R.W. (1991) *Foundations of Cognitive Grammar (Vol. 2): Descriptive Application*. Stanford, CA: Stanford University Press.
Langacker, R.W. (2001) The English present tense. *English Language and Linguistics* 5 (2), 251–272.
Langacker, R.W. (2008) *Cognitive Grammar: A Basic Introduction*. Oxford: Oxford University Press.
Lieven, E. and Tomasello, M. (2008). Children's first language acquisition from a usage/based persprective. In P. Robinson and N.C. Ellis (eds) *The Handbook of Cognitive Linguistics and Second Language Acquisition* (pp. 168–197). New York: Routledge.
MacWhinney, B. (2005) A unified model of language acquisition. In J.F. Kroll and A.M.B. de Groot (eds) *Handbook of Bilingualism: Psycholinguistic Approaches* (pp. 49–67). New York: Oxford University Press.
MacWhinney, B. (2008) A unified model. In P. Robinson and N.C. Ellis (eds) *The Handbook of Cognitive Linguistics and Second Language Acquisition* (pp. 341–372). New York: Routledge.
McEnery, T. and Wilson, A. (1996) *Corpus Linguistics*. Edinburgh, UK: Edinburgh University Press.
Odlin, T. (2003) Cross-Linguistic Influence. In C.J. Doughty and M.H. Long (eds) *The Handbook of Second Language Acquisition* (pp. 436–486). London: Blackwell Publishing.
Odlin, T. (2008). Conceptual transfer and meaning extensions. In P. Robinson and N.C. Ellis (eds) *Handbook of Cognitive Linguistics and Second Language Acquisition* (pp. 306–341). New York: Routledge.
Pavlenko, A. and Jarvis, S. (2002) Bidirectional transfer. *Applied Linguistics* 23 (2), 190–214.
Pavlenko, A. and Driagina, V. (2006) *Advanced-level Narrative Skills in Russian. A Workbook for Students and Teachers*. State College, PA: Center for Advanced Language Proficiency, Education, and Research.
Pienemann, M. (1999) *Language Processing and Second Language Development*. Amsterdam/Philadelphia: John Benjamins.
Polunenko, A. (2004) *English Past Tense Forms in Russian Speakers' Oral and Written Production*. Unpublished MA thesis, Department of Linguistics, Ohio University.
Radden, G. and Dirven, R. (2007) *Cognitive English Grammar*. Amsterdam and Philadelphia: John Benjamins.
Ringbom, H. (2007) *Cross-linguistic Similarity in Foreign Language Learning*. Clevedon: Mulitlingual Matters.
Robinson, P. (ed.) (2001) *Cognition and Second Language Instruction*. New York: Cambridge University Press.
Selinker, L. (1972) Interlanguage. *International Review of Applied Linguistics* 10 (3), 209–231.
Selinker, L. (1992) *Rediscovering Interlanguage*. London and New York: Longman.
Selinker, L. and Lakshamanan, U. (1992) Language transfer and fossilization: The multiple effects priciples. In S. Gass and L. Selinker (eds) *Language Transfer in Language Learning* (rev. edn.) (pp. 197–216). Amsterdam: John Benjamins.
Silić, J. and Pranjković, I. (2007) *Gramatika hrvatskoga jezika [Grammar of the Croatian language]*. Zagreb: Školska knjiga.
Sinclair, J. (1991) *Corpus, Concordance, Collocation*. Oxford: Oxford University Press.
Sinclair, J. (2004) *Trust the Text: Language, corpus and discourse*. London: Routledge.
Slobin, D. I. (1985) Crossligniustic evidence for the language-making capacity. In D.I. Slobin (ed.) *The Crosslinguistic Study of Language Acquisition* (Vol. 2) (pp. 1157–1256). Hillsdale, New Jersey: Lawrence Erlbaum Associates.

Taylor, J.R. (1998) Syntactic constructions as prototype categories. In M. Tomasello (ed.) *The New Psychology of Language: Cognitive and Functional Approaches to Language Structure* (pp. 177–202). Mahwah., NJ: Erlbaum.
Taylor, J.R. (2002) *Cognitive Grammar.* Oxford: Oxford University Press.
Taylor, J.R. (2004) *Linguistic Categorization.* Oxford: Oxford University Press.
Tomasello, M. (1992) *First Verbs: A Case Study of Early Grammatical Development.* Cambridge: Cambridge University Press.
Tomasello, M. (2003) *Constructing a Language.* Cambridge, MA & London; England: Harvard University Press.
Tomasello, M. (2007) Cognitive linguistics and first language acquisition. In D. Geeraerts and H. Cuyckens (eds) *The Oxford Handbook of Cognitive Linguistics* (pp. 1092–1112). Oxford: Oxford University Press.

6 Associating Temporal Meanings with Past and Present Verb Forms

Smiljana Narančić Kovač and Ivana Milković

Introduction

In their classes, primary children learning EFL are usually exposed exclusively to present verb forms, which are generally considered to be easier to adopt and understand than past forms. On the other hand, teachers of EFL to young learners often encounter situations in which it would be more logical or more natural to use either the simple past tense or present perfect. They tend to rely on their learners' personal experiences, hoping to provide natural contexts of language usage suitable for acquiring various elements of language, and such experiences are regularly closely connected with past events, no matter whether they are only mentioned, or narrated. Narratives also help improve young learners' communicative skills, and the story, 'as a vehicle for language development, appears to have much potential across a wide range of situations' (Garvie, 1990: 29).

Generally speaking, narration is essentially related to the past tense. As Wallace Martin (1986: 74) explains, 'there is an all-important feature of narration that is at once linguistic, temporal, and epistemological. Narratives concern the past'.

Children distinguish concepts of past and present rather early. It has been shown that the majority of children use the past tense consistently when telling stories by the age of five, so that children generally adopt the past tense as a convention of narratives (whether real or fictional) by the time they start school (Applebee, 1978).

Using stories and references to past events in EFL classes, while the available expressions are limited to present verb forms, results in the use of unnatural English for language instruction. Specific past events require the simple past tense, and teachers need the present perfect to at least inquire about homework having been done. The present simple tense is less concrete and more abstract; it is normally used rather for generalized statements than for specific events, and it is particularly confusing in stories.

Primary learners between ages 7 and 11 are in the concrete operational stage of cognitive development (Piaget & Inhelder, 1969/2000). Accordingly, a nine-year-old learner of EFL logically assumed that the statements 'I eat pizza for breakfast. I drink milk.' referred to a specific event (especially considering the choice of food), and not to a rule implied by the tense he did not recognize. He provided the following, contextually appropriate translation: *'Jeo sam pizzu za doručak. Pio sam mlijeko.'* [I ate pizza for breakfast. I drank milk.] (Narančić Kovač, 2007a: 183). Such a response can be expected because, at that age, it is typical to be more concerned with immediate events than with generalized statements. The concept of the past, with its concreteness and the immediacy of experience, seems easier to grasp than the concept of generalization, conveyed by the simple present tense, which is more abstract in its meaning. Also, in everyday situations similar inquiries about personal experiences are quite common, and people (children included) often ask each other questions such as 'Where did you spend your summer holidays?' or 'Did you watch the movie on Sunday?', rather than 'Where do you spend your summer holidays? or 'Do you watch movies on Sundays?', which are the kinds of questions English language teaching (ELT) materials abound in. The language of the classroom also regularly requires past and perfect tenses, which are common in any of the subjects in the curriculum, such as 'What was for homework?' or 'Have you done it?'.

This does not, of course, mean that children are not capable of understanding generalizations – quite the contrary. In their mother tongue, primary children correctly ascribe past and present meanings to the respective morphological features of specific verbs. However, young learners of EFL do not have a repertoire of correct verb forms in English because they do not adopt morphological features and their grammatical meanings through structure-based instruction, but rather spontaneously, largely relying on their experiences of the English language. As Vilke (1993: 185) points out, when children speak freely, they stick to content words to convey meaning, but show a disregard for grammatical morphemes. In the process, they manage to communicate in English and to reconstruct (i.e. understand) the meanings of specific utterances.

Previous research has indicated that young primary children do not recognize morphological indicators of present and past verb forms when reading a text in English, and that they consistently connect temporal meanings with the type of discourse – past with narration and present with description and exposition (Narančić Kovač & Lauš, 2011). Also, young learners recognize familiar lexical meanings of the verbs when they read a text in

English, but they sometimes adopt present forms, as the only ones familiar to them, instead of the past forms of the text. Thus it was noted that Croatian young learners (age 7–8) sometimes read aloud *sang* as 'sing', *had* as 'has', and *came* as 'come'. In another study, a 9-year-old Croatian learner read aloud *began* as 'begin' and *leaned* as 'leans' (Narančić Kovač, 2007b: 63). Medved Krajnović (2001: 51) has also found that 'the wrong use of the verb tense – present instead of past tense, wrong formation of the past tense, errors in subject-verb concordance' etc. are typical errors found in young learners, caused by their 'lack of morphosyntactic competence'.

Meaning is not only derived from lexis and grammar, but also from the context, and tense and aspect are 'communicative devices for getting features of context into focus, for providing a sharper definition of what words mean in relation to the external world' (Widdowson, 1990: 85). Lacking the mastery of morphology, young learners necessarily rely on a wider context to associate specific temporal meanings with the verbs in an English text.

Therefore, young children are not expected to encounter difficulties when exposed to past verb forms in class. Morphologically, both present and past forms can be expected to be equally irrelevant for them as temporal signals in EFL in classroom communication, and young learners can be expected to interpret both general and temporal meanings correctly, relying on the context and on their existing knowledge of vocabulary.

The Study

This chapter aims to describe how young EFL learners ascribe temporal meanings to present (and past) verb forms in narrative discourse, and to establish how both teachers and learners cope with the problem of the limited repertoire of verb forms when they need to express past temporal meanings in various contexts (classroom talk, sharing personal experiences, telling stories).

We performed a qualitative analysis of classroom communication in Grades 1–6, and especially of primary children's oral expression when both the first (L1 – Croatian) and the second (L2 – English) language are used in the same situation, to support the assumption that it would be beneficial to expose young learners as early as possible to L2 past verb forms in appropriate contexts of language use.

The sample consisted of seven randomly chosen classes of children (and their English language teachers), each from one of seven Croatian primary schools, which were visited twice every school year, starting in 2006/07, when the children were in Grade 1 (age 6–7 years), until 2009/10, when they were in Grade 4 (age 9–10 years). Each time, a 45-minute EFL lesson was recorded. Simultaneously, in 2006/07 fifth- and, in 2007/08, sixth-graders and their teachers were also studied. Recordings of two lessons with the fifth-graders, aged 10–11, and four lessons with the sixth-graders, aged 11–12, were inspected for useful examples. A few relevant examples were also found in recorded interviews with randomly selected children, six from each of the observed classes, conducted to check oral production, although they mostly focused on typical present-tense situations of language usage.

In order to observe the children's reactions and learn about their understanding of temporal meanings in general, the recordings of the EFL lessons were transcribed and inspected for relevant communicative situations, in which the need for tenses other than present tenses came up, for instances of the children's oral production of present and past tenses, and for instances when teachers used various tenses in their speech.

For the purpose of this chapter, each recorded period is designated in the following manner: Arabic numerals are used to designate grade in question (Grades 1–6). The recording session in any given school year is marked as 'a' if it was the first recording that year, or 'b' if it was the second recording. The schools are randomly designated by lower-case roman numerals ranging from i to vii. Individual interviews are marked as 'in'. In the material, teachers are referred to by 'T', interviewers by 'I', individual pupils (P) are numbered if there are more than one involved, and 's' is added when they speak in unison. The real names of the pupils have been replaced by invented ones.

The recordings were analysed and specific situations were grouped with respect to the strategies teachers and learners adopted in the contexts of the need for or the appearance of past meanings in the spoken discourse. Special focus has been placed on Grades 1–4, when past verb forms have not yet been fully introduced. Longer sections presenting specific episodes of classroom communication have been numbered.

Because the lessons were randomly chosen for recording, only a few focused on stories. Yet the recordings provide considerable insight into classroom communication between individual teachers and their pupils, and reveal their strategies.

Before focusing on the strategies related to past meanings themselves, it is useful to consider instances found in our corpus that give a wider overview of how tenses are used in primary EFL classes and which demonstrate the previously mentioned disregard of the morphological features of the verb by young learners, in spite of their contextual understanding of the general and temporal meanings of individual verbs.

Young learners and their clues about tenses

According to the Croatian primary-school (Grades 1–8) curriculum for English (Nastavni plan i program za osnovnu školu – NPP, 2006), tenses are gradually introduced into EFL teaching in individual grades. The plan and the levels of introduction are given in Table 6.1. It can be seen that the present simple tense is supposed to be introduced from the beginning, and that

Table 6.1 Introduction of tenses and other verb forms in teaching EFL in Grades 1–6 in Croatian schools – based upon the Croatian Curriculum (NPP, 2006)

Grade	Level of recognition	Level of correct usage
1	**Imperative** – 'orders within the scope of thematic fields'	the **Present** of the verbs *to be* and *have/has got* and of some frequently used verbs in further grades
2	**Imperative** (classroom talk) **Present Continuous Tense** of frequently used verbs	
3	**Simple Past** – to allow for spontaneous use when telling stories	**Present Continuous Tense** of frequently used verbs In further grades **Imperative** in further grades too
4	**Simple Past Tense** **Present Perfect Simple** to express the results of an action	
5	**Present Perfect Simple** to express the results of an action	*would* + *V* to express a future wish **Past Simple** – a few most frequently used verbs in further grades
6	**Present Perfect Simple** to express the results of an action	*Going-to* **Future** **Simple Future** **Past Simple** – regular and irregular verbs in further grades

the present tenses, at the level of correct usage, dominate the English curriculum in the first four grades. It should also be noted that the NPP suggests the gradual introduction of grammatical terminology only in the sixth grade, while explicit meta-linguistic explanations are not to be applied before the fifth grade, and then only concerning the present simple, the present continuous, and the past simple, and only to a limited extent, with the purpose of developing a basic awareness of their grammatical features in young learners, while the present perfect simple is supposed to be adopted spontaneously, within the context of proposed thematic units, and not explicitly explained.

As can be seen in Table 6.1, the future tenses are not supposed to be introduced before the sixth grade. Yet teachers spontaneously use them rather often, and young learners do not seem to encounter any difficulty in understanding them. For example, on one occasion a first-grade EFL teacher said, 'I have some pictures here, some cards. We will put them on the board!' (1.a.i), and another time, she introduced a guessing game by saying, 'Now somebody will come and pick one card from here...aaand show it to the class, but I must not see it, ok? I must not see the card. You must hide the card from me' (1.b.i). The children confirm they understand in Croatian, and the game proceeds smoothly.

Another example from the same class:

Episode 1. 1.b.i

T: You have a question here. Under the picture. 'Is it a tree?'
Ps: No.
T: 'Is it a tree?' Under the picture?
Ps: No!
T: No. 'Is it a balloon?'
Ps: Yes!
T: Yes. Where **are you going to write** 'yes'? Here, 'Is it a tree'? or 'Is it a balloon?'? Nena?
P1: 'Is it a balloon?'
T: 'Is it a balloon?' Yes.
And what **are you going to write**, 'Is it a tree?' **Shall we write** 'yes' or 'no'?
P2: No!
T: No.

It is obvious that the children were not confused by the verb forms used to express future temporal meanings. Instances of similar expressions by teachers can be found in other grades, as well: 'What will you write here?' (2.b.ii), 'I think it'll help to put these flashcards on the board', 'Will you please stop writing, drawing, whatever you are doing for a minute' (2.a.vii), 'Now, we are going to listen to the story' (2.b.vii); 'We are going to write dictation' (3.b.iii); 'So today we are going to learn the days of the week' (3.a.vii); 'First, I'll divide you in three groups' (4.b.iv), etc.

The next example shows how a teacher used various tenses while dramatizing the lesson from the textbook with first-graders. She did not want to miss an opportunity to teach the present continuous, either:

Episode 2. 1.b.iii

T: Now, Greg! **Will** you please **come** here? This is bathroom. This is bathroom. Now Greg is in the bathroom! OK!
Wait. Wait! Don't do anything. Just wait. OK?!
Er who is Greg's dad? Who is dad?
(Whispering to P2 what he should say to P1, 'Greg').
P2: Wash your face!
T: *Uhhum! Look children! Greg **is washing** his face! Wash your face, Greg! Yees! Greg **is washing** his face!

P3: Brush your teeth!
T: *mmm! Grandpa! Brush your teeth! Greg **is brushing** his teeth! OK! Now, Greg, come to the kitchen. Here is the kitchen. **Will** you please **sit down**¿
Who is … who is grandma¿ Who is grandma¿ You are grandma¿ Come here please!
(…)
P4: Eat your breakfast!
T: OK! Thank you. Are you hungry¿
P1: No.
T: No¿ Not any more. Greg is not hungry because he **has eaten** his breakfast. All right.
Now Jessica! Sister **is coming**. Sister **is coming**. Who is Jessica¿

As children did not respond orally to new verb structures, it is not possible to conclude whether they ascribed any particular temporal meanings to any of them, but they were not confused by any either. The communication was successful because the teacher maintained it by providing meaningful context, and the main goal of the activity was achieved: acting out the scene, and acquiring vocabulary. Another benefit of such a strategy is that communication is conducted in L2, and very little L1 is used during the English class. In the process, children are exposed to natural and accurate English, and they are not required to use structures that may be beyond their linguistic competence in EFL.[1]

When children do have problems understanding their teacher's instructions, it is usually for other reasons than problems with tenses. For instance, the following statement caused a lot of confusion because the teacher used unfamiliar words, and not because of the simple future: 'Now I will tell you the number and you have to write the number in the circle next to appropriate word' (2.b.i).

When teachers try to teach tenses directly, despite the clear instructions given in the NPP (2006) that in the first four grades grammar structures are never to be explained explicitly, but learners acquire them globally, it is usually time-consuming and not really efficient. The following example is just a short segment of an English class with second-graders, where the teacher is trying to teach the formal features of the present continuous, even though she was not supposed to introduce it at the level of correct usage before Grade 3.

Episode 3. 2.b.iii

T: … Who is dancing¿
Ps: Greg and teacher!
T: *Tko mi može reći 'Greg i učiteljica plešu'.* [Who can tell me 'Greg and teacher are dancing'¿]
P1: Greg and teacher dancing!

T: Uh-uh. (Shaking her head).
T: *Igore?*
P2: Greg and teacher is dancing!
T: Uh-uh. (Shaking her head).
P3: Greg is... teacher is
T: Uh-uh. (Shaking her head). Uh-uh. *Ovdje može još nešto ... pokušajmo.* [Here something else can... let's try]
P3: Greg are teacher...
T: *Još jednom?* [Once again?]
P2: Greg are teacher...
T: Uh-uh. (Shaking her head).
Ps: Greg and teacher...
T: *Lijepo ste počeli* [You started nicely] Greg and teacher. *To je dobro. Greg i učiteljica.* [That's fine. Greg and teacher.] Greg and teacher. *I dalje nešto mi fali.* [Something is still missing.] Greg and teacher ...?
Ps. (Unintelligible.)
T: Listen! Greg is dancing! Listen! Teacher is dancing! But Greg and teacher are dancing! Greg and teacher are dancing. *Kad je jedno onda je 'is' a kad je dvoje onda je ... ?* [When there is one, then it is 'is', and when there are two, then it is ...?]
Ps: are!
T: (talking to P2) *A ti si pobrkao?* 'Are' *staviš na pogrešno mjesto. Znači tko pleše ovdje?* [And you mixed it up? You put 'are' to the wrong position. Well, who is dancing here?] Greg and ...?
P2: Teacher.
T: *I onda?* [And then?]
P2: 'are'.
T: *Neee Igore!* [Noooo Igor!] Greg are teacher! Greg and teacher! *I onda* 'are'! *Glagol ide poslije subjekta. Jel' tako?* [And then 'are'! The verb comes after the subject. Right?] Greg and teacher...?
P2: are dancing.
T: Greg and teacher are dancing.
Ps: Greg and teacher are dancing.
(...)
P4: Sanja and Lucija are dancing.
T: Dancing! OK! Marko, Dino, Sanja, and Lucija are dancing! *Da li mi netko može reći 'oni plešu'?* [Can anyone tell me 'they are dancing'?]
P5: Children is dancing!
T: Children ...?
P5: are dancing.
(etc.)

These are the same teacher and pupils as in Episode 2, only here the adopted approach to grammar was obviously less appropriate to the needs and cognitive capacities of young learners. Episode 3 indicates that teachers of EFL sometimes ignore the NPP, instead relying only on the teaching materials. In this case, the present continuous was found in the textbook, which is in accordance with NPP, because learners are supposed to be exposed to it in the second grade. However, as mentioned above, the Curriculum emphasizes that the explicit teaching of tenses is not supposed to be applied in the first four grades at all. Episode 3 plainly illustrates that there are very good reasons for this.

In our corpus, teachers of the first four grades sometimes used the present perfect spontaneously. For example, the teacher's question 'Have you finished?' was readily answered 'No!' by her second-graders, and she could ask them to 'Please, hurry up' (2.a.i). The next two examples are questions that a teacher asked in a third-grade class: 'Have you ever seen some kind of film that er...that includes aliens in it?', 'Have you heard for (*sic!*) the *E.T.* movie?' (3.b.v). In both cases, the children understood the questions and replied properly. Finally, an example from the fourth grade: 'Now you have to listen to the tape once again and see if you've done it correctly' (4.b.iv).

It seems that tenses which are considered complicated and are thus carefully avoided when teaching EFL to young learners do not hinder their class communication in EFL, at least when used sparingly and in contextually clear situations, but that problems can be expected if those tenses are taught explicitly.

Examples of full sentences spoken by young learners are rare in our corpus. Episode 3 also demonstrates that much effort needs to be put into eliciting complete sentences by second- graders. Their productive abilities in EFL at the early stages seem to be sketchy. This concurs with the typical 'propositional simplification' found in early L2 speech, that is, with the fact that 'learners find it difficult to speak in full sentences so they frequently leave words out.' (Ellis, 1997: 21) Young learners tend to use a simplified grammatical system (Vilke, 1999: 214), and Kovačević has found that 'the key category in focus is the noun' (1993a: 81). Left-out words very often include verbs.

Accordingly, simple present sentences spoken by young learners were rarely found in this study, and most of them occurred in the reading activities of third-graders. They generally read the third person singular verbal ending correctly, having listened to the CD recording of the text previously, as in these examples: 'Holly likes...really likes dancing', 'Holly likes playing computer games' (3.b.vii), and 'Clara hits something' (3.b.v). Yet, occasionally, the *s* was omitted: 'He puts the game in his computer and **see** a message' (3.b.v).

The omission of the verbal endings by learners occurs more often when they get more opportunities to speak in full sentences, and especially in Grades 5 and 6.

The fourth-graders were asked open questions during their individual interviews. One boy, when encouraged to translate a statement he made in Croatian about his best friend, came up with 'Luka **like** football', and two girls both started describing persons using 'have' instead of 'has': 'Mate have got fair hair, he always wearing...'; 'She have, hm, a long hair and... she's wearing a pink T-shirt and jeans' (4.in.vi). In addition, the former girl also used the -*ing* participle instead of the simple present tense, while the latter used the present continuous correctly when describing a picture.

Here are some examples from the higher grades:

Episode 4. 5.a.vi

P1: A policeman **catch** burglars.
T: Er, did I hear this good (*sic!*)? A policeman **catch** burglars? Er, is it right?
P1: Yes.
T: Are you all sure it's right? Policeman **catch** burglars?
Ps: Catches, catches.
T: Bingo! Oh, come on, you know that. So, will you please repeat?
P1: A policeman **catches** burglars.
T: Good.
 ...
P2: Does a postman **repairs** teeth?
 ...
T: Nino, come on, ask another funny question, come on.
P3: Does postman **catches** a burglar?
T: Catch.
P3: Catch.
T: Catch a burglar.

In Episode 4, P1 replied 'Yes', meaning her answer was contextually correct, and she was right. The missing ending seemed to be beyond her concern at that moment, and her awareness of the grammatical structures did not seem to be very strong yet.[2] Such a statement about fifth-graders can also be supported by further examples of their oral production when talking about themselves – their use of the present tenses is generally correct, but they do stray:

Episode 5. 5.in.iv

I: Do you play with your friends somewhere?
P1: Yes.
I: Where do you play?
P1: I **go** in town.
I: Aha.
P1: We **walking**.
I: So you don't go to the park anymore?
P1: No.
 (...)

P2: (about the park) I **go** with my friends there, or my sister sometimes.
I: Aha.
P2: But I'm not in that ... that park all the day. I just **walk** in the streets and then **talking** to my friends.
I: I see. So, you don't really go to the park and play?
P2: Yes, I just **walk by**.

With some children, the habit of dropping endings persists in the sixth grade, too. For instance, describing the Tower of London, a girl said: 'It start as a fortress', and the teacher responds: 'OK, That was in the past' (6.b.vi). Another example was provided by P1 in Episode 6 below, and the examples provided by P2 show that there are pupils of that age who know well when and how to use simple present and simple past:

Episode 6. 6.in.iv

I: What do you usually do in the living room?
P1: **Watching** TV.
...
I: Aha, when does she cook her lunch?
P1: When she **come** home.
...
I: And what do you do in your free time?
P2: I **play, listen to** music, **watch** TV.
I: Do you go somewhere in your free time?
P2: Yes, I **go** with my friends outside, sometimes into the cinema.
I: Uh-huh. And always with your friends?
P2: Hm yes.
I: Uh-huh.
P2: I **went** one time with my friend to explore the city, I almost **got** lost.
I: Wow, really?
P2: Yes.
I: In the centre?
P2: No... we **went** to ..., hmm to Zagreb.
I: I see, to the east?
P2: Yes.

In the following example, a sixth-grader was so well aware of the semantic features of the tenses he used and of their temporal meanings that he resisted the inappropriate attempts by his teacher to correct him. She was distracted by the noise and was not listening to him carefully enough:

Episode 7. 6.b.iv

T: **Do** you **buy** comics?
Ps: Yeah!

T: Tell me!
P: When I **was** young I always...
T: (interrupts) Girls, please!
P: .. **bought**...
T: (interrupts) **buy**
P: I sometimes **bought**...
T: (interrupts) **buy**
P: ...*Blek Stena*.
T: You always **buy** it. That**'s** your favourite character.
P: It **was**, but I **don't read** it any more.
T: Any other characters?

Even when individual learners show an exceptional ability at using tenses, they make mistakes. Despite quite a few errors, the awareness of the need to speak accurately and use correct structures is obvious in the following responses by a sixth-grader, who often used the strategy of self-correction:

Episode 8. 6.in.vi

I: What's your favourite room in your flat?
S. My room.
I: Your room, of course. And why?
P: Because, because...
I: It's yours.
P: No, no. I**'m** that, but I**'m writing** their homework. I **am**, I**'m** on internet, I**'m looking** for some pictures. I'm... and I**'m playing** with my *bidgie. (He probably meant 'budgie')
I: Who's bidgie?!?
P: I **think**...parrot, a parrot
...
I: Do you ever go to a park?
P: Yes, I usually **go** to park. I **think**, every day.
...
I: Where else do you go in your free time?
P: I **go**...I **play** basketball.
I: Oh, OK ..
P: For six ye... I **have been playing** basketball sin... since... two thousand and second or...
I: ... and two, ok, great.
...
P: In summer I, this summer **is** very special to me hm for me.
I: Why?
P: Because my granny, grandma and grandfather **are going to visit** me. They're in America.
I: Oh, I see.

P: I **didn't saw** them eight years or ten.
I: Aha.
P: For eight years.
I: Great.
P: And I think this summer **will be** the best in my life.

Appropriate and correct usage of the past continuous was also recorded in Grade 5, when a pupil, upon being asked 'What were we talking about?', answered with a full sentence, 'We were talking about food.' (5.b.vi.)

The analysed examples show that young children easily cope with various tenses they are exposed to, and that towards the age of 12 they gradually develop their awareness and understanding of semantic (in this case temporal) values of specific verb forms. They rely on the wider linguistic context, as well as on their previous knowledge and experience to interpret the temporal meanings of individual English verbs in specific situations. However, it is mostly teachers who initiate the communication. They quite often use future tenses, and they encourage children to use present tenses properly. Generally speaking, children do not seem to speak much in class, at least not before Grade 5, when their awareness of the relation between the morphological features of verbs and their temporal meanings becomes more obvious.

On the other hand, as mentioned above, children as native speakers clearly distinguish past and present meanings and associate them correctly with verb forms. This can be seen in the following episode from our corpus, in which a teacher of a first grade class tried to avoid past tenses in a conversation in Croatian so that it would suit her teaching materials better. P4 interrupted a sequence of generalized statements with a past statement about his own birthday, but the teacher resumed with generalizations. She only switched to the past tense herself in a new context:

Episode 9. 1.a.i

T: *Što vi obično dobijete za dar za svoj rođendan? Što dobijete?* [What do you usually get for your birthday? What do you get?] Marija?
P1: *Ja dobijem paket i slatkiša i ništa više.* [I get a package and sweets and nothing else.]
T: Uhhum. Vesna?
P2: *Ja dobijem paket i ništa više.* [I get a package and nothing else.]
P3: *Ja dobijem puno slatkiša i nekad nešto od igračaka.* [I get a lot of sweets and sometimes some toys.]
T: *Dobro.* [Fine.] Matko?
P4: *Ja dobijem slatkiš i ovaj kak se zove neki poklon igračku a nekad dobijem ...(not clear).* [I get a candy and, well, you know, some gift toy, and sometimes I get...]
T: Dora?

P5: *Ja za rođendan uvijek dobijem jednu igračku i slatkiše. Puno slatkiša.* [I always get a toy for my birthday and sweets. A lot of sweets.]
P6: *Ja slatkiše errr odjeću i igračke.* [I sweets errrr clothes and toys.]
T: *A recite mi da li obično za rođendan... što errr mame naprave onda vama? Što naprave?* [And tell me, do you usually for your birthday... what do your mums make for you then? What do they make?]
Ps: *Tortu.* [A cake.]
T: *Tortu, uhhum! Jel' to nekakva posebna torta? Kakva je to torta?* [A cake, uhhum! Is that some kind of special cake? What kind of cake is that?]
P7: *Posebna.* [Special.]
T: *Kakva? Kako se zove ta torta?* [What kind? What is that cake called?] *Matko?*
P4: *Recimo moja baka je **pravila** er neki sladoled onak sladoled.* [For instance, my granny was making er some ice-cream some sort of ice-cream.]
T: *Dobro. Kako zovemo tu tortu? Kako je zovemo?* [Fine. What do we call that cake? What do we call it?]
P8: *Učiteljice! Sladoled torta!* [Teacher! Ice-cream cake!]
P9: *Učiteljice! Rođendanska torta!* [Teacher! Birthday cake!]
T: *Tako je! Zovemo ju rođendanska torta! A što obično stavimo gore na tu tortu?* [That's right! We call it birthday cake! And what do we usually put on that cake?]
P10: *Učiteljice!* [Teacher!]
T: *David?*
P10: *Stavimo svijeće.* [We put candles.]
T: *Tako je. Stavimo svijeće. Pa ja ovdje imam nekakve sličice.* [That's right! We put candles. Well, I have some little pictures here.] I have some pictures here, some cards. We will put them on the board! Vilko, come!
...
T: *A što mislite zašto **je** njoj mama **pripremila** baš surprise?* [And what do you think, just why did Mum prepare her a surprise?] *Zašto **je** **slavila** rođendan baš toga dana?* [Why did she celebrate her birthday exactly on that day?]
Ps: ***Pripremila** joj **je** daaa[r]* [She prepared her a preeeesent.]
T: ***Pripremila** joj **je** toga dana zato što je njezin tata pilot i ne može doći na njezin rođendan tada kad joj je rođendan nego **je došao** nekoliko dana ranije. Dobro!* [She prepared it on that day because her dad is a pilot and he cannot come to her birthday when it is, but he came a few days earlier. Fine!]
Ajmo sada. [Let's go now.] Let's listen once again...

The children were able to make general statements about birthday parties, but it is obvious that the specific past experience introduced by P4 was more interesting to share and talk about. Apart from that, the conversation was unnatural and artificial, just like much of ELT language. P4's interruption was unsuccessful at first, because the teacher was determined to stick to the present. About ten minutes later, towards the end of the above example, she spontaneously switched to the past when she needed it to explain the context of a story.

Teachers seem to avoid the simple past and the present perfect before Grade 5, even though it is recommended that children should be exposed to them starting in the third and fourth grades, respectively (see Table 6.1). Intentional usage of the past simple tense can be found only sporadically in the first four grades. However, as situations requiring the use of past tenses cannot be avoided, as shown in Episode 9, and particularly as one of the goals of EFL instruction as early as the third grade is to enable children to 'retell a sequence of events' (NPP, 2006: 87), the need to refer to past events persists, and this seems to be felt both by teachers and young learners. Therefore, they develop strategies to cope with such situations.

Strategies: Expressing past meanings

Typical strategies adopted by teachers and young learners in contexts requiring past tenses which have been found in the corpus are presented in Table 6.2. The grades in which specific strategies were found are presented separately in terms of learners' and teachers' strategies.

Using L1 to express past meanings is a common strategy in the early stages of EFL learning. It is frequently used by both teachers and learners, and it has been found in the recordings of all four grades before Grade 5. In addition, teachers sometimes use the simple past tense in L2 spontaneously when addressing learners, or in conversation, but none of the children were recorded using English past verbs before Grade 5 in the analysed material. Instances of adopting present verb forms in L2 instead of the simple past

Table 6.2 Strategies used to express past meanings in appropriate EFL contexts

Strategies	Grades		
	Teachers	Learners (Young Learners)	
Using L1 to express past meanings	1 2 3 4	1 2 3 4	x x*
Using past tenses in L2 oral production	1 2 3 4	- - - -	5 6
Present forms and past meanings (L2)	- - - -	- - 3 4	5 6

*Recordings of classes in Grades 5 and 6 were not inspected for expressions in L1 because past verb forms in L2 are available as a component of EFL syllabus.

tense, which seems to be typical of young learners, are rather rare, which is in part due to the above-mentioned propositional simplification and in part to the fact that the children are not given enough opportunities to express themselves orally in English. However, from the third grade on, it was possible to detect the young learners' strategy of interpreting present in L2 as past, that is, of associating past meanings with the present simple.

Present forms and past meanings (L2)

We address the latter strategy first, because it connects well with the previous analysis, further supporting the view that children disregard verbal endings as unimportant, but rely on contextual clues instead.

The examples that reveal that children ascribe past meanings to present-tense expressions in EFL are not numerous, but they support the idea well.

Interestingly, such a strategy has even been found once in a teacher's talk, when she translated her own present expression 'and nothing happens' within a narrative context, and because of it, as 'I opet se ništa nije dogodilo' [And again, nothing happened] (1.b.iii).

In the following episode, a third-grader translated a sentence from the textbook inadequately, because he interpreted the meanings of some vocabulary items incorrectly. His general understanding of the statement was acceptable, but not accurate. He also attributed past meaning to the simple present of the original, because it suited the narrative context better. His teacher corrected his vocabulary choices, but she spontaneously followed him by switching to the past herself. She read the original sentence again, and the next one, and returned to the (now contextually appropriate) present tense, seemingly completely unaware of the tense switching:

Episode 10. 3.b.v

T: (reading) 'He puts the game in his computer and sees a message.' *Niko, što to znači?* [Niko, what does that mean?]
P: *Er.. Colin **je upalio** kompjutor i **pročitao** poruku.* [Colin switched his computer on and read the message.]
T: *Colin **je stavio** igricu u svoj kompjuter, u svoje računalo. I **vidio je** poruku.* [Colin put the game in his computer, in his computer (synonym). And he saw a message.]
(reading) 'He puts the game in his computer and sees the message. Hmmm – a new code. I wonder what it means?' *Hmmm - nova šifra. Novi kod. **Pitam se** što to znači.* [Hmmm – a new code. A new code. I wonder what it means.]

It is obvious that contextual clues were crucial for the child's understanding of the statement.

The following episode comes from the same session. The children were answering questions in writing, and they were discussing clues from the story during the process. Two were past simple questions, and this seems to be the only instance in the whole corpus when the teacher introduced the simple past tense on purpose (we address this issue in more detail below). The children were supposed to write down only short answers, but in this case, everyone is happy with the full answer to the question 'What happened to Clara?' by means of a full sentence in the simple present tense: 'She hits a purple beam':

Episode 11. 3.b.v

T: *Ajmo! Na zadnje pitanje.* [Let's go! To the last question.] What **happened** to Clara? What **happened** to Clara? Miran. What happened to. ...
P1: *Što se dogodilo Klari?* [What happened to Clara?]
T: *Tako je. Što se dogodilo s Klarom? Na kraju.* [That's right. What happened with Clara? In the end.]
Ps: *Pala je.* [She fell.]
T: *A kud se je udarila? Što ju je udarilo? Krešo? Krešo, što ju je udarilo? Krešo?* [And where did she get bumped? What hit her? Krešo? Krešo, what hit her? Krešo?]
P2: *Ljubičasta zamka.* [A purple trap.]
T: *Zraka, ne zamka. Zraka.* [Beam, not trap. Beam.]
P3: *Učiteljice?* [Teacher?]
P1: Purple beam.
P3: *Kak se to veli po engleski?* [How do you say that in English?]
T: *Kak se veli?* [How do you say that?]
P3: She she **hits** on purple beam.
T: She **hits** on purple beam?
P4: Yes.
Ps: Yes.
T: Yes! *Klara je udarila u ljubičastu zraku, koja nam dođe nešto kao da je udarila u zid, a nije ju vidjela prije dok se nije udarila u nju. A (t)ko je postavio zraku?* [Clara hit a purple beam, which would be similar to hitting a wall, and she did not see it before, until she hit it. And who set up the beam?]
Ps: *Svemirci...* [Aliens...]
T: *Zado! Zado je postavio zraku.* [Zado set up the beam.] Zado.
P5: *Krešo je postavil.* [Krešo set it up.]
T: *Krešo je postavil zraku?* [Krešo set up the beam?]
P5: Aha.
Ps: (Laughing).
T: Sh! Miran. *Jesmo odgovorili na pitanja?* [Have we answered the questions?]
Ps: *Ne.* [No.]

P5: *Jesmo!* [Yes, we have.]
T: *Jesmo, Edo?* [Have we, Edo?]
P4: *Ne!* [No!]
P1: *Ma jesmo al nismo napisali.* [Well we have, but we haven't put it down.]
P4: *Učiteljice, dajte na ploču napišite ovo zadnje pitanje.* [Teacher, please write this last task on the board.]
P5: *Pa piše ti u priči...* [Well, it's in the story...]
T: *U priči piše!* [It's in the story!]
P5: ... (not clear) *stranu?* [... page?]
T: *Ne možemo sad odmah.* [We cannot right now.]
P1: *Učiteljice*, she **hits**...? [Teacher, she hits...?]
T: She **hits**... (Helping individual pupils to write down the answer)

In the following episode, the interviewer is inquiring about what kind of TV programmes the pupil likes and watches:

Episode 12. 4.in.vi

I: Something in English?
P: Films.
I: Films? You watch films? What kind of films? Tell me.
P: *James Bond, Tarzan i izgubljeni grad, Plimni val.* [James Bond, *Tarzan and the Lost City, Flood*]
I: Yes, so you watch films. Good. So these are action movies, right? Action films that you like. OK, good.

When asked about the films he watched, in the present simple, the pupil answered by reciting a list of films he had watched – at least *Flood* was shown on Croatian TV not long before the interview. Thus, he did not really answer the question 'What kind of films?' properly, he did not provide information about his habits, as was required by the grammatical context set by the present simple tense ('You watch films'), but rather relied on the wider context and understood the question as being about his specific past experiences. The interviewer provided the proper answer herself.

The analysed examples further support the notion that young learners tend to neglect the morphological features of verbs when communicating temporal meanings. In the process, they tend to ascribe past meanings to present forms of verbs if thus guided by the wider context of their appearance, and adopt this as a strategy.

Using past tenses in L2 oral production

The strategy of introducing past tenses when the context requires them has been found more frequently in our corpus than adopting present forms for past meanings, but in Grades 1–4 it was used only by teachers. Pupils were not recorded using past tenses before Grades 5 and 6. However, it is important to see how young learners react to those instances and whether they can grasp the temporal meanings conveyed by L2 past verb forms.

The transcripts render the impression that teachers tend to avoid using past tenses whenever possible. As we have already shown, they did not avoid the various future tenses when they were needed, but this did not stretch to past-related tenses (e.g. Episode 2). Whenever possible, teachers tried to turn past-related situations and contexts into present-related ones. An example of this practice is Episode 9, when a textbook lesson about families and a birthday party was introduced by a long conversation based on the learners' experiences about celebrating birthdays in general, instead of a conversation about the children's own birthday parties or those of their friends. The children would be able to talk about specific birthday presents, instead of being obliged to talk about what they 'usually' get for their birthday – packages, toys, and sweets, of course. However, such practices are generally encouraged by ELT materials for young learners, which hardly ever include past verbs, and tend to turn natural past-related contexts into present-related ones. Thus stories are regularly presented in the form of mimetic media, such as role-play dialogues and comics (e.g. Episode 10 and Episode 11). In the latter, the visual discourse takes over the actual narration, while language expression is reduced to descriptive statements and dialogues. In this manner, teachers and children are left without much support when it comes to relating stories or even 'retelling a sequence of events' required by NPP, and they are reduced to describing pictures and acting out dialogues (e.g. Episode 2), both being present-tense contexts. As a result, any serious discussion of a story encounters problems such as are demonstrated, for instance, by Episode 11. However, past-related situations cannot be avoided – narrative is an omnipresent type of discourse, and past experiences fuse with present situations in everyday life, of which teaching is only a part. Therefore, in our corpus, the teachers generally used the simple past tense spontaneously.

When teachers did switch to the simple past, it was frequently only a sentence or two within their speech, intended to give comment, repeat something, introduce a rhetorical question, react to a situation, etc. These situations happened on impulse. Examples can be found in all the grades, and the last one listed below is followed by an immediate translation into Croatian by the teacher herself, another strategy found in our corpus that was often adopted:

- I **said**, after you write *yes* or *no,* then you can colour it! (1.b.i)
- I **forgot** to check the homework all together. (1.b.i)
- **Did** you **open** five-four? (1.b.i)
- Er… I **didn't ask** you that. (2.b.iii)
- Oh, sorry, I **didn't hear** you. (2.a.iv)

- We **said** it last time. (3.b.i)
- The last time we **talked** about the zoo keepers. (3.a.v)
- Tina, once again you **did** it! (3.a.vii)
- Somebody already **mentioned** 'b'. (3.a.vii)
- Close your books and just try to remember what we… What we **did** last week, OK? (4.b.iv)
- You **gave** the answer already, you can't give the answer twice. (4.b.iv)
- We'll listen again to check you **did** it correctly, OK? (4.b.iv)
- You write the first places you **found** in her town. (4.b.iv)
- You **didn't write** this correctly. … She **didn't mention** a hotel. (4.b.iv)
- Why **weren't** you at school yesterday? *Zašto nisi bio u školi jučer?* (4.a.ii)

The above utterances were rarely followed by an immediate response by learners, which would perhaps disclose whether and how they were understood. They are useful because they document the teachers' spontaneous reaction to contexts which presuppose past meanings. Yet, young learners can only benefit from such practices, because past-tense utterances, represented here by the above examples, demonstrate accurate and appropriate English usage, and make it possible for children to be exposed to natural English more often than usual, which in turn widens their linguistic experience and enhances their L2 repertoire in the long term.

The next set of episodes, when past utterances appeared within conversations, reveals that young learners managed to respond correctly to past tenses in all the recorded cases and that their understanding of English expressions was always achieved. If there were problems, they were caused by other issues.

In the following exchanges between a teacher and her first-graders, communication ran smoothly, even though several past verbs were used:

Episode 13. 1.b.i

T: Tell me who **said** err to Liz errr what **was** the thing. Who **told** her? Matko?
P1: Polly.
T: Polly **told** her, yes!
(…)
T: **Did** you **see** when he **was picking** the card?
P2: *Vidjela je!* [She saw it!]
T: **Did you see**? No? OK…

In the second fragment of Episode 13, it is obvious that P2 switched to L1 for a reply to the question, but he kept the past meaning, using a past verb in L1. The examples in the next episode are similar:

Episode 14. 1.b.iii

- **T:** *I on ...? [And he...?]*
- **Ps:** *..vuče mrkvu! [..pulls the carrot!]*
- **T:** pulls! *Vuče mrkvu! [He pulls the carrot!]* But nothing **happened**!
- **Ps:** *Nije izvuk'o! [He didn't pull it out!]*
- **T:** *Ništa se dogodilo nije. [Nothing happened!]*
  ...
- **T** And Ronnie pulls carrot, mummy pulls Ronnie, daddy pulls mummy, sister pulls daddy, and mouse pulls sister! Aaand what **happened**?
- **Ps:** *Izvukli su! [They pulled it out!]*

As soon as the teacher used a past expression, children adopted it. Also, whenever it was possible, that is, when the children's repertoire allowed for it, they responded in English. It was necessarily by short answers, just as P1 did in Episode 13, and just as these second-graders did in Episode 15, replying to the first question:

Episode 15. 2.b.i

- **T:** OK! Somebody **said** that (he/she) is hungry. Who is hungry? Hold up your hand who is hungry! OK! **Did** you **have** breakfast today? **Did** you **have** breakfast?
- **Ps:** No.
- **T:** No? Why not? Look what I **had** for breakfast today. Look what I **had** for breakfast.
  What's this? What's this, do you know? What's this, Pavao?
- **P:** *Kornflejks.* (L1 pronunciation.)
- **T:** Cornflakes, yes!

As mentioned above, teachers sometimes translated their past utterances, especially questions, as in the next conversation. The learners did not know the answer to either the L2 or the L1 version, but they soon responded correctly to another expression including a past verb:

Episode 16. 2.a.iv

- **T:** What **was** the question?
- **P:** aaa...hmmm...
- **T:** *Koje je bilo pitanje? [What was the question?]*
- **P:** aaa... (not clear)
- **T:** No.
- **P:** Teacher!
- **T:** Which superheroes do you know? We **said** Superman, Spiderman...
- **P:** Batman!

Second-graders successfully maintained communication in English in these examples, and it was contextually appropriate:

Episode 17. 2.b.iv

T: What number **was** it?
Ps: Number nine.
T: Number nine. Who **put out** a fire?
Ps: ... elephant.

Episode 18. 2.b.vii

T: Now, open your class book at page seven, four. Seventy-four. You can see Jack, Polly and Greg, and some food is there.
P: Teacher? Class book?
T: Activity book. I **said** class book?
Ps: Yes.
T: Sorry, my mistake.

A teacher sometimes posed the question 'What **did** I **say**?' to third-graders (3.b.i) to elicit a translation of her previous utterances from her pupils, and they reacted accordingly. In the following example, there is a misunderstanding, but it is obviously caused by an unfamiliar phrase ('to learn something by heart'), and not by the verb form:

Episode 19. 3.b.iii

T: Do you know this song?
Ps: Yes.
T: **Did** you **learn** it by er by heart? **Did** you **learn** the song by heart?
Ps: No.
T: *Jeste naučili napamet?* [Did you learn (it) by heart?]
Ps: Yes.

In the next example, there was a vivid discussion, and the children did their best to use English as much as possible. As they did not know how to provide a short answer to a *wh*-question in the past, they stuck to 'yes' and 'no'. When a longer statement was required, a child turned to another strategy – using Croatian, but the teacher proceeded in English, using appropriate tenses. Thus, Episode 20 presents an excellent teaching strategy, especially for the third grade.

Episode 20. 3.b.v

T: Who **saw** E.T.?
Ps1: Yes.

Ps2: No.
P: *Ja sam gledal* E.T. [I watched E.T.]
T: And who is E.T.?
P: Alien.
T: Yes, he's an alien.
P: *Pustili su* ga roditelji na Zemlji jer su oni *prešli* u svemir .... [The parents left him on Earth because they went into space...]
T: Yes, they **did**.

The following episode demonstrates how a child, when asked about the meaning of a word, volunteered the verb as well, translated correctly:

Episode 21. 3.in.vii

I: Thank you, Tomo, you **were** excellent. *Što znači* 'excellent'? [What does *'excellent'* mean?]
P: *Bio si* odličan. [You were excellent.]

Fourth-graders are even better prepared for coping with past expressions, and here is a short example supporting this:

Episode 22. 4.b.iv

T: What **did** they **put** there?
P: Bikes!
T: A bike.

We have already shown that young learners, and even fifth- and sixth-graders, sometimes ascribe past meanings to present verb forms. However, they also gradually build up the awareness about the association between specific verb endings and their temporal meanings. In the next example, a girl grew restless when it became obvious that she needed to talk about past events, and she did not have the necessary repertoire. Finally, she switched to Croatian, and showed that she had been able to understand everything the interviewer had said, including the temporal meanings of the verbs. This example also supports earlier findings that young learners turn to L1 when they feel that they cannot express themselves in an immediate communicative situation (Kovačević, 1993b: 235).

Episode 23. 4.in.vi

I: You like the viola, OK. You **got** some awards, right, when you **were** smaller, I remember when you **were** second grade and first grade that you **won** in some competitions. Is that true?
P: Yes.

I: Aha, are you still good?
P: Yes.
I: Yes.
P: I, I have, em..., em, this year, one and, em, first place.
I: One first place. OK, very good. And what kind of competition **was** it? Is it a Zagreb competition or Republic of Croatia competition? What kind of competition?
P: Em...(pause).
I: The state competition or the city?
P: First... *Prvo* **smo** se **natjecali** *na regionalnom, to je bilo u Velikoj Gorici, a onda na državnom u Varaždinu.* [First we competed in the regional competition, that was in Velika Gorica, and then in the state competition in Varaždin.]
I: Aha, and you **won** the first prize where? In Varaždin or in Velika Gorica? Where **did** you...
P: *Obadvoje.* [Both]
I: Both. So you are very, very good. *Mamma mia!* Very good, Dora. Congratulations! I'm very happy for you. Good.

It may seem that some of the teachers in the corpus intentionally introduced past tenses in Grades 3 and 4, in accordance with the NPP (Table 6.1). However, the examples of past verb forms in the teachers' speech found in the first two grades do not differ much from those introduced later.

There was only one case of introducing the past simple in the third grade, which may have been intentional. This has been partly reproduced in Episode 11. The teacher asked her pupils to copy and to answer four questions in all, based on a comic in the textbook they were using: 'What's The End of Planet Earth?' (It's a computer game), 'Who did Colin meet in the computer game?' (Clara), 'Who is Zado?' (A spaceman) and 'What happened to Clara?' (She was hit by a purple beam). Judging from a comment expressed in L1, the children found the questions difficult, but they managed to answer all the questions, with ample help from their teacher (3.b.v). Yet we cannot be certain that the introduction of two simple past questions was in fact well planned in advance, and that it was really intentional in terms of the children's progress in L2. It was definitely not in accordance with the NPP, as the children were not simply exposed to past expressions during storytelling, but they were expected to react to them, without much previous exposure to past tenses in appropriate contexts.

While young learners seem to respond more promptly to past statements and questions and to utterances in English in general as they become older, past-tense verbs themselves never really pose a comprehension problem. Sometimes teachers use them without much thought, and the children are thus exposed to them. More often, pupils get involved in conversations initiated by their teachers and do their best to provide appropriate replies.

It seems that they gradually develop an awareness of the ways present and past meanings are conveyed by English verbs, and that they manage to ascribe temporal meanings to the appropriate verb forms with increasing certainty. Yet they still lack the repertoire and the competence to use past verb forms in English, and they adopt a logical strategy – turning to L1, which is, in this case, Croatian.

Using L1 to express past meanings

Young learners using L1
When young learners feel the need to talk about past events, or to express themselves within a past-related context, they tend to interrupt the course of communication with single past utterances in L1. Sometimes they use those statements to initiate a conversation about past events. The following examples from our corpus reveal that this strategy was applied in all four primary grades:

- *Mene je mama **pitala** jel ja moram nosit i ovu staru bilježnicu.* [My mum asked me if I have to take this old notebook with me, too.] (1.b.vi)
- *Mi smo **išli** planinariti, **penjali se**.* [We went hiking, we climbed...] (2.a.iv)
- Teacher, teacher, ***nije rekao*** 'Batman'... [He didn't say *'Batman'* ...] (2.a.iv)
- *A ja **sam** već **napisao*** 'schoolwork'. [And I have already written *'school-work'*.] (2.a.v)
- *Učiteljice, učiteljice, **napravil sam** žirafu.* [Teacher, teacher, I made a giraffe.] (2.a.v)
- *Učiteljice, vi **ste rekli** 'big'.* [Teacher, you said *'big'*.] (3.a.iii)
- *Učiteljice, ja **sam** već jednom **napisao**.* [Teacher, I have already written it once.] (3.a.v)
- *Kak **ste rekli**?* [What did you say?] (3.b.iii)
- *Ajmo vidjet **što se dogodilo**.* [Let's see what happened. (In the next lesson.)] (3.b.iii)
- *A **nisam** točno **shvatio**.* [I didn't understand exactly.] (4.a.iv)
- *Krivo **je napisao**.* [He wrote it incorrectly.] (4.b.iv)

These examples show that children used L1 to draw the teacher's attention, to share personal experiences, to inform the teacher they had finished a task, to maintain communication, etc. The utterance 'Let's see what happened' by a third grader demonstrates that the child recognized the narrative context of the story and connected it with past expression. He meant they should look at the next lesson in the textbook, which probably contained the sequel of the story. In the actual lesson, the main character had an accident, and the child was eager to find out in the next episode whether she was well.

It is a pity that teachers often carry on with the conversation in L1 when children initiate it, even when it is not necessary to do so. The following episode presents first the beginning, and then a thematic turn, both initiated by children, of a 7-minute class conversation in L1:

Episode 24. 3.b.v

P1: *Ja bi trebal biti sad četvrti.* [I should be the fourth grade now.]
T: *I kaj **se dogodilo**?* [And what happened?]
P1: *A niš. **Ostal sam** još jednu er godinu u vrtiću.* [Well, nothing. I stayed one more er year in kindergarten.]
(etc.)
(...)
P2: *Kad sam **se** jučer **šminkao** za maškare, još mi **je ostalo** crno oko očiju.* [When I put some make-up for the masked parade yesterday, it still remained black around my eyes.]
T: *A **nisi** si **oprao**?* [And you did not wash it?]
P2: ***Nisam stig'o**.* [I didn't have the time.]
T: *A kaj **si bio** za maškare?* [And what were you in the parade?]
(etc.)

On the other hand, such behaviour corresponds to our finding that in our corpus, using L1 was definitely the most frequently adopted and most widely used strategy not only by young learners, but also by teachers, in past-related contexts, that is, when situations came up that naturally or logically incorporated past meanings and demanded past verbs.

Teachers using L1

Teachers often started individual activities in their lessons by speaking L1, or asking questions in L1. Typically, they initiated utterances in L1 in several contexts to perform various functions, such as talking about previous lessons, revising, checking task accomplishment, giving feedback, maintaining communication, establishing a friendly atmosphere, explaining, and, of course, discussing or retelling stories.

References to previous lessons appeared frequently in our corpus:

- *Sjećam se da **smo** prošli, u stvari pretprošli put **pričali** o wild animals.* [I remember that last time, in fact the time before that, we talked about wild animals.] (2.b.iv)
- *Prošli put mi **smo naučili** kako ćemo reći kako net.. kakvu netko ima kosu.* [Last time we learned how to say how som... what kind of hair someone has.] (2.a.v)
- *Da vidimo što **smo radili** prošli tjedan. Da li se sjećate što **smo** mi to **radili**?* [Let us see what we did the last week. Do you remember what we did?] (3.b.iv)

- *Koje smo životinje prošli tjedan naučili?*
  [Which animals (animal words) did we learn last week?] (3.a.v)
- *Nismo to prošli put pisali?* [Didn't we write it last time?] (3.a.vi)
- *Prije tjedana smo počeli s mjesecima, sad ćemo ih malo nastaviti.*
  [Before weeks (words for the days of the week), we started with months, now we are going to continue with them a bit.] (3.b.vi)

In most cases, such statements or questions were useful introductions to revising:

Episode 25. 2.a.iv

T: *Prošli sat. Prošli sat smo govorili o jednom gospodinu koji se zove Mysterious Mike....* [In our last class. In our last class we talked about a gentleman whose name is Mysterious Mike...]
Do you remember what is his job?
P: Superhero!
T: Well he is not (a) superhero, he is something... no.
P: OK. Detective!
T: A detective... that's right!

Episode 26. 3.b.v

T: *Pošli sat smo obrađivali* 'What's on TV today'. *Sjeća li se itko o čemu smo razgovarali? A što smo rekli koliko programa imaju Englezi?* [In our last class we did 'What's on TV today'. Does anyone remember what we talked about? And what did we say, how many channels do the English have?]
Ps1: *Tri.* [Three.]
Ps2: Three.

Revision was sometimes initiated by a single question, such as 'Koje boje sve smo naučili?' [Which colours have we learned?], followed by pupils' replies in L2 (1.a.v), and sometimes it involved more utterances, and turned into a teacher's monologue about features of English, rather than into a dialogue in English:

Episode 27. 3.a.v

T: *Što smo rekli da je hippo?* [What did we say a hippo was?]
P: *Veliki ali slon je veći.* [Big, but the elephant is bigger.]
...
T: *I tu smo dodali još jedno 'g' tako je. Onda* tall. *Rekli smo da je giraffe* very tall, *jel'da?*
[And here we added one more 'g', that's right. Then 'tall'. We said that giraffe is very tall, didn't we?]
...

T: *Što **smo rekli**?* [What did we say?] Sim is ... shorter! Sim is shorter than Sam, *jel'da?* [..didn't we?] ***Rekli* smo** *da je Sim niži od Sama. I još* **smo rekli** *da je Sim ...* [We said that Sim is shorter than Sam. And we also said that Sim is. ...] Sim is fatter than Sam.

To check task accomplishment, teachers would ask, for instance, *'Provjerimo kako ste vi to napisali'* [Let's check how you wrote it] (3.a.iv), or ask questions similar to those in the following episode. Checking homework, the teacher was talking in L1, and the children joined in:

Episode 28. 2.a.iii

T: *I vi **ste trebali** sličice izrezati i nalijepiti. ... Da li **ste** to svi **napravili**?* [You were also supposed to cut out the pictures and glue them on. ... Did you all do that?]
Ps: *Da.* [Yes.]
T: *Tko to **nije napravio**?* [Who didn't do it?]
P1: *Mate **nije napisao** u bilježnicu.* [Mate did not write it in the notebook.]
T: *Jesam tebe nešto Sonja **pitala**? Tko to **nije napravio**?* [Have I asked you, Sonja, anything? Who did not do it?]
P2: *Slavko.*
T: *Slavko, zašto?* [Slavko, why?]
P3: ***Zaboravio sam**.* [I forgot.]
T: ***Zaboravio si** što?* [You forgot what?]
P3: *Napisati.* [To write.]
T: *Znači **nisi** ni **nalijepio** sličice?* [So you didn't even glue on the pictures?]
P3: *Jesam, **nalijepio sam**.* [Yes, I did, I glued them on.]

Checking was sometimes accompanied by giving feedback to the children, as in the following example:

Episode 29. 4.b.vii

P1: She has got a book, she doesn't... she hasn't got a watch.
T: She hasn't got a watch. Very good. *Bravo, sjećate se. To **smo radili** kao prošli put.* [Bravo, you remember. We did that, like, the last time.] (noise) Has got, hasn't got. Have got, haven't got. *Domaću zadaću **smo** mi već **pogledali** ...* [We checked the homework already. ...] (noise) *To ćete završiti ... Idemo još malo ... pogledati.* [You will finish it ... Let's look at it ... a bit more.] Have you got a cat? I have got a dog. And erm... Have you got a dog?
(...)

T: *I onda ćemo umjesto 'he' staviti samo 'has'. Da čujemo, Marko.* [And then we will put only 'has' instead of 'he'. Let us hear it, Matko.] (noise) *Ništa **nisi učio**.* [You didn't study at all.]
P2:   *Pa **nisam**....* [Well, I didn't.]
T: Aha, Nora!
P3:   Has Sam got a mobile?
T: Has Sam got a mobile? *A Nora **nije bila** u školi i već zna, aha!* [But Nora was not at school and she knows already, aha!]

Sometimes teachers praised, saying, for instance: 'Vi ste stvarno naučili' [You have really learned it] (2.a.iii), and sometimes they gave individualized feedback using past utterances in L1 in the following manner:

Episode 30. 3.b.iii

T: *Dobro. Ali **nisi** ovo baš dobro **napisao**. Dobro **si** mislio ali **nisi** dobro **napisao**.* [Fine. But you didn't really write this very well. You thought correctly, but did not write it well.]
...
T: *A zašto ti **nisi napisao**?* [And why didn't you write it?] Stop Matko! Stop. *Zašto ti **nisi napisao**? A šta **sam** ja drugo **rekla**? Dobro. Ajde dobro. Ova grupa **nije** baš dobro **čula**. Da vidimo što si ti ...* [Why didn't you write it? And what else did I say? Fine. Well, OK. This group did not hear well. Let us see what you...]
P: *__Nisam__ ni ja __čuo__ ovaj ...* [I didn't hear it either this...]
T: *Pa evo Sanja **je** dobro **razumjela**.* [Well, here, Sanja understood it well.]

The following episode incorporates a teacher's past statements in L1 which are used mainly to maintain communication:

Episode 31. 3.a.vi

T: What can you ahhah! My favourite! What can you ride?
P1, P2: Horse.
T: *Cijelu rečenicu.* [A whole sentence.] Nora?
P2:   I can ride horse, camel, er
T: and a...? Look at the map! Horse camel and a...? Nela?
P3:   a bike
T: And a bike of course! ***Zaboravila si ha?*** [You forgot, ha?] Horse. I can ride a horse, camel and a bike.
...
P4:   Robbie can't fly.
T: Robbie can't fly, OK. Ivana?
P5:   Robbie Robbie can't er drive a car.
T: ..drive a car. ***Što si rekla?*** [What did you say?]

P5:   drive
T: ***Nisam čula***. [I didn't hear.] Sorry. Drive a car.

Teachers showed interest in individual pupils' situations, and sometimes asked them questions in L1 about their past experiences primarily to establish a friendly atmosphere. For instance, when a teacher asked a new pupil which school he had attended previously (*Gdje si u školu išao*, 2.a.iii), or as in the following episode:

Episode 32. 3.b.iv

T: *Jel' vam **bilo** drago jučer što **nije bilo** škole?* [Were you glad yesterday because there were no classes?]
Ps: *Daaa!* [Yeees.]
T: *Čekaj da čujemo. Nena, jel' tebi **bilo** hladno jučer doma?* [Wait so that we can hear. Nena, were you cold at home yesterday?]
P: *Ne.* [No.]
T: *Jel' ti **bilo** malo žao što jučer **nije bilo** škole?* [Were you a bit sorry because yesterday there were no classes?]
P: *Ne.* [No.]

Teachers also used past utterances in L1 when they needed to explain something, or give instructions. In the following example, a teacher referred to her previous communication with her pupils, trying to help them understand an activity in which they were supposed to combine words into a correct sentence.

Episode 33. 3.b.iii

T: *Kako **sam** ja vama **govorila**? **Rekla sam** prvo 'write', jel' tako? Onda **sam rekla**?* [What did I tell you? I said 'write' first, didn't I? Then I said?]
P1:   'can'
T: 'can'
P1:   *Onda* 'Robbie' *i onda* 'a story'. [Then 'Robbie' and then 'a story'.]
T: *Onda **sam rekla** 'Robbie' i onda **sam rekla** 'a story' i vi **ste** prvo **pisali** riječi i onda **ste napravili** rečenicu.* [Then I said 'Robbie' and then I said 'a story' and you were first writing the words and then you made a sentence.]
...
T: *Ja **nisam rekla** 'a drum', nego? Kako **sam** ja **rekla**?* [I didn't say 'a drum', but? How did I put it?]
P1:   'the drums'!
T: 'the drums'! *Tako je!* [That's right!] Who can play the drums? *Znači prvo **sam** vam **rekla** 'play', pa onda 'who', pa onda 'the drums' i onda*

'can'. [So I first told you *'play'*, then *'who'*, after that *'the drums'* and then *'can'*.] 'Who can play the drums?' Question mark!

In the next episode, the same teacher told a story, an anecdote from her own experience, to help the children distinguish between and remember the words 'fifteen' and 'fifty' better. The teacher used English for the dialogues in the anecdote, and past utterances in L1 for the narrative discourse itself.

Episode 34. 3.a.iii

T: *Jesam vam pričala priču kad sam ja kupovala čokoladu u Danskoj?* [Have I told you the story about when I was buying chocolate in Denmark?]
Ps: *Daaaa!* [Yeees.]
T: *Kako me nije razumjela trgovkinja, jel' da?* [How the shop assistant did not understand me, right?]
Ps: *Da.* [Yes.]
T: *Ja sam njoj rekla* 'I want Milka chocolate', *a ona je meni rekla*, If you buy two – one chocolate is ten kruna, and if you buy two, you will pay fifty'. *A ja sam rekla*, 'I can buy five and then pay fifty' – 'Oh, my English, I think fifteen'. *Znači što je meni rekla?* [I told her '...', and she told me, 'If ...'. And I said, 'I ...' – 'Oh, ...'. So what did she tell me?]
Ps: *Oh, moj engleski!* [Oh, my English!]
T: *Znači u čemu je bio nera.. nesporazum?* [So, what was the mis... misunderstanding about?] (noise)
T: *Što je ona meni htjela reć'?* [What did she want to tell me?]
P: *eerrr Da je jedna čokolada 10 kruna, a ako kupimo dvije da će biti petnaest.* [That one chocolate is 10 krunas, and if we buy two, that will be fifteen.]
T: *Tako je.* [That's right.]

In the following episode, a teacher started speaking in L2, and then switched to L1. She wanted to explain something about her copy of the textbook, and its former owner, and to give instructions based on the explanation. She needed to use the past to be able to explain the situation in a logical way, and then she could turn to using future verb forms for the instructions themselves:

Episode 35. 3.b.vii

T: Playing computer games. That's one thing she doesn't like to do. Mo doesn't like playing computer games. OK! er Now please take a look for a moment! This isn't my activity book. This is Dina's activity

book. Dina is in class four, four c. Take a look at her text. What can you see¿ Is it in some colours¿ OK. Red here! White.
*Zašto **je** Dina ovo ovako **isprešarala**¿ Zato jer **je** ona **išla** na malo drugačiji način. Ona je **uzela** bojicu i ono što **se je odnosilo** na djevojčicu, na primjer Mo, **podcrtala je** tom bojicom. Pa ajde da vidimo sad kako bi mi to primijenili na Holly. Ona je sljedeća prijateljica.*
[Why did Dina underline this so much (in different colours) in this way¿ Because she did it in a slightly different way. She took a coloured pencil and underlined everything that referred to a girl, for instance to Mo, with that pencil. So let's see now how we would apply that to Holly. She is the next friend.]
Take your coloured pencils. *Uzmi bilo koju bojicu koju ti želiš i da vidimo. Ovaj put ćemo samo podcrtavati, nećemo odmah prepisivati nego samo ćemo podcrtati ono što se u tekstu odnosi na Holly.*
[Take any of the coloured pencils you want, and let's see. This time we will only underline, we won't copy right away, we will only underline everything that refers to Holly in the text.]

Finally, when a discussion was based on or related to stories, teachers frequently used L1 to retell or discuss the narrative elements of the story, or at least to refer to past events. We have already encountered such practices in Episode 11 and Episode 34, with third-graders. Both examples given below come from classes with first-graders, and, in both, pictures from the textbooks are used to help children focus on the story. They demonstrate two different approaches to using L1 as a strategy of storytelling with young learners. In the first case (Episode 36), the conversation is conducted entirely in L1, and in the second case (Episode 37), the teacher and the children try to use as much L2 as possible, combining sentences from elements in both languages. The former episode does not seem to contribute to the English language skills of the young learners much, and the activity is in fact focused on improving the children's general abilities to interpret visual discourse and retell stories in L1:

Episode 36. 1.b.vii

T:	Ja ću početi. Spike i Ruby **bili** su na rubu kade pokraj žute patkice. I Spike **se naslonio** na žutu patkicu. Tko će sad drugu sličicu¿	[T:	I'll start. Spike and Ruby were at the edge of the tub next to the yellow duck. And Spike leaned on the yellow duck. Who will now take the second picture¿
P1:	Ja!	P1:	Me!
T:	Tomo!	T:	Tomo!
P1:	Spike **je** onda **paaal**...i onda je...hm¿...	P1:	Spike feeeell down then, and then......hm¿...
T:	(not clear)...**je** Spike **pao**¿	T:	(not clear)...did Spike fall¿

P1:	(not clear)...i žuta patkica i onda je...	**P1:**	(not clear)... and yellow duck and then...
T:	Samo to *je bila*... znači, njih dvoje *su pali*? To nam je bitno. Znamo tko *je pao*.	**T:**	Only that was... So the two of them fell. That is important to us. We know who fell.
	...		...
T:	I što *se dešava* na četvrtoj sličici? Za sad vam jako dobro ide! Hm? Pogledajte.	**T:**	And what is going on in the fourth picture? You are doing very well, for now. Hm? Have a look.
P2:	Spike *se popeo* na patkicu!	**P2:**	Spike climbed on the duck!
T:	A zašto *se* Spike *popeo* na patkicu? (etc.)	**T:**	And why did Spike climb on the duck? (etc.)]

It should be noted that both teacher and learners used past verb forms to talk about the story. The teacher used present statements only to give feedback ('You are doing very well, for now'), and to provide a comment ('That is important to us'), and a present question to ask about the picture: 'What is going on in the fourth picture?' That choice is logical, because the events presented by a picture are primarily experienced as present-related ones, unless they belong to a sequence of pictures which make up a visual narrative. As the events in the picture obviously belong to a wider narrative, a comic, P2 answered using a past verb form, which is again a logical choice. The teacher referred to the picture in isolation, and the child reacted to it in a wider context.

The teacher in the next example encountered a similar problem. She tried to retell a story with first-graders, and she used L1 abundantly, as well. However, her approach was different, because she managed to incorporate as many English expressions as possible, and to motivate her pupils to do the same. The story is, obviously, 'Three Billy Goats Gruff', and the fragment is only a short section of a rather long class discussion.

Episode 37. 1.a.iv

Ps: Troll.
T: Troooll, yees! Of course! *Što je on učinio kada je lijepo* billy goat *došao negdje na pola mosta?*
[What did he do when *billy goat* nicely came somewhere to the middle of the bridge?]
P1: *On je ga.. On ga je zaustavio-* [He him... He stopped him...]
T: Aahaa... *Zbog?* [Because?]
P1: *Zbog zato što ga je htjeo pojesti.* [Because of because he wanted to eat him up.]
T: Ahaaa. *Što je rekao?* [What did he say?] 'I'm hungry and I'm going to eat you up!' Aha! Time out! *Jel se sjećate vi još da je netko nekoga* **htio** *pojesti?*

	[Do you remember that someone else also wanted to eat someone¿]
Ps:	*Ja, ja, ja!* [Me, me, me!]
T:	Yes.
P2:	*I on je **je**, još pojest ovog* [And he (wanted), also to eat this]... er... *datte¿*
T:	Daddy and...
P2:	... and brother.
T:	Ok. *Ali nešto još prije što **smo radili**. Jel' netko nekoga **htio pojesti**¿* [But something else we did even earlier. Did someone want to eat someone¿] Yes, Grga.
P3:	er... Big Bad Wolf¿ ... *je **htio pojest'** Crvenkapicu*. [... wanted to eat the Little Red Riding Hood.]
T:	A yeees. ***Je** li on isto **bio*** hungry¿ [Was he also *hungry*¿]
P3:	Yes.
	(etc.)

The children were involved, and they used quite a few items of L2 vocabulary they had acquired. Even though L1 was used very much, the exchange was fast and dynamic, and the English language was in the focus. By the reference to Little Red Riding Hood, a story the children had obviously encountered earlier in their English classes, the teacher established links with the learners' previous experiences in the language classroom and thus made the activity even more meaningful in the context of EFL instruction. Such an approach might enable young learners to transfer their storytelling skills from L1 into L2 more easily, which may in turn be beneficial for their further progress in EFL. Another interesting detail from Episode 37 is the way in which the teacher introduced a digression about the story they did before; she used the expression 'Time out', a formula which helped her conduct the course of the lesson, and made it possible for her to avoid long explanations, which would probably have been given in L1.

It is evident that the need to meet the requirements of past-related situations in primary EFL classes enhances the quantity of L1 used in class, and that it very often leads to excessively long episodes of using L1 instead of L2 in classroom communication.

Discussion and Conclusions

Our analyses of the oral production of children and teachers in primary EFL classes seems to support previous findings that young learners primarily rely on the wider context in their interpretation of temporal meanings, and less so on the formal features of the verbs. This can be considered a general characteristic of young learners which materializes in formal instructional contexts. Therefore, it needs to be considered an element of the process of acquiring EFL by primary children. As children grow older, they gradually develop the understanding of the association between specific verb forms and their respective temporal meanings in L2. In this process, they rely on their early acquired understanding of equivalent links between the formal and semantic aspects of the verbs in their mother tongue, and of the contextual relevance of temporal meanings in various situations (i.e. present-related and past-related contexts).

We have also shown that, from the very beginning of formal language instruction, young learners react positively and in a meaningful way to various English verb forms and tenses used by their teachers. Verb structures do not hinder learners' overall comprehension of L2. Children manage to respond correctly to past-, present-, and future-related utterances in English, owing to their ability to associate temporal meanings with appropriate contexts, to use their previous lexical and contextual knowledge, and to rely on previous experiences.

On the other hand, children generally do not use verb forms accurately in their oral production in English during the first four grades. However, their productive potential increases towards the later primary years, and by the sixth grade they seem to be generally capable of accurate and conscious production of past and present tenses in English.

Our research has also shown that typical past-related contexts of language use (narratives, past experiences, references to previous lessons, etc.) frequently occur within the process of EFL teaching and learning. Because past verb forms are not formally introduced in EFL teaching to young learners, both teachers and learners encounter the problem of how to adequately cope with past-related situations. Typical strategies adopted in such situations are using L1 (by both teachers and learners), using past verb forms in L2 (by teachers) and associating past meanings with present verb forms (by learners). Yet, the most appropriate strategy, using past verb forms when they are necessary, is not readily embraced by teachers because of the limitations of the ELT materials which systematically avoid them, and because of the deeply ingrained belief that those structures would be too difficult for children.

The 'difficult past tense' issue has its roots in the widespread, and sometimes unconscious, misconception that children need to understand the formal grammatical features of certain structures to be able to use them properly, i.e. that children learn foreign languages with a conscious awareness of structures, and through explicit grammar instruction. This is, in turn, probably based on the outdated belief about foreign language learning in general, that 'the ability to communicate in a language is equated with the ability to form grammatical paradigms and syntactic patterns' (Beaugrande & Dressler, 1981: 218). Such attitudes were criticized already 30 years ago because they lead to instructional practices in which learners lack 'thorough exposure to the actualization strategies without which these virtual systems of grammar/

syntax and lexicon are of little practical value: how to relate texts to situations or to plans and goals' and because then 'learners are forced to act as if grammatical perfection were the highest priority for saying anything' (Beaugrande & Dressler, 1981: 218). However, although it would be hard to find anyone today who would shun this critique, the basic ideas about the necessity of the mastery of grammar and the importance of explicit grammar instruction still seem to persist when it comes to young learners and past tenses: the majority of the EFL community is reluctant even to discuss the topic, and the 'difficult past tense' issue still rules. ELT materials for early stages of primary instruction banish past verb forms almost completely, and even the Croatian primary-school curriculum for English, which is rather advanced regarding the treatment of tenses, confines past verb forms to higher primary classes, and does not offer sufficient support for better practices.

Thus, even when teachers do adopt the strategy of using past verb forms in their oral production when teaching young learners, this is usually done spontaneously, almost against their better judgement. On the other hand, children, who are not offered tools to express past meanings, being rarely exposed to past forms of the English verbs in class, either use the more familiar present forms or L1, sometimes provide short, but contextually adequate utterances in L2. Once they get exposed to the needed verb forms in an appropriate way, they add them to their repertoire.

However, both young learners and teachers most frequently and most extensively use L1 to cope with past-related situations and contexts. Such practice generally results in spending precious class time on listening to and speaking the mother tongue, and not English. Vilke (2001: 18) insists that 'class interaction of all kinds should be conducted in the target language with the first language coming in as a welcome help to prevent the breach of communication'. While L1 should not be excluded from EFL primary classes, it should definitely not dominate them, which is frequently the case. This occurs much too often only because it is the teachers' preferred strategy to avoid using English past verb forms.

The fact that they are not exposed to appropriate past tenses during their early years of learning EFL may not reduce learners' understanding of the past tenses later on, or at least not to everyone. However, the lack of past verb forms in their teaching materials unnecessarily deprives young learners of the exposure to natural expression in EFL, as well as of the opportunity to associate appropriate temporal meanings with specific verb forms and adopt them as a component of their interlanguage as soon as they are individually ready for that. Also, a vast amount of class time is unnecessarily spent on using L1 to express past meanings, time that could be much better used to communicate in English. This is also true of the present perfect tense, and perhaps even more so.

In order to reduce the negative consequences of the practices established in this research, it would be essential to change the present policy regarding appropriate verb forms necessary for essential communication of the basic temporal meanings. It would be crucial to encourage teachers to use contextually appropriate tenses in classroom communication whenever needed (ensuring thus also the conditions for contextualized teaching of grammar – cf. Medved Krajnović, 2007: 188), rather than using L1 instead. ELT materials should include past forms of a selection of verbs familiar to learners in narrative contexts at each level of instruction. However, it is vital, of course, not to introduce past forms as a goal of EFL instruction, and not to teach them at all in the first four grades. Children should not be required to adopt the past forms, or to use them, but they should not be discouraged from doing so, either. Above all, the acquisition of any verb forms should not be tested or graded in primary classes. Caution is necessary. Unfortunately, according to our findings, it seems that some teachers do not always adopt appropriate teaching strategies and approaches when working with young learners, and the appeal of explicit grammar teaching is often too strong to resist, in spite of the futility of such endeavours (e.g. Episode 3). It is also possible, as Vilke (1991: 172) remarked, that teachers of young learners often unnecessarily insist on grammatical accuracy out of fear that the children might permanently adopt incorrect structures. Therefore, special efforts should be made by educational authorities and EFL teacher educators to ascertain that knowledge about the ways in which young learners acquire linguistic structures related to temporal meanings really gets adopted by primary EFL teachers, which can then lead to necessary changes in teaching practices regarding verb forms.

In addition to that, some English expressions and utterances needed in primary EFL classes, which require past or perfect tenses, should be regularly used by teachers from the first grade on. For instance utterances such as 'Have you finished?', 'Have you done your homework', 'What did we do last time?', and 'We did that last week.' can easily become part of classroom language. They can be considered fixed expressions: multi-word units in the context of classroom interaction (Medved Krajnović, 2001: 46). Research has supported the usefulness of 'a systematic introduction of such units into early English language teaching' (53). Children would be able to understand and even acquire them without difficulty as meaningful wholes or formulas. It is well known that 'ready-made' formulaic chunks of language are easily remembered and correctly used by children (Ellis, 1997: 20). Besides, the introduction of suggested English utterances would notably reduce the portion of L1 in classroom interaction, because they appear frequently and repeatedly in classroom talk, but now almost always in L1.

The initial assumption that it would be beneficial to expose young learners to past verb forms as early as possible during the EFL instruction has been confirmed.

Using past verb forms would not in any way hinder the process of EFL learning in young primary children, as long as they are not taught explicitly.

On the other hand, past-related contexts are common in EFL instruction from the first grade on, so that the introduction of some basic past forms in the initial grades of EFL, such as 'was', 'were', and the past forms of familiar verbs, as well as the freedom to turn to them when they are necessary, would largely reduce the pressure to use L1 in EFL classes. Thus, children would be able not only to encounter English at school much more than they do now, but also to reach for appropriate verb structures and use them in appropriate contexts themselves when the time comes, because they would be available.

Finally, there is a concern that must not be neglected – the present practices can be improved only through the cooperation of interested and well-informed teachers.

Notes

(1) Interestingly, the recordings include a single example when a first grader uses simple future. Asked by his teacher to pick a colour, he responds: 'Orange I'll pick' (1.b.iv).
(2) Third graders provided a useful example too, even though it is not related to verb forms, but to the plural ending 's'. After some explicit grammar teaching, P2 had difficulty understanding the grammatical value of the ending, and referred to it as to a letter, turning the whole thing into a spelling issue (i.3.a):

T: OK. Tell me when do we say 'there is', and when do we say when do we use 'there are'? Matko?
P1: 'There are' *govorimo kad je nešto više, a* 'there is' *kad je jedno.* [We say *'there are'* when there is more than one, and *'there is'* when there is one.]
P2: *Učiteljice, a što ako fali jedno* **slovo**? [Teacher, and what if one **letter** is missing?]
T: *Gdje?* [Where?]
P2: *Ovdje je* 'desk' *netko napis'o ... a ne* 'desks' *nego* 'desk'. [Someone wrote 'desk' here ... not 'desks', but 'desk'.]

References

Applebee, A.N. (1978) *The Child's Concept of Story: Ages Two to Seventeen*. Chicago and London: The University of Chicago Press.
Beaugrande, R. de and Dressler, W. (1981) *Introduction to Text Linguistics*. London and New York: Longman.
Ellis, R. (1997) *Second Language Acquisition*. Oxford: Oxford University Press.
Garvie, E. (1990) *Story as Vehicle: Teaching English to Young Children*. Clevedon and Philadelphia: Multilingual Matters.
Kovačević, M. (1993a) Foreign language acquisition in children: some evidence from testing English with first graders. In M. Vilke and Y. Vrhovac (eds) *Children and Foreign Languages I* (pp. 72–86). Zagreb: Faculty of Philosophy.
Kovačević, M. (1993b) Usvajanje jezika na morfo-sintaktičkoj razini u djece rane dobi [The acquisition of morphosyntax at an early age]. *Strani jezici* 22 (3–4), 224–238.
Martin, W. (1986) *Recent Theories of Narrative*. New York: Cornell University Press.
Medved Krajnović, M. (2001) The lexical approach in early foreign language learning. In Y. Vrhovac (ed.) *Children and Foreign Languages* III (pp. 43–55) Zagreb: Faculty of Philosophy, University of Zagreb.

Medved Krajnović, M. (2007) How well do Croatian learners speak English? *Metodika* 8 (1), 182–189.
Narančić Kovač, S. (2007a) Spona jezika i kultura: kako uklopiti književnost u nastavu engleskoga jezika [Linking langauges and cultures: how to incorporate literature in English language teaching]. In Đ. Blažeka (ed.) *Dijete i jezik danas: Zavičajnost u nastavi hrvatskog jezika; interkulturalnost u nastavi stranih jezika* (pp. 173–186). Čakovec-Osijek: Učiteljski fakultet Sveučilišta u Zagrebu – Središte u Čakovcu i Učiteljski fakultet u Osijeku.
Narančić Kovač, S. (2007b) Literacy in English as a Foreign Language: Reading Readers vs. Reading Literature. In G. Shiel, I. Stričević, and D. Sabolović-Krajina (eds) *Literacy without Boundaries: Proc. 14th European Conference on Reading,* 2005 (pp. 62–67). Osijek: Croatian Reading Association.
Narančić Kovač, S. and Lauš I. (2011) Razumijevanje vremenske strukture narativnoga teksta u ranom učenju engleskoga jezika [Understanding temporal structure of narratives in early EFL learning]. In I. Vodopija and D. Smajić (eds) *Dijete i jezik danas: dijete i tekst, zbornik radova s međunarodnoga znanstvenoga skupa* (pp. 203–226). Osijek: Sveučilište Josipa Jurja Strossmayera u Osijeku, Učiteljski fakultet.
Nastavni plan i program za osnovnu školu – NPP [Primary school curriculum] (2006) Zagreb: Ministarstvo znanosti, obrazovanja i športa.
Piaget, J. and Inhelder, B. (1969/2000) *The Psychology of the Child*. New York: Basic Books.
Vilke, M. (1991) *Vaše dijete i jezik: materinski, drugi i strani jezik [Your child and language: first, second and foreign]*. Zagreb: Školska knjiga.
Vilke, M. (1993) Djeca i strani jezici [Children and foreign languages]. *Strani jezici* 22 (3–4), 178–188.
Vilke, M. (1999) Učenici mlađe školske dobi i gramatika engleskog jezika [Young language learners and English language grammar]. In Y. Vrhovac *et al.* (eds) *Strani jezik u osnovnoj školi* (pp. 214–216). Zagreb: Naprijed.
Vilke, M. (2001) Should we teach children grammar? In Y. Vrhovac (ed.) *Children and Foreign Languages III* (pp. 13–20). Zagreb: Faculty of Philosophy, University of Zagreb.
Widdowson, H.G. (1990) *Aspects of Language Teaching*. Oxford: Oxford University Press.

7 What Vocabulary Networks Reveal about Young Learners' Language

Renata Geld

Introductory Word and Theoretical Framework

A few weeks ago my 22-month-old daughter was playing on the beach. At one moment she came up to me smiling and shouting, 'na-na-na'. Naturally, my brain started to search for all the words containing that particular syllable, and I responded with several options, but her face was telling me I was not on the right track. It turned out that her little mind (mis)construed the palm trees along the beach to be giant pineapples. Being a big pineapple fan and familiar with its basic features, my daughter had no reason to doubt that the palms around her were huge specimens of pineapple, and she seemed quite impressed by their varying sizes along the beach.

When my older daughter was five years old, she had been attending an English kindergarten for about 1.5 years. One day we were reading *The Little Mermaid*. When I read the sentence, 'the mermaid lived in a kingdom under the sea,' she stopped me right away and asked me with a serious frown on her face: '*Under* the sea? What do you mean? How can something be *under* the sea?' I explained that it meant under the surface of the water; then she nodded, smiled, and asked me to go on with the story.

These two stories exemplify several fundamental and interrelated phenomena pertaining to both first- and second-language acquisition: experience and conceptualization; general cognitive processes as aspects of conceptual structure; and the subjective process of meaning construal. In the early 1990s, Larsen-Freeman and Long (1991: 227) noted that there were 'at least forty' theories of SLA. Since then, the number of approaches and theoretical frameworks has probably doubled, but the most fundamental theoretical 'battle' between the primacy of innateness vs. the primacy of experience in the broadest possible sense has still remained. The history of

SLA has witnessed a gradient continuum of approaches ranging from those rooted in aspects of linguistic environment to those developed out of the basic premise that human beings are endowed with a language faculty that supplements their interaction with the environment.

However, what has gradually become difficult to dispute, irrespective of one's specific theoretical perspective, is the fact that the quality of experience and the learner's interaction with the world cannot be ignored. The focus has somehow shifted from the innate language acquisition device *per se* to the processes responsible for language acquisition, or, in other words, the various specific processes occurring in the overall process of language acquisition. What seems to have become obvious is that language learning is only partially predictable, and thus it is not significantly different from other types of learning. As suggested by Ellis (2003: 63) in his overview of constructivist[1] approaches to SLA, language representations result from 'simple learning mechanisms operating in and across human systems of perception, motor action, and cognition while exposed to language data in communicatively rich human social environment'. This theoretical framework is also assumed in the analysis that is going to be presented in this chapter. Children make sense of the world by comparing old and new experiences and building categories, and their cognitive domains are constantly changing and growing. In the process, they attend to certain aspects of their reality, and thus make particular features temporarily or consistently more salient than others. For a two- or four-year-old child, the specific surface of the palm tree trunk and its fan-leaved top may be temporarily much more salient than its exact shape and size.[2] This is how a palm tree compares to a pineapple, and this is how it gets to be categorized as such. Naturally, as they grow and develop, children learn more about the world, and their categories become more detailed and refined. It is almost certain that, at some point in the future, my younger daughter will realize that palm trees are not giant pineapples. However, we cannot be absolutely certain that this early-childhood conceptualization will not be coded in her mental representation of the concepts in question and create permanent mental links between these two concepts and a number of others. Consequently, what researchers investigating both children's L1 and L2 are bound to face are predictable cognitive processes interacting with language on the one hand, but highly subjective meaning construal on the other. The interaction between language and other cognitive processes is more than evident in the second story as well. What is it that enabled a five-year-old child to understand the meaning of *under the sea*? First, in the process of language acquisition, children develop a variety of cognitive processes that are in constant interaction with language. In this particular example, the girl's language reasoning reflects topological schematization (Talmy, 1988, 2000) that includes image schemas such as containers and surfaces. Depending on the nature of attention (or salience), the sea can be construed either as a container or as a surface. Second, the child's personal experience of diving into the water, or keeping her head above the surface while learning to swim, is part of her encyclopaedic knowledge that enables her to select only the surface of the sea to represent the referent scene (Geld, 2006a). This focal adjustment of selection is responsible for the ability to attend to those elements of experience that we find relevant at a particular moment. In experiencing the world, our sensory capacities provide a variety of basic domains. Basic domains such as TIME, SPACE, MATERIAL, FORCE, COLOUR, HARDNESS, HUNGER, PAIN, LOUDNESS, etc. are rooted in directly embodied human experience, and they represent the base for the semantic characterization of concepts (Langacker, 1987).

As already suggested, the theoretical framework assumed in the analysis that follows is constructivist in nature and assumes the following (see Figure 7.1): first, that language is an experiential phenomenon, and second, that it is intimately related to other cognitive processes (such as attention, comparison, perspective, and gestalt). Thus, language is not viewed as an independent faculty separated from other aspects of cognition. Furthermore, meaning construal is dynamic and subjective, and construal operations (e.g. various aspects of attention, categorization, perspective, etc.) are viewed as instances of the above-mentioned general cognitive processes as aspects of conceptual structure. Finally, strategic meaning construal, that is, meaning construal in L2, and second-language acquisition inevitably depend on whatever precedes them. Being entangled with L1 and experiential knowledge of the world, L2 both relies on and mirrors various cognitive processes that constitute conceptual structure in L1. However, this specific cognitive state of L2 learners, burdened with prior linguistic knowledge and experience (MacWhinney, 2001, 2006), functions also as a constraint in the process of language acquisition and strategic meaning construal. Naturally, the nature of this constraint depends on the learners' age. For example, young learners' experience and knowledge of the world are somewhat less complex than the experience and knowledge of older L2 learners. We can easily imagine a young learner of English acquiring a new form and effortlessly attaching it to the conceptual content she had acquired in her L1. Her cognitive domains are still growing and changing, and they are likely to contain mental representations simpler than those found in adults. This is in accordance with MacWhinney's (2005) unified competition model, which suggests that the L2 is somewhat parasitic in terms of its relation to the L1 when it comes to lexical learning – in the initial stages of learning, L2 learners rely on the conceptual structure constructed in the process of acquiring their L1. Furthermore, young learners' experience does not shape motivation related to long-term plans and the benefits of learning – they are motivated by what is enjoyable and accessible at a particular moment or in the immediate future. Thus, they tend to be more carefree and less anxious about how much they are going to attain.[3] At this point it is important to note that both naturalistic and instructed settings have their constraints in the process of second-language acquisition. For the

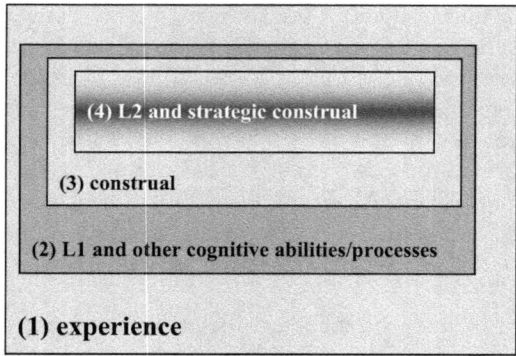

Figure 7.1 Integrated model of second-language acquisition (taken from Geld 2006b: 108)[4]

purpose of this chapter, we are going to mention several aspects of the instructed setting that are likely to bear relevance for our central discussion.

Let us now return to the integrated model of SLA (Figure 7.1) and discuss the concept of experience with young language learners. They enter their classrooms with a variety of objects, people, relations, and events shaping their knowledge. They make sense of whatever new things they experience in class by comparing it to what they have already learnt. In the process of comparing old and new experiences, they are helped by whatever context is provided by their teachers. These contexts are created and/or enriched by objects, gestures, pictures and photographs, drawing and acting, defining, analyzing, translating, etc. (Nation, 1990). However, a large portion of what they need to learn has already been selected, classified, and organized for them. For example, textbooks and teachers organize vocabulary thematically and focus on basic level concepts. What is more, textbook authors and teachers often assume that 'children will only learn simple language, such as colours and numbers, nursery rhymes and songs, and talking about themselves' (Cameron, 2001: xii). However, children are capable of much more, and, even when exposed to rather simple and structured input, they often acquire more. How does that happen? The answer lies in the fact that no matter how limited their classroom linguistic experience is, it does not happen in a vacuum – the learners' out-of-class experience, their L1, and their cognitive abilities that communicate with language enable them to go beyond what is taught in class. For example, a seven-year-old who watches cartoons in English or hears her older brother chanting lyrics from the world charts is likely to recognize more readily what is said in class or create useful links from one item to another in her mental lexicon. Similarly, a child with a richer L1 lexicon is more likely to recognize cognates. Generally, our learners' overall experience and knowledge of the world will determine what they find more salient, which connections they are going to make, and how they are going to categorize new input. On the other hand, it would be unreasonable to claim that the fact that certain clusters of words and semantic fields have already been sorted out for learners does not facilitate their acquisition. Textbooks and teachers introduce and reinforce certain thematic word and construction clusters (such as e.g. *breakfast / cereals / milk* or *Hello! / How are you today? / Sit down, please!*), and these clusters get to be acquired like prefabricated, formulaic expressions. In sum, instructed settings frequently provide limited and pre-organized vocabulary input, and, thus, somewhat constrain learners' natural tendencies to compare, analyze, and categorize. However, these processes still happen at all times even though they may not result in the same depth of processing as one expects to find in natural settings. As a matter of fact, pre-organized and systematic input is a necessary shortcut in educational circumstances with insufficient/limited time of exposure to language. Naturally, such input represents a true challenge for our young learners' memories. As suggested by Szpotowicz (2008: 102), 'the role of memory in vocabulary acquisition is absolutely vital because it is responsible for lexical coding, storage and retrieval'. This takes us to the central operational concept of our discussion – the mental lexicon, which Richards and Schmidt (2002: 327) define as 'a person's mental store of words, their meaning and associations'.

The Aim of the Study

As suggested by a number of authors, the lexicon has been a relatively neglected area of SLA research. However, a body of relevant research has emerged over the last two decades (e.g. Bogaards & Laufer, 2004; Meara, 1997; Nation, 2001; Pavlenko, 2009; Singleton, 1999). In the sections that follow we examine what our young learners' vocabulary networks might tell us about the overall organization of their mental lexicons. Even though many authors believe that the real nature of mental lexicon is still somewhat of a mystery (e.g. Aitchison, 2003; McCarthy, 1990) and that there is no consensus about the differences/similarities between L1 and L2 mental lexicons (e.g. Meara, 1982 vs. Wolter, 2001), we believe that investigating early vocabulary networks in L2 could be quite informative about certain aspects of this intricate system.

In this study we investigate what kind of meaning relations our early learners form and what seem to be their conceptual preferences. More precisely, in discussing representative answers of the participants in our study, we examine the following: (a) the nature of relations (taxonomic vs. thematic: see, for example, Bauer & Mandler, 1989; Smiley & Brown, 1979) which reflect organizational principles of our learners' lexicon (e.g. reliance on event schemas rather than hierarchies); (b) the continuum of grammar and lexicon through syntagmatic and paradigmatic choices (e.g. Coultard *et al.*, 2000); and (c) idiosyncratic relations that are based on the learners' personal experience, and subjective and dynamic meaning construal. We also hope to demonstrate that certain characteristics of young learners' early L2 may be indicative of network-like organization of both lexicon and grammar, as is generally suggested by various cognitively-oriented authors (e.g. Hudson, 1984, 2007; Langacker, 2000).

In the part describing the results obtained from the entire sample, we discuss our learners' preferences in terms of the complexity of the items recalled (words vs. constructions / sentences), and differences in the number of items pertaining to out-of-school topics.

In Section 2 (immediately below), we introduce our research protocols and instruments, as well as exemplify and discuss our participants' individual productions. In Section 3 we describe quantitative and qualitative results pertaining to the entire sample, as already explained above.

Research Sample, Instruments, Protocols and Representative Answers

The sample comprised 42 Croatian young learners of English whose vocabulary retrieval and production was elicited at the end of school year in Grades 1, 2 and 3.

The instruments described below were taken from the ELLiE project (for details see Chapter 1).

First year

At the end of the first year of their EFL learning, our participants were asked to name specific groups of items that were shown to them in two pictures. In Picture 1 they could see four different rooms: (1) a children's room with a wardrobe, shelves full of books, a picture on the wall next to one of the bookshelves, a boy sitting at his computer desk playing a computer game, some sports equipment around the boy (a racket, a skateboard, and a pair of roller blades), a bed, a box with two little animals (presumably a hamster and a guinea pig), and some toys grouped together in the bottom right corner (a plane, a doll, a train, a teddy bear, and a kite); (2) a living room with a big window, a small bookshelf, a picture on the wall, a TV set, a fish tank, a box with a little rabbit, a parrot in a cage, a lamp, and a woman sitting on a sofa and reading a book; (3) a bathroom with a toilet seat, a bath with a shower, a sink with a bar of soap, and a mirror with a toothbrush in a cup in front of it; and (4) a kitchen with kitchen units (one unit open and revealing some cups and presumably some plates), a cooker and a fridge, a table with two chairs, a bowl with four apples and two bananas on the table, and a mouse and a cat in the bottom right corner. There was also a fragment of the garden shown outside of the main frame of the picture, with a portion of garden fence, and a dog and four flowers in the garden. In Picture 2 they could see a scene from a zoo with seven children at different places in the central part of the picture (a boy and a girl eating ice-creams, a boy and a girl eating cotton candy, a boy eating an ice-cream, a girl eating an ice-cream, and a boy eating an ice-cream and accompanied by an adult) and 17 different animals (a monkey, a hypo, a crocodile, an elephant, a zebra, a rhino, a pelican, a polar bear, a panda, a fox, a wolf, a bear, a snake, a lion, a kangaroo, a tiger, and a giraffe). With Picture 1 the interviewers prompted the learners by pointing to pets and fruit, all one by one. After that they were asked to take a look at the toys in the bedroom, and name all the toys they knew how to name in English. The interviewers had been instructed to help by pointing to those which the learners were not able to find. Finally, they were asked to name whatever other object they could see and name in English. In the case of Picture 2 the learners were first asked to name all the animals and objects, and if they were not able to answer, the interviewer tried to elicit the following seven animals: a monkey, a crocodile, a snake, a bear, a lion, a giraffe, a hippo.

Let us consider two individual answers (see Tables 7.1 and 7.2):

These two examples have been chosen for several reasons. First, they are quite representative in terms of the number of items recalled by individual learners and, also, a considerable number of children (32) started their production with either the word *dog* or the word *cat*, usually both, one immediately after the other. Second, mistakes were very infrequent and most of them stem from the participants' cognitive strategies that reflect certain aspects of conceptual overextensions or underextensions. For example, as in ex. 1, the brand name Barbie is used to denote an ordinary doll, which is

Table 7.1 Elicited vocabulary production: An individual answer (ex. 1)

Picture 1
dog / cat / mouse / fish / plane / train / teddy bear / Barbie (for the doll) / orange / banana / apple / house / window / picture / tv / books / racket / chair
Picture 2
monkey / hippo / zebra / bear / snake / lion / red / yellow / orange / blue / black / white

Table 7.2 Elicited vocabulary production – an individual answer (ex. 2)

Picture 1
cat / mouse / apple / banana / orange / book / computer / teddy bear / balloon (for the kite)
Picture 2
tiger / lion / bunny (for the kangaroo) / elephant / crocodile / bear / red / yellow / pink / blue

probably due to the fact that the known is used for the unknown, that is, an early acquired word, in this case *Barbie*, for a later word that could not be recalled at a particular moment, i.e. *doll*. Furthermore, how individual learners named certain items reveals a great deal about how particular cognitive processes, such as categorization and attention, communicate with language. In ex. 2, the learner uses the word *bunny* to stand for 'kangaroo'. Even though it is difficult to say whether the learner simply did not recognize the animal in the picture and mistook a kangaroo for a bunny, or he could not recall the right word, his choice still gives us certain insight into how the process of categorization relates to language acquisition. The learners' selective attention, that is, their attention to particular elements of what needs to be communicated, coupled with their knowledge of the world, their L1 and L2, synergically affect their lexical choices. Thus, their strategic construal (Geld, 2006b; Geld & Letica Krevelj, 2011) reflects their knowledge of the world, the strategies they employ while processing the language, and their linguistic knowledge. In this particular case, the learner might have gone through several stages of comparison and selective attention, first in order to recognize the animal, and then in order to find a substitute animal close enough to the animal that had been recognized but could not be appropriately labelled in English. The learner searched his cognitive domains loaded with experience and knowledge (including his L1 and L2), and opted for *bunny*.

Second year

In their second year of EFL learning, the learners' knowledge of vocabulary was measured with free and stimulated vocabulary retrieval. The learners were first asked to try to remember whatever they had learnt up to that point and say the words aloud. The interviewer was not allowed to prompt or elicit, but simply write down words in the computer in a large font so as to make the words visible for the learner to check them. After this free, non-elicited production, the learners were given prompts that had been obtained from their respective teachers as recently covered topics in English classes. Let us consider three individual examples of free and stimulated production (see Tables 7.3, 7.4 and 7.5).

As is evident from the data in Tables 7.3, 7.4 and 7.5, the vocabulary in free production is quite diverse. The most obvious difference between the first two productions (ex. 3 and ex. 4) and the third one (ex. 5) is that the first two are considerably richer. The difference may be attributed to the fact that the vocabularies in examples 3 and 4 were produced by the learners evaluated as excellent by their English teachers, whereas the learner who produced the vocabulary in ex. 5 was evaluated as poor. Another interesting difference is the nature of the vocabulary produced by the two excellent learners. The learner from ex. 3 seems to build her vocabulary network in a somewhat systematic manner. She starts with a rich associative chain at the

What Vocabulary Networks Reveal about Young Learners' Language 157

Table 7.3 Free and stimulated production: An individual answer (ex. 3)

Free production
Listen and repeat! / Stand up! / Sit down! / Hello children! / Good morning, teacher! / How are you today? / Fine, thanks! / Open your book! / summer / T-shirt / skirt / shorts / shoes / boots / trainers / raincoat / jogging suit / jeans / scarf / dress / spider / rabbit / penguin / monkey / zebra
Stimulated production (topics: *Uncle Phil's Pet Shop*; food; family members; seasons and weather; school objects; vehicles; actions - *Super Suzy*)
owl / fox / dog / cat / monkey / snake / turtle / fish / parrot / kangaroo // orange / cocoa / sandwich / carrot / apple / coca-cola / banana // mummy / daddy / sister / brother / me / grandpa / grandma // spring / summer / autumn / winter / sunny / cold // book / pencil box / school bag / school / teacher / classroom / car / bus / helicopter / plane / bike / skateboard // roller-skating / drawing / driving a car / swimming / flying / She is drinking super milk.

Table 7.4 Free and stimulated production: An individual answer (ex. 4)

Free production
flowers / lion / juicy (instead of juice) / please / thank you / goodbye / bear / owl (mispronounced) / ball / zebra / doll / parrot / fish / sandwich / tree / grass / swimming / bike / a letter / roller-skating / ice-cream / big / mummy / sister / sun / Ronnie / open / close / door / window / teacher / crocodile / frog / pullover / school / pig / dog
Stimulated production (topics: greetings; colours; school things; toys; my family; Ronnie's room; my body; clothes; activities happening now; numbers; pets; food)
hello / goodbye // black / yellow / pink / red / blue / green // pencil / pencil box / book / notebook/ school // ball / doll / car / teddy bear // mummy / daddy / sister / brother / grandma / grandpa // bed / wardrobe / tv / skateboard / dvd // eyes / ears / shoulders / fingers / face / nose / neck / mouth // cap / T-shirt / dress // Jessica is roller skating. / Greg is talking on the phone. / Miss Lemon is riding a bike. / Uncle Phil is washing his car. / Susan is eating a banana. / Luke is playing the guitar. / Jessica is playing the piano. / one / two / three...../ thirteen (skipped) / fourteen / fifteen (mispronounced) / sixteen.../ twenty // dog / cat / frog / spider / turtle / fox / snake / fish / parrot // sandwich / pizza / chocolate / juicy (instead of juice) / coca-cola / cornflakes / milk / cake / butter (mispronounced) / cheese

syntagmatic level - frequently used imperative statements typical for classroom discourse. She proceeds with the word *summer*, which seems to represent a thematic link to three closely related words that follow (*T-shirt, skirt,* and *shorts*), and then continues first with plural nouns denoting shoes, and nouns denoting clothes. She finishes with a cluster of nouns denoting animals. In sum, the learner's associations run the gamut from fixed multi-word

Table 7.5 Free and stimulated production: An individual answer (ex. 5)

Free production
woman / girl / man / baby / dog / Sit down! / an arm

Stimulated production (topics: in the street; at school; numbers; fruit; at the park; at home; clothes; body parts)
car // (no production for the topic 'at school') // one / two / three / four / five / six / seven / nine // an apple / an orange / a banana / a cake // ball // table // trousers / jumper / a T-shirt / skirt // a head / a body / a hat

items at the syntagmatic level to noun clusters at the paradigmatic level. On the other hand, the other learner in ex. 4 seems to be a bit less systematic. She starts with the noun *flowers*, proceeds with *lion*, and then produces the word *juicy*, which actually stands for the noun *juice*. What is interesting is the fact that the mistake is not that unusual because the word *juicy* is a well-known Croatian brand name for fruit juices, and it frequently makes problems for young learners. Thus, in this girl's lexicon the word *juicy* is temporarily coded to represent fruit juice, so it is reasonable to assume that it thematically links to the cluster that follows: *please, thank you,* and *goodbye*, which belong to the event schema of buying and/or having a drink. She goes on with a mixed string of nouns belonging to two very popular categories: animals and toys. This is followed by a seemingly unrelated noun (*sandwich*) and a paradigmatically and thematically related noun pair (*tree* and *grass*). The two nouns seem to introduce a cluster of words related to outdoor life and activities (*swimming, bike, roller-skating, ice-cream*...). A very interesting group of five words comes close to the end of this free production, and these are: *open, close, door, window,* and *teacher.* The string starts with a paradigmatic contrastive pair of verbs (*open* and *close*) which both syntagmatically relate to the noun that follows (*door*). The noun *door* triggers the noun *window*, and the string ends with the noun *teacher*. The last word is particularly interesting because it belongs to an event schema pertaining to classroom life, but it is not grammatically related to the preceding words. It seems like a kind of after-thought that represents the source of these words (it is the teacher who gives classroom directions containing the words in question). Contrary to the above described productions, the production in ex. 5 is rather poor and much less informative. After four co-ordinated nouns semantically linked on the basis of belonging to the same category (HUMAN BEING), the learner produces the noun *dog*, which is followed by the imperative statement *sit down*. Even though one might assume that the noun *dog* is syntagmatically linked to *sit down*, it is much more likely that *sit down* is an independent item whose salience in the boy's mental lexicon comes from its repeated use by the teacher (the boy's profile reveals that he has a hard time concentrating in class, tends to get quite restless, and has serious learning difficulties).

As has already been explained, the vocabulary in stimulated production was prompted by recently covered topics in class. The most obvious difference between the free and stimulated production is that learners were more likely to recall multi-word items and sentences when prompted. However, this is not too surprising if we take into consideration that in addition to simple superordinates, such as *fruit* or *clothes*, the learners were also prompted with topics that associate complex relations rather than simple and concrete things. Thus, when prompted to say what she remembers from the topic 'actions – Super Suzy', the girl from ex. 3 recalled *roller-skating, drawing, driving a car, swimming, flying,* and *She is drinking super milk.* Likewise, when prompted with 'activities happening now', the girl from ex. 4 produced the following: *Jessica is roller- skating; Greg is talking on the phone; Miss Lemon is riding a bike; Uncle Phil is washing his car; Susan is eating a banana; Luke is playing the guitar; Jessica is playing the piano.* What is evident is that the learners had been exposed to grammar. As expected, it was contextualized and reinforced with a variety of examples. However, what these answers also reveal is that the learners were either not encouraged or simply not ready to abstract and extend the use of the grammatical construction in question. In other words, they stored constructions of various lengths in particular places in their network, and they seem to have stored them as multi-word units that are specific rather than schematic. In all 42 free and stimulated productions, there was only one instance of the Present Continuous tense in the first person singular. It was produced by a learner prompted with the topic 'activities happening now'. As a matter of fact, there are only five instances of the personal pronoun *I* (three of which belong to a single learner). What this is likely to suggest is that the learners are still at the concrete and specific level of acquisition – they simply reproduce what they have learnt (in this particular case the Present Continuous for specific actions performed by specific people) and they do not tend to extend its use to other people and actions.

Third year

In the third year, the focal learners' knowledge was tested with the following two tasks: (a) free vocabulary retrieval (the learners were instructed to say whatever comes to their mind: words, phrases, etc.); and (b) stimulated vocabulary retrieval. The stimulated retrieval consisted of two parts: (1) retrieval prompted by recently covered topics in class; and (2) retrieval prompted with three out-of-school topics (computers and the internet, songs/lyrics, and films and TV). Here are three representative examples of the answers for both types of tasks.

There are two aspects of free and stimulated production in the third grade that we wish to exemplify with these three representative answers (see Tables 7.6, 7.7 and 7.8). First, in comparison to the second year, the learners tended to produce more constructions that are part of classroom discourse

160 Early Learning and Teaching of English

Table 7.6 Free and stimulated production: An individual answer (ex. 6)

Free production

lion / tiger / school / home / sister / queen / crown / zebra / elephant / crocodile / fox / Buckingham Palace / Mr. Cocopolus / Croatia / bike / computer / book / notebook / clock

Stimulated production (school topics: animals; *Little Red Riding Hood*; London; in the city)

whale / dolphin / squirrel / nuts / grass / polar bear / rabbit / giraffe // teeth / eyes / wood / wolf / hunter / granny / mum / Little Red Riding Hood /ears / bed // bus / bus stop / pet shop / theatre / book shop

Stimulated production (out-of-school topics: computers and the internet; songs/lyrics; films and TV)

web / Puma / Dock Ock / griffin / demon / Elizabeth / archer / footman / grunt // (no production for songs/lyrics) // ten thousand volt ghost / crazy / cool / car / control panel / door / upside / street / money / gun / boat / cop

Table 7.7 Free and stimulated production: An individual answer (ex. 7)

Free production

yellow / tiger / good night / good morning / castle / girl / ghost / white / mirror / lamp / lighting / parrot / dad / sister / brother / mum / cat / who / water / fire / colours / trousers / skirt

Stimulated production (school topics: weather; sports; in the city; animals)

What's the weather like? / foggy / sunny / hot / windy / cloudy / raining / coat / hat / shoes / boots // volleyball / football / tennis / basketball / handball / swimming / ball // restaurant / supermarket / post office / library / train station / police station / giraffe / penguins / lion / dog / horse / crocodile / snake

Stimulated production (out-of-school topics: computers and the internet; songs/lyrics; films and TV)

windows / Google / games / bookmarks // eye of the tiger / rival / wild boys / final countdown // love / animals / fight

(as in ex. 8, free production), and it is reasonable to assume that this tendency might be an important indicator of learners expanding their vocabulary from single-word clusters related to their textbook topics to construction clusters pertaining to classroom discourse. Second, it becomes obvious that children differ in their amount of exposure to English out of school (see productions related to out-of-school topics in examples 6, 7 and 8). As for out-of-school exposure, there are two easily observable elements: first, children vary noticeably in the number of items related to out-of-school topics (see

Table 7.8 Free and stimulated production: An individual answer (ex. 8)

Free production
Hello, children! / Hello, teacher! / Have you today.../ Thanks, sit down! / Open the book!
Stimulated production (school topics: animals; in the city; describing people; clothes)
dog / cat / elephant / tiger / monkey / lion / squirrel / crocodile / snake / giraffe / dolphin // bookshop / museum / pet shop / supermarket / newsagent's / bus stop / post office // happy / sad / hungry / big / short / fat / thin / plump / old / young // short / T-shirt / jacket / jeans / dress / cap
Stimulated production (out-of-school topics: computers and the internet; songs/lyrics; films and TV)
play / continue / reading / loading / help // (no production) // (no production)

Section 3.3 for details), and second, the vocabulary acquired is frequently highly specific and contextualized. For example, when prompted with the topic 'computers and the internet', the learners recalled proper names of fictive characters (e.g. Dock Ock) as well as common nouns denoting very specific and narrow categories (e.g. footman, archer, etc.).[5] As has already been suggested for the grammatical construction of the Present Continuous in the previous section, the learners were still at a specific level of acquisition, that is, the words they produced refer to a very specific category acquired in a very limited context (in this case the context is a popular computer game). However, these specific items are invaluable components of both vocabulary and grammar networks - they serve as a foundation for abstraction, a cognitive process that is likely to lead to the acquisition of less specific members of the category. Thus, for example, when they encounter *Footmen*, computer games fans also deal with an accompanying body of language describing their characteristics, weapons, actions, and foes. Even though children do not need to acquire all this in order to play the game, the language to which they are exposed, often on a daily basis, is bound to establish at least some provisional links from one concept to another, and/or pave the way for words and concepts that come later.

Quantitative and Qualitative Analyses: The Entire Sample

First year

As has already been explained, in the first year of EFL learning, the participants were asked to name particular groups of items in two pictures (see

162 Early Learning and Teaching of English

detailed descriptions of Pictures 1 and 2 in Section 2.1). The items belong to the following categories: pets, fruit, toys, and animals. The interviewer first prompted the learners by pointing to different items from the abovementioned categories. After that, they were asked to say whatever other object they could see and name in English. The children produced a total of 98 words and only 3 multi-word items. Table 7.9 shows their individual frequencies in the entire sample (the frequency is given in brackets and refers to the preceding string of words).[6]

What is evident from Table 7.9 is that the most frequently produced words belong to the category of colours and animals, except for the word *banana*. The children's favourites among animals are not surprising – the two most frequently kept pets (*cat* and *dog*), and the two animals whose specific characteristics are loved by cartoon makers and authors of textbooks and stories for children (*snake* and *mouse*). On the other hand, a large number of words (33) were produced only once. There were two nouns denoting brand names (Barbie and Coca-Cola), three nouns that were strategically used for something they do not actually denote (*balloon* for 'kite', and *bunny* for 'kangaroo', *dragon* for 'kite' – the Croatian word *zmaj* denotes both the imaginary fire-breathing creature and the tethered aircraft loved by children), two nouns denoting animals that are difficult to account for (*frog* and *turtle*), and five nouns (*sandwich, hamburger, hot-dog, spaghetti* and *juice*) denoting food/drink items that are not present in the pictures, but may have been triggered by either the cotton candy or the ice-cream eaten by the children in the zoo, or by the interior of the kitchen. An associative, thematic link to the kitchen could also be assumed in the case of adjectives *thirsty, hungry*, and *sweet* – the last possibly standing for the collective noun *sweets*. It is also reasonable to

Table 7.9 Elicited vocabulary production: Frequencies of particular words/constructions – entire sample – year 1

Pictures 1 and 2
fox / frog / balloon / wash your teeth* / cup / turtle / pig / dragon / trees / ice-cream / boy and girl / dad and boy / sandwich / Coca-cola / thirsty / hungry / juice / hamburger / spaghetti / hot dog / game / flamingo / panda / bathroom / woman / mummy / rhino / hippopotamus / sweet / radio / shampoo / Barbie / bunny **(1)** // girl / racket / house / hamster / table / flowers / wolf / kangaroo / ball / milk / cow / pudding / soap / hairbrush **(2)** // bed / sheep / dad / pizza / towel **(3)** // horse / picture / desk / car / toothbrush **(4)** // window / hippo / teddy **(5)** // chair / television / giraffe **(6)** // crocodile / zebra / boy / purple **(7)** // kite / bunny / computer **(9)** // rabbit **(10)** // brown / train / mum / bird **(12)** // elephant / white **(14)** // parrot **(15)** // apple **(16)** // lion / bear **(17)** // fish **(18)** // orange **(20)** // plane / black **(21)** // teddy bear / monkey / red **(23)** // doll **(24)** // tiger **(25)** // book **(27)** // snake / green / pink / yellow **(28)** // mouse **(29)** // banana **(30)** / cat / dog **(32)** // orange **(36)** // blue **(37)**

speculate that the word *shampoo* is automatically triggered by the interior of the bathroom, even though the item itself is not visible in the picture, as well as the construction *wash your teeth** which is a direct translation from Croatian (*wash* instead of *brush*) and relates to the toothbrush in the bathroom. Finally, the noun *mummy*, in the same manner as the noun *dad*, which was produced three times, may indicate our previous assumptions that children are still at a very specific level of acquisition – *dad* stands for the man in the zoo, and *mummy* for the woman sitting in the living room. As many as five nouns (*ball, milk, cow, pudding,* and *hairbrush*) denoting objects that cannot be directly identified in the pictures were produced by two different learners. This points to two potentially important phenomena in early L2 processing – the strength and salience of well-entrenched concepts and the associations they bear, and compensatory strategies of substituting, that is, overextending or underextending. For example, there is no ball in the pictures used for elicitation; however, the word *ball* seems to be salient in the children's lexicon and it thematically belongs to the toys found in one of the pictures, which explains its existence among the elicited words. The same processes might be responsible for the occurrence of the nouns *milk* and *hairbrush* – their salience in the vocabulary network, and their respective associative links to the 'kitchen' and 'bathroom'. As for the noun *cow,* which is used to mean for 'guinea pig', it represents a sort of strategic, compensatory overextension, at least in the case of the learner who was asked by the interviewer to point to the animal, which enables us to speculate about the processes activated in the learner's attempt to name the animal in question. Finally, the salience of the word *pudding* for Croatian learners is primarily in its strength as a cognate. The Croats use the word *puding* for a variety of milk and starch based dessert (sometimes served with toppings such as whipped cream or fruit).[7]

In addition to *cow*, there were two other words denoting animals that do not have corresponding referents in the pictures - *sheep* (produced three times) and *horse* (produced four times). The interviewer encouraged the learners to point to the referent on two occasions in both cases, and the referent was always the above-mentioned guinea pig. Thus, in four out of seven occasions we may claim that the learners either did not recognize the animal or they simply approximated and overextended from what they already knew to what they did not know. The problem with this particular animal may be attributed to the following: first, in real life it resembles a hamster, but this is not the case in the picture (i.e. it is a typical rodent but its teeth are not visible in the picture); second, its head seems a bit too prominent and too big; and third, in comparison to the bunny situated in the box in the living room, both the hamster and the guinea pig in the children's room look more like cartoon animals than real-life pets.

What the elicited vocabulary production in the first year suggests may also be quite relevant for discussions on the nature of breadth vs. depth of L2 learners' vocabulary (Anderson & Freebody, 1981). Even though the instruments used stimulated mostly simple one-word productions, it was obvious that the children went beyond what was visually accessible and produced vocabulary that suggests complex interdependence between concepts/words. For example, when a learner produces the word *hairbrush* after being stimulated with the picture of a bathroom, this reveals something about where this particular concept is situated in the learner's network, that is, what kind of interconnections and knowledge of the world might be activated in the process of its recognition. This is in accordance with what has been proposed by Meara and Wolter (2004), who suggest that the depth of lexical knowledge needs to be discussed not only in terms of single words as separate items but also in terms of their interconnectedness. Thus, within the theoretical framework outlined at the beginning of this chapter, and in accordance with what has been proposed by other authors, it is reasonable to conclude that young learners' vocabulary depth stems from subjective meaning construal, and depends on the following: experience and knowledge pertaining to L1, experience and knowledge pertaining to L2, and cognitive processes interacting with language. On the other hand, measuring the breadth of vocabulary knowledge seems less complex than determining its depth. Even though our focus was not the investigation of the breadth of young learners' vocabulary, the data obtained is quite indicative of individual differences related to this particular aspect of vocabulary acquisition. The data in Table 7.10 shows the lowest and highest number of words produced in a single production, and, thus, relative differences in the number of words produced by individual learners in the study. It also shows the frequencies of all the productions.

Table 7.10 Elicited production: Frequencies – entire sample – year 1

Number of words / constructions per single production	Frequency	Number of words / constructions per single production	Frequency
1	2	20	3
6	1	21	1
8	2	23	1
9	1	29	3
10	2	31	2
12	1	32	2
13	3	34	2
14	1	35	1
15	2	39	1
16	2	41	1
18	3	47	1
19	3		

From this data it is evident that there are considerable differences in the number of items produced: 6 learners produced less than 10 items, 17 learners produced between 10 and 20 items, 8 learners produced from 20 to 30 items, and 10 learners produced more than 30 items. As shown in Table 7.10, the lowest number of produced items is 1, and the highest 47.

Second year

As previously mentioned, in the second year the learners' knowledge of vocabulary was measured with both free and stimulated vocabulary retrieval tasks. Since the topics employed to prompt the learners' stimulated production differed depending on what the teacher had provided in class, in the first part of the analysis we shall focus only on the language produced in free production. This will be followed by the quantitative results for both free and stimulated production for the entire sample.

Let us first consider the overall free production (see Table 7.11) by looking at the produced words and constructions separately.

What the qualitative data in Table 7.11 shows is that learners in the second year produced mostly the following two types of constructions: (a) typical formulaic expressions (e.g. *Good morning!* or *How are you today?*); and (b) both correctly and incorrectly reproduced, rote-learned sentences from their textbooks (e.g. *Jessica is playing the piano.* or **Parrot is swinging.*). As for single-word productions, they seem to be quite diverse. For example, 165 items were produced only once (including several article-plus-noun constructions that were not categorized as constructions but as words), and 58 items were produced only twice. Furthermore, as shown in Table 7.12, there are considerable differences in the number of word items produced by individual learners – 11 learners produced up to 10 words, 12 learners produced from 10 to 20 words, 5 learners from 20 to 30 words, and 4 learners produced more than 30 (including one learner with a remarkable 128 items). These numbers also differ from the number of constructions produced in this task (see Table 7.13). A total of 15 learners did not produce a single construction, 14 learners produced from 1 to 5 constructions, and only three learners produced more than 5 constructions. The maximum number of constructions produced was 11.

Let us now take a look at the stimulated production. The data in Table 7.14 shows the production of word items, and the data in Table 7.15 shows the production of constructions. As already explained, this production was stimulated by particular topics that were covered in class, and they differed from one school to another. Since the topics overlapped only partially, it is not possible to do thorough qualitative analyses. However, these results are still indicative of how well the learners tended to recall recently covered vocabulary, and to what extent they differed individually. Five learners produced up to 10 words, 9 learners produced from 10 to 20 words, only four produced from 20 to 30, and 11 learners produced within a range of 34 and

Table 7.11 Free production: Entire sample – year 2

Free production – words

a pear / kite / jump / train / pink / yellow / one / two / eleven / Otto / children / beaver / trousers / bathroom / living room / mouse / cake / white / purple / rubber / read / toybox / balloon / boots / trainers / raincoat / scarf / spider / dress / bananas / salad / spaghetti / fingers / fat / sad / bored / thirsty / cold / knees / cheese / tea / sharpener / this / Mick / bike / sea / wolf / bin / Daisy / crab / bookcase / body / a banana / apple / teddy bear / bear / blackboard / TV / DVD / computer / juice / monster / jumping / like / box / a dress / butterfly / please / roller-skating / bike / a letter / big / mummy / sun / open / close / door / pullover / pink / swinging / bear / Garry / turtle / dolphin / autumn / winter / butter / thanks / ride / sheep / hen / presents / bag / Christmas / Santa Claus / sandals / cloud / basket / camera / binoculars / boyfriend / glasses / river / picture / rainbow / Croatia / fishing / match / girlfriend / hot / thinking / Greece / mouth / nose / holidays / homework / professor / suitcase / grandfather / grandmother / baby / Tracy / Greta / Mick / Kiki / pleasure / funny / no / yes / daddy / game / motorbike / after / football / potato / tomato / Orc / Germany / cigar / cars / cool / soldier / pirate / firefighter / umbrella / glass / sun / chocolate / heart / behind / in front of / rice / Africa / bird / smoke / near / clock / ring / wall / on / in / soap / film / cartoons / jump **(1)** // bird / jumper / doll / skateboard / Polly / Jack / Daisy / plane / house / shoulders / socks / sitting room / wardrobe / woman / green / pig / reading / jogging suit / elephant / sandal / mango / milk / clock / notebook / eraser / bikini / sky / man / cap / an arm / dog / book / leg / summer / Miss Lemon / Elliot / spring / water / hair / desk / baby tiger / frog / grass / window / crocodile / school / brother / Monday / Thursday / Wednesday / Friday / Saturday / pen / ship / eyes / ears / teeth / fire **(2)** // skirt / bedroom / foot / mum / kitchen / bag / baby / book / giraffe / penguin / shorts / tree / goodbye / swimming / a tiger / Luke / sister / Tuesday / Sunday **(3)** // tiger / lion / head / girl / fine / thanks / snake / kangaroo / sandwich / ice-cream **(4)** // fish / ball / dad / hello / red / boy / monkey / zebra / jeans / flower **(5)** // pizza / car / shoes / table / orange **(6)** // pencil / pencil case / blue / parrot **(7)** // chair **(8)** // T-shirt **(10)** // cat **(12)** // teacher **(13)** // dog **(14)**

Free production – constructions

Goodbye, teacher! / Good morning. / This is / Listen and repeat! / Stand up! / Good morning, teacher! / Open your book! / Open the book! / It's five o'clock. / washing his car / It's five o'clock. / *Teacher is reading a book. / Jessica is playing the piano. / Greg is talking on the phone. / Ronnie is eating a carrot. / Good morning, children! / Thank you! / I had two / I had an ice-cream. / I was / jumping like a frog / Dog, sit down! / *Flower is pink. / *Bear is sleeping. / I am speaking English. / *Parrot is swinging. / *Lion is eating a carrot. / *Tiger and lion is eating a fish. / teacher and children / clock and six / I don't / too short **(1)** // Hello, teacher! / Hello children! / Listen! / Please! / Come on! **(2)** // Fine, thanks! / Sit down **(3)** // Hello! **(4)** // How are you today? **(5)**

Table 7.12 Free production (words): Frequencies – entire sample – year 2

Number of words per single production	Frequency	Number of words per single production	Frequency
0	2	17	1
4	1	18	1
5	4	19	1
6	2	21	1
8	1	22	1
9	1	27	1
10	1	28	1
11	1	29	1
12	1	37	1
13	2	38	1
14	2	43	1
15	1	128	1
16	1		

Table 7.13 Free production (constructions): Frequencies – entire sample – year 2

Number of words per single production	Frequency
0	15
1	6
2	2
3	3
4	2
5	1
8	1
9	1
11	1

96 words. These results seem to suggest the following: (1) there are substantial differences among learners in how much they are able to retain and recall; and (2) learners' vocabulary knowledge is still concentrated around specific topics that contextualize individual items. As for constructions, their production was as follows: 10 learners did not produce anything, 18 learners produced up to 5 constructions, and 4 learners produced more than 5 constructions. The maximum number of constructions produced by one learner was 11. If we compare this to their free production, we shall see that the stimulated production does not seem to be too different from the free production. The only difference that stands out is the difference in the number

Table 7.14 Stimulated production (words): Frequencies – entire sample – year 2

Number of words per single production	Frequency	Number of words per single production	Frequency
2	1	34	1
4	1	36	1
6	1	45	1
7	2	47	1
10	1	52	1
14	1	54	1
15	2	62	2
17	4	74	1
18	1	79	1
21	1	96	1
23	1		
28	2		

Table 7.15 Stimulated production (constructions): Frequencies – entire – year 2

Number of words per single production	Frequency
0	10
1	6
2	4
3	4
4	4
6	1
7	1
9	1
10	1

of learners who did not produce a single construction (15 in free vs. 10 in stimulated production).

Third year

Since the time allocated for free productions in the third year differed substantially from the time allocated for this task in the second year, it was not reasonable to compare the two productions. Likewise, the classroom topics did not correspond to those employed in the instrument used in the second year. Thus, we will concentrate only on the production prompted with out-of-school topics – the part of the instrument employed only in the third year.

Table 7.16 Stimulated production: Frequencies – (out-of-school topics) entire sample – year 3

Number of words per single production (computers/internet)	Freq.	Number of words per single production (songs/lyrics)	Freq.	Number of words per single production (films/TV)	Freq.
0	13	0	22	0	18
1	7	1	7	1	5
2	7	2	3	2	4
3	3	3	2	3	8
4	4	4	2	4	2
5	2	5	2	6	1
6	2	6	2	7	1
7	1	8	1	8	1
8	1			11	1
9	1				

Let us then consider the results pertaining to the above-mentioned topics - computers and the internet, songs/lyrics, and films and TV (see Table 7.16).

This data seems to reveal that music and TV vocabularies are somewhat less prominent in young learners' lexicons than the vocabulary they tended to relate to computers and the internet. First, the totals of the three productions differ (99 words related to computers and the internet, 56 words related to songs and lyrics, and 77 words produced for films and TV). Second, a total of 22 learners did not produce a single word when encouraged to recall words they had learnt from songs and their lyrics, and the same result was reached when 18 learners were asked to produce some words related to films and TV. On the other hand, only 13 learners did not produce a single word when asked about what they had learnt via computers and the internet. Naturally, it cannot be claimed that the words they did produce had been acquired exclusively through the medium used here as a prompt, but it is reasonable to assume that the words produced and their association to a particular topic represent important links in our learners' mental lexicons. Considering the young age of our research participants, it is not surprising that songs and lyrics seemed to be less prominent sources of language input. This particular source of language is likely to gain importance as they enter the (pre-)puberty age.

Conclusions

Young L2 learners' mental lexicons seem to consist of a variety of networks that show a continuum of words and constructions, that is, a continuum of lexicon and grammar, and its foundations rely on the learners' prior experience and knowledge. Young learners start with single words and their clusters, highly contextualized and specific (thematically linked and pertaining to event schemas), proceed with simple constructions of the same specific nature, and then gradually take small steps towards acquiring units of classroom language used by their teachers more as a medium and less as the content of teaching. It is important to stress that each of these stages is likely to have its separate and unique contribution to the overall acquisition. For example, specific items serve as foundation for abstraction, a cognitive process that is likely to lead to the acquisition of less specific members of the category. As a matter of fact, going through the above-mentioned stages, learners activate various cognitive processes, such as categorization and attention, and use them strategically to make inferences, compare, select, overextend, underextend, etc. Thus, their subjective, dynamic, and strategic meaning construal reflects their prior knowledge, the strategies employed while processing the language, and their actual linguistic knowledge.

Furthermore, individual lexicons seem to vary in size, shape, and content. Some networks are built in a rather systematic manner with rich associative chains and intersecting paradigmatic and syntagmatic levels, whereas others exhibit seemingly unrelated elements whose salience is most probably determined by highly individual factors. In addition, it is reasonable to assume that a variety of items found in the network are only temporarily coded and represent provisional links in the system. These are often words and constructions traditionally treated as errors. Finally, our learners' lexicon networks also suggest that certain items are favourites with a vast majority of learners, whereas others are individual preferences, sometimes even unusual and idiosyncratic. This is due to the fact that children simultaneously share particular aspects of their experience as well as live their individual lives determined by a variety of internal and external factors. Whatever the case may be, we believe that the findings of this study support the idea that the vocabulary of young learners and its meaning construal needs to be discussed in terms of interconnectedness in vocabulary networks, and, perhaps more importantly, in terms of general cognitive processes activated as language is being acquired.

Notes

(1) These include connectionists (Christiansen & Chater, 2001; Christiansen *et al.*, 1999), functional linguists (Bates & MacWhinney, 1981; MacWhinney & Bates, 1989), emergentists (Elman *et al.*, 1996), cognitive linguists (Croft & Cruse, 2004; Lakoff, 1987; Langacker, 1987, 1991), constructivist child language researchers (Slobin, 1997; Tomasello, 1992, 1995, 2000), and many others.
(2) Due to yearly pruning, palm trees often have fat, rounded trunks. However, some people may be familiar only with their 'Californian' image – very tall with narrow tree trunks.

(3) The complexity of factors affecting the process of vocabulary acquisition in L2 has been nicely put forward by Hall and Ecke (2003) in their discussion and elaboration on the model of vocabulary acquisition based on the detection and exploitation of similarity between novel lexical input and prior lexical knowledge, i.e. the model representing the processing and storage mechanism named 'parasitic learning strategy' (Hall, 1992). Hall and Ecke list the following factors conditioning CLI (cross-linguistic influence): (1) learner (psychotypology and metalingustic awareness, motivation, attitude, age, learning style and strategy use, and degree of anxiety), (2) learning (e.g. proficiency in each language, fluency in each language, amount of exposure to each language, learning context, etc.); (3) language (e g. typological distance, historical distance, degree of contact, etc.); (4) event (e.g. language mode, language control, style, task, etc.); and (5) word (e.g. degree of form similarity with competitors, number of form competitors, degree of frame (lemma) similarity with competitors, number of frame (lemma) competitors, degree of concept similarity with competitors, number of concept competitors, etc.).
(4) See also Geld and Letica Krevelj (2011).
(5) The examples in brackets are characters from a computer game popular with children and teenagers who like violent games featuring strong, courageous, but bloodthirsty characters.
(6) The production is shown in the form of frequencies of words rather than by the type/token distinction because children were prompted to produce single words and their productions do not involve semantic differences pertaining to grammar/syntax.
(7) In American English *pudding* has the exact same meaning as *puding* does in Croatian.

References

Aitchison, J. (2003) *Words in the Mind: An Introduction to the Mental Lexicon* (3rd edn). Malden, MA: Blackwell Publishing.

Anderson, R.C. and Freebody, P. (1981) Vocabulary knowledge. In J.T. Guthrie (ed.) *Comprehension and Teaching: Research Reviews* (pp. 77–117). Newark, DE: International Reading Association.

Bates, E. and MacWhinney, B. (1981) Second language acquisition from a functionalist perspective. In H. Winitz (ed.) *Native Language and Foreign Language Acquisition, Annals of the New York Academy of Science* Vol. 379 (pp. 190–214). New York: Academy of Sciences.

Bauer, P.J. and Mandler, J.M. (1989) Taxonomies and triads: conceptual development in one- to two-year-olds. *Cognitive Psychology* 21 (2), 156–184.

Bogaards, P. and Laufer, B. (2004) (eds) *Vocabulary in a Second Language*. Amsterdam: John Benjamins.

Cameron, L. (2001) *Teaching Languages to Young Learners*. Cambridge: Cambridge University Press.

Christiansen, M.H. and Chater, N. (2001) Connectionist psycholinguistics: capturing the empirical data. *Trends in Cognitive Sciences* 5 (2), 82–88.

Christiansen, M.H., Chater, N. and Seidenberg, M.S. (1999) Connectionist model of human language processing: progress and prospects. Special issue of *Cognitive Science* 23 (4), 415–634.

Coultard, M., Knowles, M., Moon, R. and Deignan, A. (2000) *Lexis*. Birmingham: Centre for English Language Studies.

Croft, W. and Cruse, D.A. (2004) *Cognitive Linguistics*. Cambridge: Cambridge Univesity Press.

Ellis, N.C. (2003) Constructions, chunking, and connectionism: The emergence of second language structure. In C. Doughty and M. Long (eds) *The Handbook of Second*

Language Acquisition (pp. 63–103). Malden/Oxford/Melbourne/Berlin: Blackwell Publishing Ltd.
Elman, J.L., Bates, E.A., Johnson, M.H., Karmiloff-Smith, A., Parisi, D. and Plunkett, K. (1996) *Rethinking Innateness: A Connectionist Perspective on Development*. Cambridge, MA: MIT Press.
Geld, R. (2006a) Konceptualizacija i vidovi konstruiranja značenja: temeljne kongitivnolingvističke postavke i pojmovi [Conceptualization and aspects of conceptual structure: fundamental cognitive linguistic premises and concepts]. *Suvremena lingvistika* 62 (2), 183–211.
Geld, R. (2006b) Strateško konstruiranje značenja engleskih fraznih glagola [Strategic construal of English phrasal verbs]. *Jezikoslovlje* 7 (1–2), 67–111.
Geld, R. and Letica Krevelj, S. (2011) Centrality of space in the strategic construal of *up* in English particle verbs. In M. Brdar, M. Omazić, G. Buljan, V. Bagarić and T. Gradečak-Erdeljić (eds) *Space and Time in Language* (pp. 145–166). Frankfurt/New York: Peter Lang Verlag.
Hall, C.J. and Ecke, P. (2003) Parasitism as a default mechanism in L3 vocabulary acquisition. In J. Cenoz, B. Hufeisen and U. Jessner (eds) *The Multilingual Lexicon* (pp. 71–85). Dordrecht: Kluwer Academic.
Hall, C.J. (1992) *Making the right connections: Vocabulary learning and the mental lexicon*. Universidad de las Américas – Puebla. (ERIC Document Reproduction Service No. ED 363 128).
Hudson, R. (1984) *Word Grammar*. Oxford: Blackwell.
Hudson, R. (2007) *Networks of Language: The New Word Grammar*. Oxford: Oxford University Press.
Lakoff, G. (1987) *Women, Fire and Dangerous Things: What Categories Reveal About the Mind*. Chicago, London: University of Chicago Press.
Langacker, R.W. (1987) *Foundations of Cognitive Grammar (Vol. 1): Theoretical Prerequisites*. Stanford: Stanford University Press.
Langacker, R.W. (1991) *Foundations of Cognitive Grammar (Vol. 2): Descriptive Application*. Stanford: Stanford University Press.
Langacker, R.W. (2000) A dynamic usage-based model. In M. Barlow and S. Kemmer (eds) *Usage-based Models of Language* (pp. 1–63). Stanford: Center for the Study of Language and Information.
Larsen-Freeman, D. and Long, M.H. (1991) *An Introduction to Second Language Acquisition Research*. New York: Longman.
MacWhinney, B. (2001) The competition model: The input, the context, and the brain. In P. Robinson (ed.) *Cognition and Second Language Instruction* (pp. 69–70). Cambridge: Cambridge University Press.
MacWhinney, B. (2005) New directions in the competition model. In M. Tomasello and D.I. Slobin (eds) *Beyond Nature–Nurture: Essays in Honor of Elizabeth Bates* (pp. 81–110). Mahwah, NJ: Lawrence Erlbaum.
MacWhinney, B. (2006) Emergent fossilization. In Z.-H. Han, and T. Odlin (eds) *Studies of Fossilization in Second Language Acquisition* (pp. 134–156). Clevedon: Multilingual Matters.
MacWhinney, B. and Bates, E. (eds) (1989) *The Crosslinguistic Study of Sentence Processing*. New York: Cambridge University Press.
McCarthy, M. (1990) *Vocabulary*. Oxford: Oxford University Press.
Meara, P. (1982) Word associations in a foreign language: a report on the Birkbeck Vocabulary Project. *The Nottingham Linguistic Circular* 11 (2), 29–38.
Meara, P. (1997) Towards a new approach in modeling vocabulary acquisition. In N. Schmitt and M. McCarthy (eds) *Vocabulary: Description, Acquisition and Pedagogy* (pp. 109–121). Cambridge: Cambridge University Press.

Meara, P and Wolter, B. (2004) V_links: Beyond vocabulary depth. In D. Albrechtsen, K. Haastrup and B. Henriksen (eds) *Angles on the English speaking word (Vol. IV): Writing and Vocabulary in Foreign Language Acquisition* (pp. 85–97). Copenhagen: Museum Tusculanum Press and University of Copenhagen.

Nation, P. (1990) *Teaching and learning vocabulary.* New York: Heinle and Heinle.

Nation, P. (2001) *Learning Vocabulary in Another Language.* Cambridge: Cambridge University Press.

Pavlenko, A. (ed.) (2009) *The Bilingual Mental Lexicon, Interdisciplinary Approaches.* Bristol/Buffalo/Toronto: Multilingual Matters.

Richards, C. and Schmidt, R. (2002) *Dictionary of Language Teaching and Applied Linguistics* (3rd edn.) London: Longman.

Singleton, D. (1999) *Exploring the Second Language Mental Lexicon.* Cambridge: Cambridge University Press.

Slobin, D.I. (1997) The origin of grammaticizable notions: beyond the individual mind. In D.I. Slobin, (ed.) *The Crosslinguistic Study of Language Acquisition* (Vol. 5) (pp. 265–323). Mahwah, NJ: Lawrence Erlbaum Associates.

Smiley, S.S. and Brown, A.L. (1979) Conceptual preference for thematic or taxonomic relations. A nonmonotonic trend from preschool to old age. *Journal of Experimental Child Psychology* 28 (2), 249–257.

Szpotowicz, M. (2008) *Second Language Learning Processes in Lower Primary Children.* Warsaw: Wydawnictwa Uniwersytetu Warszawskiego.

Talmy, L. (1988) The relation of grammar to cognition. In B. Rudzka-Ostyn (ed.) *Topics in Cognitive Linguistics* (pp. 165–205). Amsterdam: John Benjamins.

Talmy, L. (2000) *Towards a Cognitive Semantics (Vol. 1): Concept Structuring Systems.* Cambridge, Mass.: MIT Press.

Tomasello, M. (1992) *First Verbs: A Case Study of Early Grammatical Development.* Cambridge: Cambridge University Press.

Tomasello, M. (1995) Language is not an instinct. *Cognitive Development* 10 (1), 131–156.

Tomasello, M. (2000) Do young children have adult syntactic competence? *Cognition* 74 (3), 209–253.

Waxman, S. and Gellman, R. (1986) Pre-schoolers' use of superordinate relations in classification and language. *Cognitive Development* 1, 139–156.

Wolter, B. (2001) Comparing the L1 and L2 mental lexicon. *Studies in Second Language Acquisition* 23 (1), 41–69.

8 Receptive Skills in the Linguistic and Non-linguistic Context of EFL Learning

Renata Šamo

Introduction

Listening and reading have often been subordinated by speaking and writing due to the general belief that they are secondary language skills without being ends in themselves but 'means to other ends' (Nunan, in Richards & Renandya, 2002: 238). Such an approach to language proficiency consequently implies the idea of second-/foreign-language knowledge primarily related to the ability of producing language (receptive vs. productive language skills). This sharp division by reference to the activity of the language user – passive vs. active (Widdowson, 1978) – was seriously questioned in the 1980s with the emphasis on comprehensible input seen as 'the essential ingredient for second-language acquisition' (Krashen, 1985: 4). This was the time when SLA researchers started paying attention to listening in particular because they considered listening crucial for providing the learner with input in the language classroom. In other words, his/her failure in understanding input makes learning hardly possible. Making sense of the message by relating it to background knowledge is one of the main demands not only for the listener but also for the reader, so listening and reading are viewed as very similar processes.

The Processes of Listening and Reading

According to the bottom-up processing view, which is strongly influenced by structuralism in linguistics, both listening and reading are linear decoding processes, ranging from the smallest contrastive units (phonemes/graphemes) to complete (spoken/written) texts with their meaning construction as the last stage in the process. On the other hand, the top-down interpretation view, under the considerable influence of psycholinguistics, suggests a reconstruction process, in which the listener or the reader actively (re)constructs the original meaning of the speaker/writer with the use of incoming sounds/letters as clues. To be able to make sense of what is heard or read, s/he also needs prior knowledge of situational context (Brown, 1990; Nuttall, 1996). Today it is known that decoding or code-cracking ability is as important as context-based guessing ability, so what is needed is the integration of the two.

The interactive model of listening and reading based on the use of information processing strategies has thus been proposed, suggesting that listeners and readers play a highly responsible and independent role in their own language learning (Cohen, 1998; O'Malley & Chamot, 1990; Oxford, 1990). According to this theoretical framework, which has been dominant in the context of cognitive processing for the last thirty years, the listener/reader first tries to recognise phonemes and graphemes before s/he is able to understand the messages, i.e. s/he primarily needs to extract distinctive features from incoming audio/visual stimuli (sounds or letters) and to transfer them into meaningful units (words, phrases, sentences/utterances). Identifying what is distinctive in speech or writing requires some general recognition processes, such as perception and attention. Although some unconscious and rapid filtering of data registered by the senses[1] as, for instance, patterns of letters in reading or sounds at different frequencies in listening takes place in the process, we can still consciously direct our attention to some aspects of data. This is very important in the case of second/foreign language learners because they need to develop a system for sorting out distinctive features in the new language in contrast to fluent first language speakers whose recognition process has become automatic. In other words, until they are able to automatically recognise the new combination of features in the second/foreign language, they will need to make conscious efforts to detect it and consequently spend more capacity on processing bottom-up information than top-down information.

Once the basic individual units have been identified and assembled in larger chunks through using rules from the Long Term Memory (a more serious problem for second-/foreign-language learners), they should be given the meaning. Background knowledge, also stored in the Long Term Memory upon the acquisition of individual and socio-cultural experiences, is very significant at this stage of text comprehension. In comparison with first-language speakers, second-/foreign-language learners will have more difficulties making sense of data because they will generally lack the adequate schema to interpret messages in the new language (Randall, 2007).

The Skills of Listening and Reading with Young Learners

The term 'young learners' covers some of the crucial years of their intellectual, physical, emotional, and social development, so the age of 10 or 11 fits here.[2] Learning a foreign language is also a part of this developmental process, and that is why it is very important to take into consideration certain features of young learners. Among other things, rather mature children such as ten- or eleven-year-olds have the basic concepts formed, differentiate between fact and fiction, rely on both the spoken word and the physical world to construct and understand meaning, can decide on their own learning, etc. In terms of their language development, by that age, they are quite competent in their mother-tongue use (the main rules of L1 syntax are already familiar to them). They also understand abstracts, understand symbols (e.g. words), generalize, and systematize. Most of young learners at this age have some sort of L1 awareness, that is, they know that other clues – apart from the spoken or written word – are needed and helpful in the process of meaning construction (see Scott & Ytreberg, 1990). More intellectual, motor, and social skills, as well as a wider knowledge of the world, are also brought into the process of learning another language as children mature. These sources should be, therefore, used to make a language relevant and communicative, which implies the development of all four skills (Phillips, 1993).

Learning to listen to a foreign language is hard work, just as learning to read in a foreign language is very demanding. In the early stages of learning, much time is spent on listening to the teacher while playing simple games, singing songs, saying rhymes, or reading simple stories. The so-called classroom language (e.g. instructions, questions, praise) is mainly in the learner's mother tongue, but this changes as time goes on. A wide range of carefully selected activities from 'listen and remember' to 'listen and do' motivate children and give their listening some purpose, making them actively engaged in the process and helping them develop their listening strategies. Their confidence also increases with the use of support materials (e.g. visuals) because they know what is important to concentrate on. Actively encouraging learners to use comprehension strategies (e.g. using pictures, working out the meaning of unfamiliar words from context, guessing, etc.) helps them understand spoken as well as written passages effectively. In the initial stages of learning, children may also be at an early stage of L1 reading development. However, usually they have already learnt how to read in their mother tongue, so they have a working knowledge of the Roman alphabet but still should be trained to spot similarities and differences between alphabets (e.g. Croatian vs. English). Although this initial work on language awareness mostly refers to word attack skills which are based on learning/recognizing sound and letter correspondences, usually with the use of pictorials, it is extremely important to organize reading so that it includes a variety of activities from traditional (gap-filling and answering comprehension questions) to more alternative (reading for meaning, developing concepts, or enhancing thinking ability). Listening and reading tasks are very important in the primary school classroom, as they provide a rich source of language data from which children draw their own conclusions about how the language functions and how to learn the language (as well as how to learn in general) (see Brewster et al., 1991; Gabrielatos, 1998; Goh & Taib, 2006).

Assessment is also of great significance in any discussion about young foreign language learners. In order to decide which tasks and techniques are suitable for young learners, again we need to take into account their special characteristics setting children apart from older learners. McKay (2006) identifies three general categories, such as: growth, literacy (reading and writing), and vulnerability. Without understanding them, she claims, effective assessment is not possible. Why are these characteristics so special and relevant? The answer lies in the following: children are in a state of constant cognitive, social, emotional and physical growth; they are developing literacy knowledge, skills and understandings with or without possible transfer from their first language; in comparison with older learners, they are more vulnerable to criticism or failure. Primary education is based on the main principles of child growth, realizing that children have different developmental rates, experiences, emotions, and learning styles to bring into their learning; they best learn when they are actively engaged with their environment and motivated to be creative and reflect upon their learning. There is no doubt that language is a crucial element in this process.

Listening is rather difficult to assess because it is not accessible to direct observation. A child's listening ability is influenced by the nature of spoken texts, varying with the purpose, topic, and context. The spoken text may be supported by gestures, pictures, and actions. Stress and intonation may help a child understand it just as different accents, while fast speech and long stretches of input may hinder his/her understanding. Other information from the context or listener's background knowledge may compensate for a gap in understanding, which is often a problem for a foreign language learner who lacks the appropriate schemata. Reading, like listening, can be only assessed through other skills: the child's actions, speaking, or writing, reveal his/her reading ability. According to McKay (2006), children's listening and reading skill development requires organisational knowledge on the one hand and pragmatic knowledge on the other. The former includes grammatical and textual knowledge, whereas the latter consists of functional and sociolinguistic knowledge. The scope of abilities in both cases is wide, so assessors need to carefully consider L1 literacy, oral language in L2, and cultural and background knowledge, as the key factors of L2 literacy development before they select tasks and interpret performance in them (see Alderson, 2000; Buck, 2001; McKay, 2006).

A Study of Young Croatian EFL Learners' Listening and Reading Skills

Aims

The aim of the present study was to see whether or not listening and reading are equally developed skills by end of the fourth year of learning EFL, as well as how this development is related to relevant individual and contextual factors. It was hypothesized that the participants would be successful in both skills and that their results would positively correlate, whereas these were assumed to be better developed in more beneficial individual and contextual settings.

Methodology

Sample, instruments, and procedure

The study was conducted during the 2009/2010 school year and involved fourth-graders ($n = 100$) from seven primary schools (groups 1–7) located in the east and north-west of Croatia. The schools were attended by local children except for one school (group 7), where children of foreign diplomats and businessmen followed an international curriculum, together with some local children. Apart from the village schools (groups 3–5), all the other schools were very well equipped.

In all seven schools English was learnt (at the time of testing, English was a compulsory school subject for all participants), but in some of them other foreign languages such as German, Italian, French and Hungarian were offered, as well. In Grade 4, young learners in this study were taught by qualified teachers, four teachers had a university degree in primary education with a minor in English, two teachers (groups 3 and 6) were holders of a university degree in English language and literature, and only one teacher (group 5) had a college degree in English. However, some of the groups (1 and 3) had unqualified teachers during different periods of Grades 1–3.

The participants were asked to perform paper-and-pencil tasks probing into their listening and reading skills, while information about their EFL learning/teaching context was elicited with the help of questionnaires in L1. The tasks were taken over from the ELLiE project (for details see Chapter 1). The listening task consisted of two separately administered parts, followed by a post-listening questionnaire. The first part (listen and tick the correct picture) contained 12 items, and the second part (listen, look at the picture, and tick the correct/incorrect box) comprised 20 items. The post-listening questionnaire included five[3] questions eliciting their reflections on both parts of the listening tasks, such as difficulty levels, comprehension clues, comprehension problems, and emotional factors. The story-based reading task (read and write a letter in every bubble[4]) contained three rows of pictures, some pictures had empty bubbles, but their options were provided below each row to help the participants complete the text. It was followed by a questionnaire asking the participants to explain in L1 the reasons for their choices. In addition, the information on a wider context of their EFL learning was obtained through smiley questionnaires administered to them and questionnaires targeted at their parents.

Results and discussion

Listening and reading comprehension

We first computed the total score on the listening and reading tasks. The scores were high in both cases, which clearly confirmed our first hypothesis about the learners being successful in both skills.

More specifically, the total performance on the listening task revealed that the ability of the participants was quite developed comprehension, as was especially demonstrated in the first part. According to the statistics, 38.4% of the participants answered all the questions correctly, while 25.8% answered just one incorrectly, 21.2% got two wrong, and 9.3% had three incorrect answers. In other words, the majority of them achieved very high scores. The performance on the second part indicates that the percentage of the participants who provided all the correct answers was considerably smaller (17.1%); the percentage of those who answered one or two questions incorrectly was very similar (20.4% and 21.1%, respectively), while the percentage of those who had three incorrect answers was almost the same (9.2%). This was followed by the percentage of those who had four (8.6%) incorrect answers, so we can say that the majority of the participants still had high scores.

The total performance on the reading test additionally indicated the participants' developed comprehension ability. The statistics show that it was not so difficult for them to interpret the given context, in particular at the very beginning, because 85.8% and 80.9% chose correct answers for the first and the second bubble, respectively. However, the middle part of the story revealed certain comprehension problems, especially in terms of one particular bubble with a larger percentage of incorrect answers (50.9%) compared to the percentage of correct ones (38.9%). The next two bubbles were accurately understood by 64.2%, i.e. 61.7% of the participants. Almost the same percentage of correct answers referred to the story's end, which also covers three (62.3%, 65.4%, and 62.3%) bubbles.

In order to gain deeper insights into their language proficiency in the two skills, we also looked into how the participants differed in the acquired level of listening and reading comprehension by group (each group being drawn from a different school), which is presented in Figures 8.1 and 8.2 below.

A significant difference ($F = 5.967$, $p < 0.001$) was only found between group 1, with the lowest score, and groups 6 and 7, with the highest scores

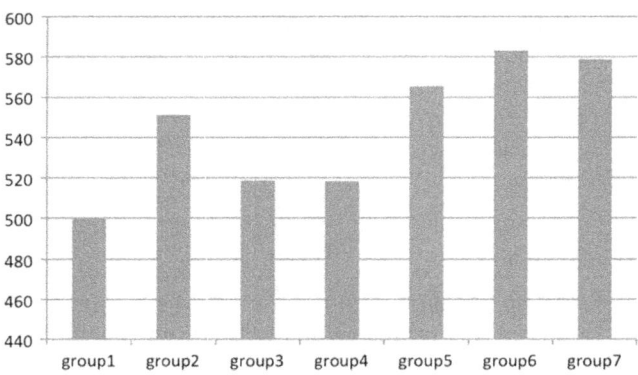

Figure 8.1 Total listening scores in the seven groups

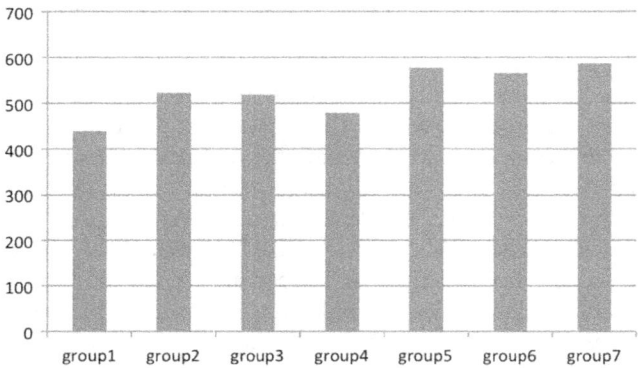

Figure 8.2 Total reading scores in the seven groups

on listening comprehension. The ANOVA analysis also confirmed that the mean scores for other groups (2–5) were not significantly different.

In the case of reading comprehension (see Figure 8.2), group 1 scored significantly lower than groups 6, 5 and 7, while group 4 scored lower than group 7 (F = 7.205, $p < 0.001$).

It is necessary to say that group 1 was drawn from a small town school in the western part of Croatia, while groups 6 and 7 were drawn from city schools (located in a working class area and a prestigious area respectively). Group 5 came from a village school in the east of Croatia.

The correlation coefficients ($r = 0.558$, $p < 0.001$) between the listening and reading task scores was found to be statistically significant, that is, there was a significant positive relationship between the participants' listening and reading comprehension. This finding consequently proves our second hypothesis, according to which listening and reading comprehension develop to similar extents in the early years of EFL learning.

Receptive Skills in the Linguistic and Non-linguistic Context of EFL Learning   181

With regard to the data obtained from the smiley questionnaires, listening and reading were the participants' favourite skills, as reported by a total of 65.6% participants. Moreover, 14.2% said that listening was their first favourite activity, while 12.3% saw reading as their first favourite activity, and another 12.3% considered singing their first favourite activity. Most participants (29%) ranked playing as their favourite activity. In addition, the percentage of those who reported reading and listening as their second favourite activity is almost the same (16.7% and 16.0%, respectively), to be compared with singing, which comes next (13.6%). Asked about how they felt about listening, 46% answered that they liked it, and 37.4% answered that they liked it a lot. There was no explicit question about reading, but it may be interesting to mention here that 42.9% liked learning new words a lot, while 31.9% reported that they liked it. We mention these results knowing how important the knowledge of vocabulary is for learning to read as well as in the activity of reading. Generally speaking, the participants in our study seemed to be enthusiastic about listening and reading activities in the classroom, which has certainly contributed to their successful achievement in both skills.

Metalanguage awareness about listening and reading

Metalanguage awareness data were collected with the help of post-listening and post-reading questionnaires. In this section we report our descriptive findings of the former and qualitative analysis of the latter.

Metalanguage awareness about listening

Figure 8.3 clearly presents how the learners perceived the first part of the listening task.

The majority of the participants reported that the first part of the listening task was very easy and easy, whereas a smaller percentage of them thought that it was neither easy nor difficult. Nobody thus perceived it as

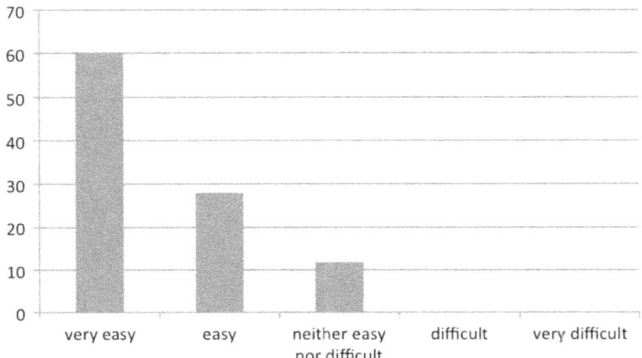

Figure 8.3 Learners' perception of the first part of the listening task

difficult or very difficult, probably due to the pictures supporting the context in each of the 12 items. In addition, the utterances covered language that is generally included in the EFL programme(s) at that age: familiar concepts (e.g. spatial relations, possession, weather conditions, everyday/current school and home activities, games and sports, physical descriptions, clothes, etc.) and grammar forms or structures needed to express them (e.g. prepositions and prepositional phrases, possessives, the present continuous tense, imperatives, modal *can/can't*, plurals of nouns and pronouns, *there is*, etc.). The language also contained some chunks or fixed phrases, usual in formal or informal communication, whose function is already known to EFL learners in the fourth year of exposure to English (e.g. *Sit down, please!, Come on, let's go! It's late., Here you are!, What is the weather like today?, What are you doing this weekend?,* etc.). We therefore suppose that the participants efficiently combined their linguistic (grammar) and non-linguistic (presented through the context of family, school, environment, and geography) knowledge. We could say that their knowledge of language was added to the socio-cultural schemata they possessed and that they knew how to adjust to the pragmatic requirements of communication in EFL. There is something else that should be mentioned in connection with the presentation of the listening material itself. Except for the above-mentioned visual support, each recording was played twice, which enabled better listening and comprehension checking, as well. However, what really helped the participants or discouraged them during information processing will be clear later, in the analysis of the subsequent post-listening (as well as post-reading) questions.

In terms of the second part of the listening task, the obtained results were a bit different. They are shown in Figure 8.4 below.

We can see that the majority of the participants considered the second part of the listening task either very easy or easy, but the percentage of those who reported that it was neither easy nor difficult was higher this time.

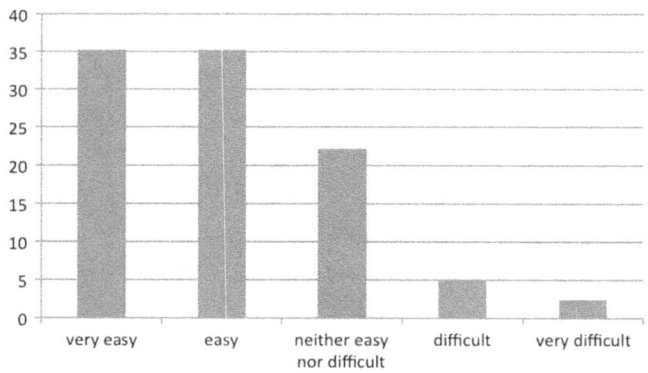

Figure 8.4 Learners' perception of the second part of the listening task

Nevertheless, they did experience difficulties in doing the task – despite the very small percentages of answers in the two last categories. The task was again based on textual (spoken code) as well as on non-textual information processing, as it was also supported by a picture depicting a situation in a familiar family context and home setting. The concepts and grammar items were mainly the same as in the first part of the task, with an emphasis on family members, their activities, and spatial relations (consequently, the present continuous, prepositions and prepositional phrases, possessives, etc. were needed). This time, however, the task at hand was slightly longer (20 items in total) and included almost any detail about people and objects all around (inside and outside), which means that better perceptual control over the whole situation was needed. The utterances presented the details at random, which required faster reactions to both linguistic and non-linguistic cues. The listeners were thus expected to integrate all the available sources of information as quickly and efficiently as possible to be able to follow the recording successfully and feel more confident. This is actually what happens in the real conversation or authentic exposure to spoken utterances in L1 or L2, so it contrasted with the first part of the task, in which the listeners were simultaneously exposed to a set of three small pictures, which enabled them to concentrate on particular situations or fewer details more easily and to narrow their attention span. This is the main reason, we assume, why the performance was slightly better on the first part of the listening task, although it should be noted that in both cases the recording was played twice, helping the listeners understand better, correct possible mistake(s), and do the task more successfully. Another reason may lie in the fact that the second part of the task was presented in the form of a dialogue including two different speaking models, which may not be easy to follow. Moreover, in this sequential question-asking and -answering procedure, the statements were not correct every time, so the listeners were additionally burdened with the necessity to detect the utterances that could not be matched with the pictures presented. In brief, the second part of the task was largely based on listening abilities, perceptual skills, problem detection, and quick responses to the given stimuli.

It now seems interesting to see how the scores on both parts of the listening tasks are interrelated with the participants' own perception of task difficulty. As Figure 8.5 presents, the participants who achieved above-average scores perceived the first part as very easy/easy as well as neither easy nor difficult in comparison to the ones with scores below the average, who reported serious task difficulty. In other words, they were quite aware of how demanding the task was or was not to them.

Almost the same trend was noticed in the case of the second part of the task, because above-average scores again revealed an interaction with the lack of difficulty as perceived by the learners themselves. However, those whose achievements were below the average reported some difficulties, as well, that

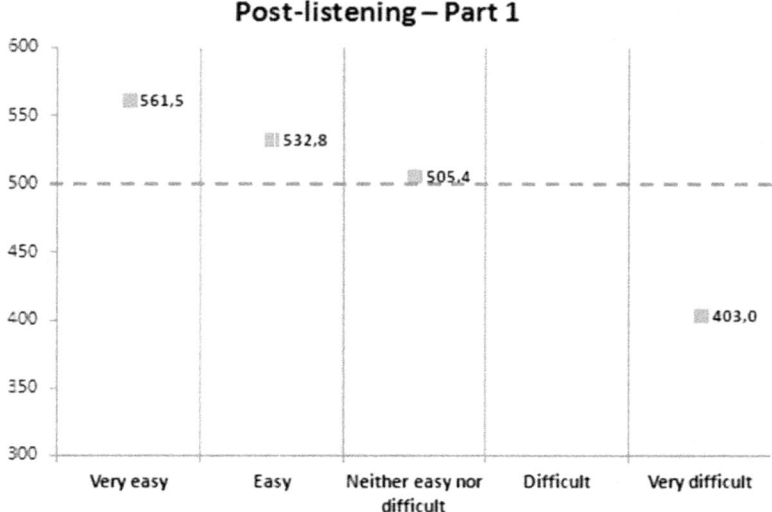

Figure 8.5 Interaction of scores on listening task – part 1 and learners' perception of task difficulty.
Note: The broken line represents the average score.

is, task difficulty (both serious and not-so-serious) was reported more frequently this time (see Figure 8.6).

Additionally useful insights into the procedures of meaning construction and message interpretation were provided by the answers to other questions in the post-listening questionnaire, covering comprehension clues and comprehension problems in both listening activities.

Asked about what helped them understand the recordings better, the participants were provided with some clues (pictures, sounds, known words, concentration, others) and were required to mention not more than three answers, ranking them 1–3. Available pictures were reported most frequently (being the first clue for 58.4% of the participants and the second clue for 27.2%), followed by recorded sounds and utterances (the first clue for 34.3% of the participants and the second clue for 42.6%). Familiar words used in the materials were also helpful (the first clue for 25.9% of the participants, the second clue for 31.9% of the participants, and the third clue for 42.2% of the participants). Interestingly, the issue of concentration was reported by 47.9% of the participants as the third clue, 31.5% of the participants considered it as the second clue, and 20.5% of the participants stated that it was the first clue they relied on. 'Something else' was also rather frequently reported (ranging from 14.3% (the first clue) to 42.9% (the second and the third clue) of the participants), but the participants rarely stated what had helped them choose the answers. Instead, they generally mentioned clues that had already been provided.

Receptive Skills in the Linguistic and Non-linguistic Context of EFL Learning 185

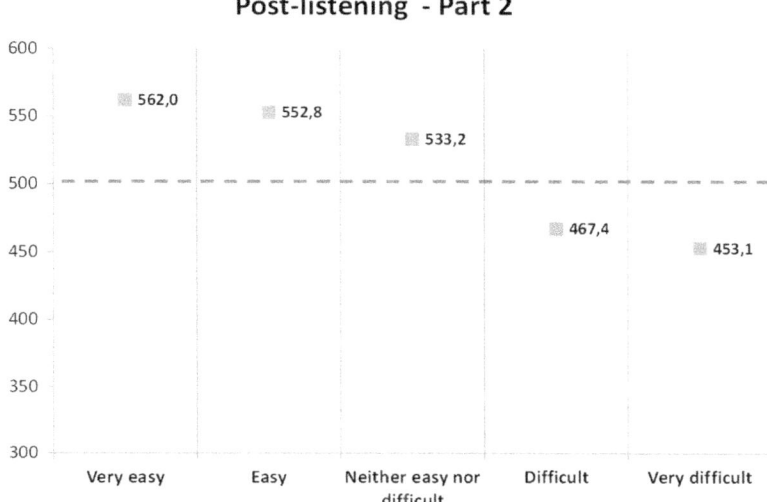

Figure 8.6 Interaction of scores on the second part of the listening task and learners' perception of task difficulty
Note: The broken line represents the average score.

On the other hand, the answers to the question about comprehension difficulties (pictures, sounds, unknown words, noise, lack of concentration, recording speed, others)[5] showed that unfamiliar words was the main comprehension problem of the participants, reported by 56.4% as the first problem and by 33.3% as the second problem. Quite interestingly, pictures were reported as the first problem by an overwhelming 71.4% of the participants, along with the 14.3% of the participants who reported this as the second problem, followed the vocabulary problem. Noise as one of the crucial environmental factors in listening comprehension (and perception, as well) was reported next, so that 46.4% saw this as the first problem and 34.8% saw this as the second problem, i.e. 81.2% in total. Another interesting finding concerns the recorded sounds and utterances, because 43.8% of them recognized this auditory input as the main cause of their comprehension problem (in addition to 34.4% for whom this was the second problem). In the case of 51.2% of the participants (the first problem in the case of 18.6% and the second problem in the case of 32.6%), lack of concentration caused serious problems and prevented them from understanding the recordings better. Besides, 45% of them reported the speed at which the recordings were played (too fast or too slow) as the third problem, 35% recognized this as the second problem, while the rest (20%) saw this as the first problem. Finally, 'something else' was also reported as the first (11.1%) and the second problem (11.1%) but, again, the participants were not quite specific about the precise nature of the difficulty – despite a high percentage who reported this as the third problem (77.8%). However, even when they stated what had hindered their listening, they actually mentioned previously provided options (e.g. picture(s); one, two, or more unknown words; the tape was incomprehensible, etc.).

The last, open-ended question regarding their listening experiences in this particular situation and feelings about the task was not answered by the majority of the participants. The answers that were provided revealed mostly positive attitudes (e.g. super, good, interesting, entertaining) because they stated that they felt, for instance, curious, excited, comfortable, and happy due to the task not being demanding and their self-confidence about learning English. However, there were also some negative attitudes (e.g. confusing, bad, boring) as they felt distracted, tense, or even afraid due to their lack of knowledge or inappropriate technical conditions including the quality of the recording or the general classroom atmosphere.

To sum up, the participants were generally aware of the fact that successful listening comprehension requires all the available sources – linguistic and non-linguistic ones. Their dynamic interaction can help listeners construct appropriate meanings and interpret messages to match situational contexts, just as they can negatively affect their listening abilities. Vocabulary knowledge is of great significance in this information processing. When auditory input is simultaneously supported by visual input, the task is likely to be easier to accomplish, in particular provided that enough concentration (largely based on the learner's attention span) is invested in this demanding process. Consequently, a lack of required vocabulary; simultaneous availability of audio and visual stimuli or perhaps their quality in terms of expected contextual support; noise, speed, or some other environmental and technical factor; and a loss of concentration may be inhibiting from the listener's point of view and lead to incomplete comprehension.

Metalanguage awareness about reading

What can be said about the learners' perception of reading as another meaning construction process? According to the answers obtained from the post-reading questionnaire, it is quite clear that the participants tended to rely on linguistic and non-linguistic sources, as well as both, to reach an interpretation of messages (in complete or empty bubbles). It seems that the most helpful information for guessing what was missing included explicitly stated key words (e.g. *eat, banana, chocolate, wait, think, aha, hi, yum, mmm*), phrases (e.g. *clever girl, where is, caught you, let's go, and watch TV, oh, it's you*), and sentences (e.g. *Something very strange happened., I think we've got ghosts!, oh, it's you!*). Apart from reporting the linguistic clues in English, just as they were used in the text, the participants paraphrased in L1 (e.g. ... *zato što je njoj trebala banana* [because she needed the banana], ... *uz to kaže da je fino* [she also says it's delicious], ... *jer je rekao da je pojeo* [because he said that he ate it], ... *i rekla mu je hvala* [and she thanked him]) or translated from English (e.g. *Uhvatili smo te!, Ja sam gladan.* [Caught you! I'm hungry.]). They did not, however, use only the explicit portions of text but referred to them in L1, instead (e.g. *ponuđene riječi* [the provided words], *cijela rečenica* [the whole sentence], *rečenica prije* [the previous sentence], *ove zadnje dvije upitne rečenice* [the last two interrogative sentences], *slaže se s rečenicom* [it matches with the sentence], *vidi se iz rečenice* [it's obvious in the sentence], *zaključila sam iz rečenice po tome što Tina govori* [I concluded from the sentence what Tina is saying]). Meaning was also mentioned, more or less explicitly, confirming that the participants knew about its significance in the reading (e.g. *značenje rečenice* [the meaning of the sentence], *smisao rečenice* [the meaning of the sentence], *ponuđene rečenice i smisao* [the given words and the meaning], *razumio sam rečenicu* [I understood the sentence], *slaže se s rečenicom* [It fits into the sentence], *jer su najbolje išli uz rečenice* [because they go best with the sentences]). Some answers additionally revealed their awareness of text as a coherent unit above the sentence level, such as *pročitala sam tekst i slaže se* [I've read the text and it fits], *pročitala sam tekst i paše* [I've read the text and it goes well here], *mislim da to najviše paše tekstu* [I think that this best matches the text], *jer se slaže s cijelom pričom* [because it fits into the whole story]). A smaller number of the participants paraphrased some text segments in L1 (e.g. ... *jer je prepričao što se dogodilo* [because he retold what happened], *logično je da on počne pričati o svom događaju kada mu dođe prijateljica a da ona smisli plan kako uhvatiti kradljivca* [it's logical that he starts speaking about the event when his friend comes to see him, and she suggests a plan for how to catch the thief], *pitala ju je što joj treba pa mu je odgovorila* [she asked her what she needed and she answered], *zahvalila mu je pa je morao nešto prije reći* [she thanked him, so he must have said something before], *pomogao mi je tekst koji priča djevojčica* [the girl's text helped me], *zato što je nastavila njegovu rečenicu* [because she continued his sentence]). Interestingly, a few of the participants reported a punctuation mark as one of the linguistic clues in the process of reading (e.g. *upitnik* [a question mark], *upitnici* [the question marks]).

The second group of clues the participants found very useful in meaning construction and text completion included non-linguistic, that is, visual clues (e.g. *namigivanje* [winking], *položaj ruke* [position of the hand/arm], *njihov položaj* [their position]; *stavila je ruku i začuđeno izgleda* [she put her hand there and looks surprised]; Toni pokazuje prstom [Tony is pointing]; *vidlli su majmuna, majmun je uživao* [they saw a monkey, the monkey was enjoying itself]; *gleda što ima u frižideru, nosi čokoladu i sav je iznenađen – iznad glave su crtice* [he looks to see what's in the fridge, takes the chocolate, and he's all surprised–there are short lines above his head]; *zato što se vidi na slici* [because you can see it in the picture]). This is in accordance with the use of situational context in message interpretation, which is largely dependent on the reader's background knowledge. These clues were less often reported than the other two groups.

The most interesting clues belong to both groups and prove that EFL learners-readers at that age knew how important it is to integrate all the available sources of information, regardless of their origin, in order to understand a text better. These are some of the most encouraging examples that were reported: *ponuđene riječi, slika, smisao rečenice* [the given words, the picture, the meaning of the sentence]; *fridge i sličica* [the fridge and the small picture]; *pomogao mi je smisao i začuđenje na dječakovom licu* [the meaning and the boy's surprised face helped me]; *nestala je hrana, a ovo je upitna rečenica* [the food vanished and this is an interrogative sentence]; *on uzima čokoladu, a tu piše čokolada* [he's taking the chocolate and here it says 'chocolate']; *vidim na slici da ga nešto pita* [I can see in the picture that she's asking him something]; *vidi se po slici i slaže se s rečenicom* [you can see in the picture and it matches with the sentence]; *po tome što majmun uzima bananu, po tome što Tina govori, po Tininom pokretu ruke* [because the monkey's taking the banana, because of what Tina's saying, the movement of Tina's hand]; *uhvatili smo te – zar nije očito* [we've caught you – isn't it obvious]; *na slici je stvar smeđe boje, a čokolada je smeđe boje, uz to kaže da je fino, čudi se* [there is some brown thing in the picture, and chocolate is brown, he also says that it's delicious, he's surprised]; *pomogao mi je tekst od djevojčice (...) vidio sam da razmišlja* [the girl's text helped me (...) I saw that she was thinking]; *značenje rečenice, odgovor, namigivanje* [the meaning of the sentence, the answer, winking].

Therefore, we could say that similar trends can be found in listening and reading comprehension: explicit and implicit vocabulary knowledge was again reported as extremely important, in particular when word recognition was purposefully supplemented with the identification of syntactic features to help the reader reach the sentence level and proceed beyond it. When attention was paid to almost every detail presented in more than one mode (e.g. text as well as a picture), the context could be understood more accurately and the message interpreted more comprehensively.

Listening and reading in a wider context

Significant differences in listening and reading comprehension were found among the studied groups, indicating that school and class environments are distinctive contextual factors. Only one group (1), however, performed significantly worse than groups 6 and 7 (city schools). This may be attributed to the fact that the learners from this small town school were generally less exposed to English outside the classroom and, importantly, their second grade teacher was replaced by an unqualified and less experienced colleague.

According to their parents' reports, the young learners in this study had considerable out-of-school exposure to English. For instance, over 70% of them spent between one and four hours a week listening to music, about 60% read books or comics for an hour a week on average, over 70% used the internet for playing computer games or watching videos, close to 80% had met someone who did not speak Croatian, etc.

Parents or other family members helped the young learners with their English, so that 87% reported on this help. The parents' support seemed very important because only two fourth-graders claimed that their parents were not happy about their English because of their low grades in this school subject.

From the young learners' perspective, their increase in knowledge could be an advantage for watching TV programmes/films or using the internet in English. It is interesting to note that learning new words was a bit less encouraging for them in Grade 4 than in the previous grades, but new activities – reading being one of them – became more appealing to them instead. Fourth-graders also reported that, apart from reading and learning new words, listening, playing games, and speaking were their favourite classroom activities – activities which are typically associated with proper language learning (with the exception of games, of course).

Discussing reading comprehension in a wider context, it is interesting to note that significant positive correlations were found between reading scores and the amount of time spent watching TV programmes in English ($r = 0.205$, $p = 0.017$), playing video or computer games in English ($r = 0.423$, $p < 0.001$), and listening to music in English ($r = 0.228$, $p = 0.010$). However, correlations with the amounts of time spent on reading or speaking in English were not significant.

Conclusion

Apart from being code-cracking and information-evaluating activities, listening and reading are unavoidable skills in the teaching of foreign languages. Their portion, presentation, practice, and assessment in the stated process should be seriously taken into account and necessarily based on the crucial theoretical background.

On the other hand, in this modern world, exposure to foreign languages (particularly English) also occurs far beyond the school setting, so that the teacher's role is not the only important factor in their acquisition. The power of using the internet and other mass media is increasingly encouraging in the process of learning, since young learners spend large amounts of their time playing video and computer games, watching TV programmes and films, listening to music in a foreign language, etc. (Mihaljević Djigunović, 2011). However, further research is needed to provide multi-faceted insights into the development of listening and reading skills. To have a clearer picture of foreign-language learning and teaching, it is not enough to present the outcomes, but also to find out the paths that have led to such outcomes.

The study presented in this chapter is just a contribution to these endeavours, confirming that listening and reading are to an equal degree successfully developed skills after four years of exposure to English as a foreign language.

Moreover, listening and reading comprehension performances, as shown by the results of this study, are positively correlated. Both skills are generally better developed in individuals with positive attitudes and favourable contextual settings, although the impact of these factors may vary in certain cases, which is something that should be especially targeted in future studies.

Notes

(1) The linguistic symbols are selected and filtered in the Sensory Register.
(2) Our study participants belong to this age group.
(3) The first four questions were structured, but the last one was open and optional.
(4) There was an extra bubble; there were 8 empty bubbles.
(5) Asked about what made their understanding difficult, as in the previous question, they were required to choose not more than three answers and to rank them 1–3.

References

Alderson, C. (2000) *Assessing Reading*. Cambridge: Cambridge University Press.
Brewster, J., Ellis, G. And Girard, D. (1991) *The Primary English Teacher's Guide*. London: Penguin English.
Brown, G. (1990) *Listening to Spoken English*. London and New York: Longman.
Buck, G. (2002) *Assessing Listening*. Cambridge: Cambridge University Press.
Cohen, D.A. (1998) *Strategies in Learning and Using a Second Language*. London and New York: Longman.
Gabrielatos, C. (1998) Receptive skills with young learners. In A.S. Gika and D. Berwick (eds) *Working with Young Learners: A Way Ahead* (pp. 52–60). Whitstable, Kent: IATEFL.
Goh, C. and Taib, Y. (2006) Metacognitive instruction in listening for young learners. *ELT Journal* 60 (3), 222–232.
Krashen, S.D. (1985) *The Input Hypothesis: Issues and Implications*. London and New York: Longman.
Mihaljević Djigunović, J. (2011) *Early EFL Learning in Context. Evidence from a Country Case Study*. London: The British Council.
McKay, P. (2006) *Assessing Young Language Learners*. Cambridge: Cambridge University Press.
Nunan, D. (2002) Listening in language learning. In C.J. Richards and W.A. Renandya (eds) *Methodology in Language Teaching. An Anthology of Current Practice* (pp. 238–241). Cambridge: Cambridge University Press.
Nuttall, C. (1996) *Teaching Reading Skills in a Foreign Language* (2nd edn). Oxford: Heinemann.
O'Malley, J.M. and Chamot, A.U. (1990) *Learning Strategies in Second Language Acquisition*. Cambridge: Cambridge University Press.
Oxford, R. (1990) *Language Learning Strategies. What Every Teacher Should Know*. Boston, MA: Heinle and Heinle Publishers.
Phillips, S. (1993) *Young Learners*. Oxford: Oxford University Press.
Randall, M. (2007) *Memory, Psychology and Second Language Learning*. Amsterdam, PA: John Benjamin Publishing Company.
Scott, A.W. and Ytreberg, H.L. (1990) *Teaching English to Children*. London and New York: Longman.
Widdowson, H.G. (1978) *Teaching Language as Communication*. Oxford: Oxford University Press.

9 Early EFL Development from a Dynamic Systems Perspective

Stela Letica Krevelj and
Marta Medved Krajnović

Introduction

A dynamic systems perspective, so well established in the natural sciences, has taken some time to make its entrance into the field of second language acquisition research (SLA), despite the fact that it was advocated by some of the most prominent researchers in the field (e.g. Herdina & Jessner, 2002; Larsen-Freeman, 1997, 2002), and already present in the works of psychologists, psycholinguists and cognitive linguists (e.g. Cooper, 1999; Van Geert, 1991; Van Gelder, 1998).

The primary goal of dynamic systems theory (DST) is to try to predict and explain the developing dynamism of a system in which two or more variables constantly interact. Even the interaction of only two variables creates a complex system the development of which cannot be explained simply as the sum of these two variables; therefore, second language acquisition or foreign language learning processes, which always imply the interaction of numerous variables, are excellent candidates for the application of DST or, as it has been also called, complexity theory (Larsen-Freeman, 2012). This application has occurred in the last decade in numerous works written by some of the leading scholars in the field (e.g. de Bot *et al.*, 2005, 2007a, 2007b; Larsen-Freeman & Cameron, 2008; de Bot & Larsen-Freeman, 2011).

Initially, one might pose the following questions: what are the basic postulates of DST when given from an applied linguistic perspective, and what makes them so applicable (or at least attractive) when, for example, trying to explain the process of foreign language learning in young learners? Here are some of the postulates:

- language is a dynamic system, i.e. a set of variables that are in constant and changing interaction during language development.

- language possesses some of the key characteristics of dynamic systems that we encounter around us (e.g. climate systems, ecosystems, social systems); these characteristics are as follows: sensitivity to initial conditions of development, complete interconnectedness of all the subsystems, predictable and unpredictable variability, the existence of so-called attractor states, the ability of internal re-structuring and constant interaction with the environment, sensitivity to even minor changes in the environment.
- for language development to occur, there should be something that can be developed further; this could be either an inborn language capacity or just a general learning capacity, the further development of which is triggered by language input and by interaction with the environment.
- in order for language to continue developing, there should be a constant source of 'energy' that will support that development; this source can be internal, such as the ability to learn, time to learn, and motivation, or external, such as language input, organized time and space for learning, material means such as books, and the media; internal and external sources can compensate for each other, so that, for example, with high motivation a learner can overcome problems such as poor learning space conditions.
- the development of a language system is more or less chaotic, but it is not completely random, since there is also a great deal of similarity among individuals (e.g. developmental stages) that can be explained by the combination of internal and external sources.
- language development is creative and individual, but it is also a reflection of communicative needs, i.e. it is triggered by the need to satisfy these needs.

If we apply all the above in describing a young EFL learner, we could point out the following: a young language learner is one dynamic system within two other dynamic systems: the context of the school where foreign language learning and teaching is happening and the wider social context of family, friends, occasional FL interlocutors, the internet, etc. The young learner language system consists of numerous subsystems which interact with numerous outside (sub)systems. The young language learner has his or her own cognitive ecosystem, which consists of concepts, L1 knowledge, possibly additional L2 knowledge, language learning aptitude, attitudes, and motivation. This cognitive ecosystem is connected with the degree of input and the already mentioned educational and social ecosystem that can be found within the school and outside the school. All parts of these ecosystems continuously interact, causing sometimes unpredictable reactions and non-linear development of the foreign language system. This variability is especially present when the language system is moving from one attractor state to another, that is, from one developmental stage of the interlanguage to the next. However, if enough energy is continuously fed into the system, the final outcome, despite ongoing unpredictability and variability, is predictable. This predictability is manifested in the fact that quality language input over a period of time will result in higher language proficiency. We believe that the data analysis and discussion presented in the rest of this chapter support this conclusion.

The Study

To investigate the development of L2 English in young learners from a DST perspective, we will concentrate on the variation and interaction of different aspects of language development through time. We will describe the language development of Croatian young learners of English based on their oral production of English over a four-year period. The progress of the whole sample in terms of five measures of oral production will be presented and discussed, and later on compared and contrasted with the actual paths of development of four individual learners in terms of each of the measures of language development. The data used and the units and methods of analysis are explained in more detail in the sections that follow.

Participants

The participants were 42 learners from seven schools participating in the project described in Chapter 1. Additionally, for the purpose of this study, we selected four participants, based on their achievement in the fourth and last year of the study: two participants (male and female) who had the best scores on vocabulary complexity and two participants (male and female) who had the lowest scores on vocabulary complexity at the last data collection point in the study.

Instruments and Procedures

The participants were asked to carry out three different oral tasks within the four-year period. Because we were dealing with young learners of English, it was not possible to employ the same tasks throughout the testing period of four years. We used stimulated recall tasks in Grades 1, 2, and 3, a controlled role-play task in Grades 2 and 3, and an interactive controlled role-play task in Grade 4. All the tasks were performed at the end of the each year. The participants were interviewed individually, and their oral performance was recorded and transcribed.

Stimulated recall tasks were used in the first three years of the study in order to measure the growth of the young learners' vocabulary. In Grade 1 the participants were given two pictures where they had to name the words they knew in English. The pictures depicted objects which were mentioned during their English lessons and covered the following four categories: animals, colours, food, and toys.

In Grades 2 and 3 the participants were asked to recall all the words they knew, and four topics that had been covered in their English classes were used as prompts for the recall. The participants had one minute to list the vocabulary for each prompt. Categories varied from school to school, but the most common ones were clothes, colours, and school in Grade 2 and animals, weather, and clothes in Grade 3. Furthermore, as an addition to the English lesson prompts in Grade 3, three prompts related to TV, music, and computers/internet were used in order to see the influence of exposure to out-of-class English.

In Grades 2 and 3, the participants' oral production was tested through a controlled role-play task in which they were asked to respond in English to situations that were explained in participants' L1. The situational exchanges were placed in a restaurant context. It was expected that the task would elicit both formulaic language and vocabulary items that had been covered in their English lessons.

The speaking task in Grade 4 consisted of a more advanced task, a guessing game which elicited more interactive exchange and this time entirely in the foreign language on the part of the interviewer. The students were asked to describe people, give locations, and ask questions about such items as people's appearance and their location in a picture.

Data Analysis

Given that none of the tasks was used throughout the four-year period, in order to provide a dynamic description of the young learners' progress, the production data from the stimulated recall tasks in Grades 1 through 3, and the data from the role-play tasks in Grades 2 through 4 will be presented separately.

Therefore, the L2 English language development will be described through two repeated-task designs employed within the four-year period.

The number of vocabulary items produced in Grades 1 through 3 was used as the measure of vocabulary growth in the stimulated recall tasks. In the role-play tasks, on the other hand, we tried to measure both vocabulary and grammatical complexity. Vocabulary complexity was measured using Giraud's Index (i.e. the total number of word types divided by the square root of the total number of tokens), a measure that is less sensitive to the length of analysed production than the regular type-token ratio.

Grammatical complexity was operationalized by two measures: noun phrase syntactic complexity (i.e. the total number of determiner tokens divided by the total number of noun tokens), and verb phrase syntactic complexity (i.e. the total number of auxiliary verbs divided by the total number of clauses).

Quantitative measures, at the whole-sample and individual participant level, were used to see how the system changes over time, and qualitative data on the performance of four selected individuals was provided in order to explain the variation in the individual participants' performance in more detail. Profiles of each of the four participants are provided; these include some of the individual differences and contextual variables that we thought could have been related to the differential developmental paths taken in the course of their learning English as a foreign language.

Results and Discussion: Quantitative Whole Sample Analysis

Out of the 42 participants data for some of the participants were missing at particular data collection points. Therefore, ANOVA repeated measures were performed to exclude the participants pair-wise. Thirty-six participants were included in the analysis of stimulated recalls, and 25 were included in the analysis of role-play tasks.

The results on mean number of words produced in stimulated recall tasks across the three years (Grades 1, 2, and 3) are presented in Figure 9.1.

The mean number of words produced in Grade 1 was 22.4, in Grade 2 it was 32.8, and in Grade 3 it was 32.2. Paired samples t-tests showed that there were statistically significant differences between the performances within the three years, but the differences in performance were significant only between Grade 1 and Grade 2 ($F(1) = 6.63$, $p = 0.015$), and between Grade 1 and Grade 3 ($F(1) = 32.31$, $p = 0.000$). The participants produced significantly more words in Grades 2 and 3 than in Grade 1, but there was no statistically significant difference in the mean number of words produced between Grades 2 and 3, where the means were almost the same.

It is necessary to point out that certain differences in performance could have been brought about by the nature of the categories of prompts used in the elicited production tasks across the three years. One of the prompt categories used in Grades 1 and 2 was the numbers prompt, which allowed the participants to list all the numbers up to 20, which is much easier to recall than 20 items in any other prompt category. This may explain the lack of significant increase in the mean number of words produced between Grades 2 and 3.

However, when the mean scores are plotted together with standard deviations within the three-year period, it is obvious that there was a substantial standard deviation from the mean number of words produced in Grade 2 compared to those in Grades 1 and 3 (Figure 9.1). This might be attributed to higher developmental variability at particular stages of interlanguage development. Grade 2 might have been a period when EFL system that our

196 Early Learning and Teaching of English

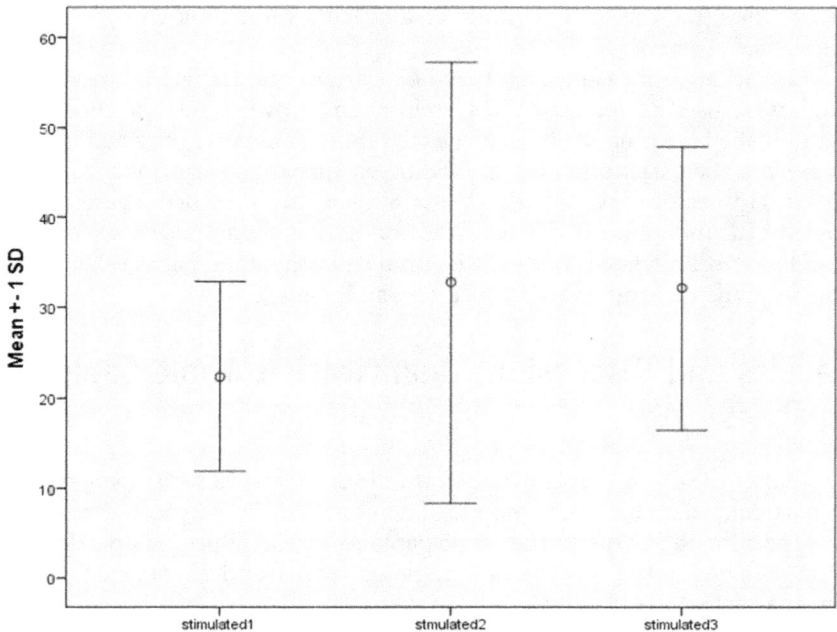

Figure 9.1 Mean number of words (+/− 1 SD) produced in stimulated recall tasks in Grades 1, 2, and 3

participants were developing was undergoing significant restructuring, but this restructuring was not happening for all the participants at the same time and rate.

Vocabulary complexity measured by Giraud's index in Grades 2, 3, and 4 was the only measure that showed linear progress across the three years, and a statistically significant difference was found in performance from Grade 2 through 4. Mean values and ANOVA repeated measures are presented in Table 9.1, and the means with standard deviations are presented in Figure 9.2.

The results show that there was a linear increase in the ratio of total number of words and total number of word forms used with similar standard deviations at each data collection point.

Table 9.1 Mean values for vocabulary complexity and ANOVA repeated measures

Vocabulary complexity	N	Mean	StD	Giraud	F	df	Sig.
Giraud 2	25	2.97	0.78	2 vs. 3	15.11	1	0.001
Giraud 3	25	3.38	0.93	3 vs. 4	31.89	1	0.000
Giraud 4	25	4.27	0.75	2 vs. 4	75.44	1	0.000

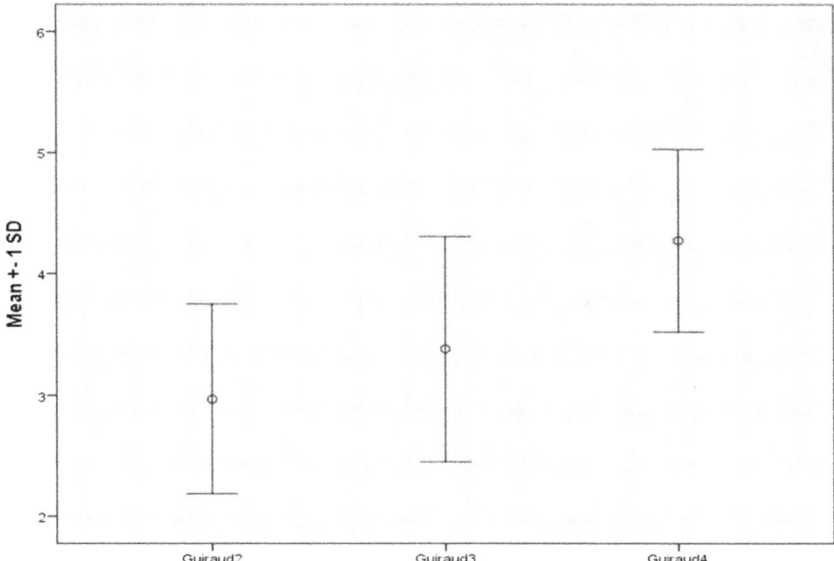

Figure 9.2 Vocabulary complexity means (+/− 1SD) in grades 2, 3, and 4

The mean indices of grammatical complexity (the determiner-noun ratio and the auxiliary-clause ratio) throughout the three years showed different patterns of development. The means of the determiner-noun ratio were expectedly low in Grade 2 (M = 0.37, SD = 0.42), and they remained so through Grade 3 (M = 0.42, SD = 0.30) and Grade 4 (M = 0.37, SD = 0.26). No statistically significant difference was found across the three data collection points (F(2) = 0.371, p = 0.692).

The mean indices of the auxiliary-clause ratio in Grades 2, 3, and 4 were even lower than the indices of the noun-determiner ratio. The means were 0.04, 0.08, and 0.12 respectively, but the repeated measure ANOVA showed that there was a significant increase in grade 4 over grade 2 (F(1) = 12.10, p = 0.002). The means obtained in Grade 3, when compared to those of Grade 2 (F(1) = 1.26, p = 0.272), and Grade 4 (F(1) = 2.171, p = 0.154) did not constitute a significant difference. The mean indices of the two measures of grammatical complexity (determiner-noun and auxiliary-clause ratio) with standard deviations are presented in Figure 9.3.

Conclusion: Quantitative Whole Sample Analysis

We can conclude that since there was a continuous foreign language input, some progress could be seen over the three years, especially in the lexical domain, which is in accordance with general predictions about early EFL.

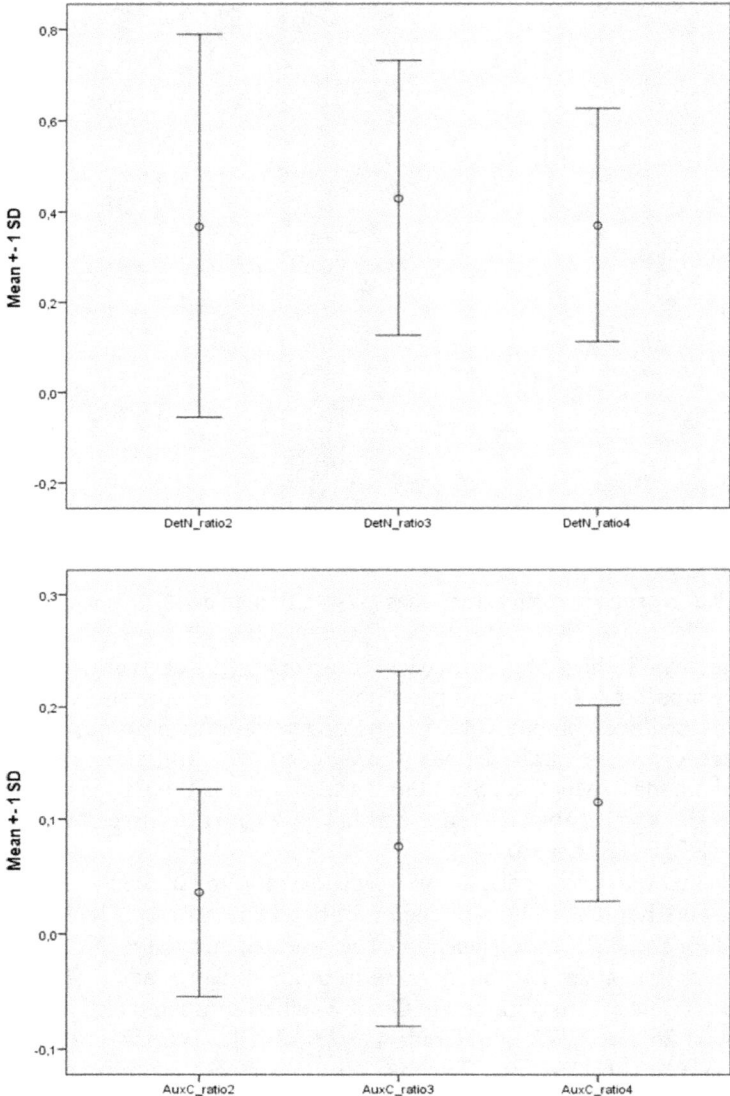

Figure 9.3 Means (+/−SD) for two indices of grammatical complexity (noun-determiner and auxiliary-clause ratio) in Grades 2, 3, and 4

On the other hand, and also in accordance with these predictions, grammatical development was lagging. While there appeared to be a linear progress in the ratio of the total number of words to the number of different word forms from Grade 2 to Grade 4, the use of determiner tokens (articles, demonstratives, possessives, or quantifiers) in relation to nouns was underdeveloped at this stage of language learning, and there were no signs of increase by the end of Grade 4. The use of auxiliaries per clause was also very low, but it did show a statistically significant increase in Grade 4 in comparison to Grade 2.

However, we have to stress again that sometimes rather high standard deviations within a particular data collection point across all measures used in the study (presented in Figures 9.1, 9.2 and 9.3) point to great variation in the performance of young learners through time. Furthermore, progression was not obvious from one data collection point to the next, which is all in accordance with the DST postulates.

Results and Discussion

Interindividual variation

We wanted to tap into the progress at the individual level by taking the two most successful and two least successful participants in terms of their vocabulary complexity indices at the end of Grade 4. More specifically, we wanted to see the paths of development of the two most successful and two least successful learners in terms of vocabulary and grammatical complexity (interindividual variation) as well as the interrelatedness of the development of vocabulary and grammatical complexity within individual learners (intra-individual variation).

The two participants with the highest scores were participants A and B, and those with the lowest score were participants C and D. Interindividual variation, presented in raw scores, on three measures used in the role-play tasks used in Grade 2 through to Grade 4 is depicted in Figure 9.4.

The first graph with raw indices of vocabulary complexity clearly depicts the criteria used for the selection of the four participants (A & B clearly above, and C & D below the average). While the whole sample average is represented by the clear ascending line, the means of all but one (participant A) of the individual participants show a different path of development from Grade 2 to Grade 4.

The second and third graph with raw indices of noun and verb phrase syntactic complexity show different patterns in the development of the two most successful and two least successful individual learners. While the participants C and D remain below the whole sample average on all data collection points, participants A and B show peculiar variation with both participants falling below average at some point within the three-year period.

However, it seems that the development of different aspects of language of those participants with the lowest score at the end of Grade 4 was practically non-existent from Grade 2 through 4.

We might conclude here that external factors, such as exposure to English outside school and parents' attitudes towards EFL, which can be deduced

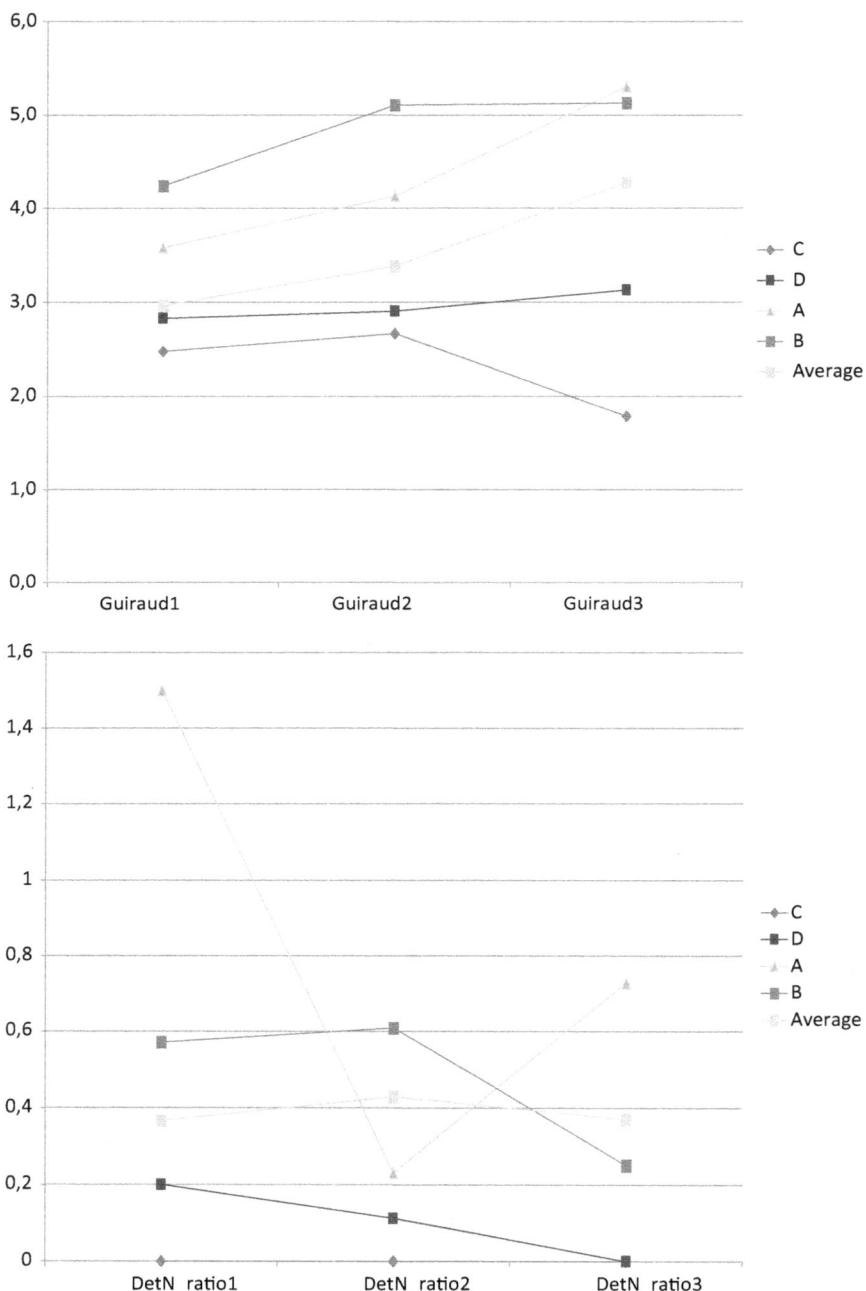

Figure 9.4 Interindividual variation from Grade 2 through Grade 4 and the average values of the whole sample on three indices in the controlled role-play tasks

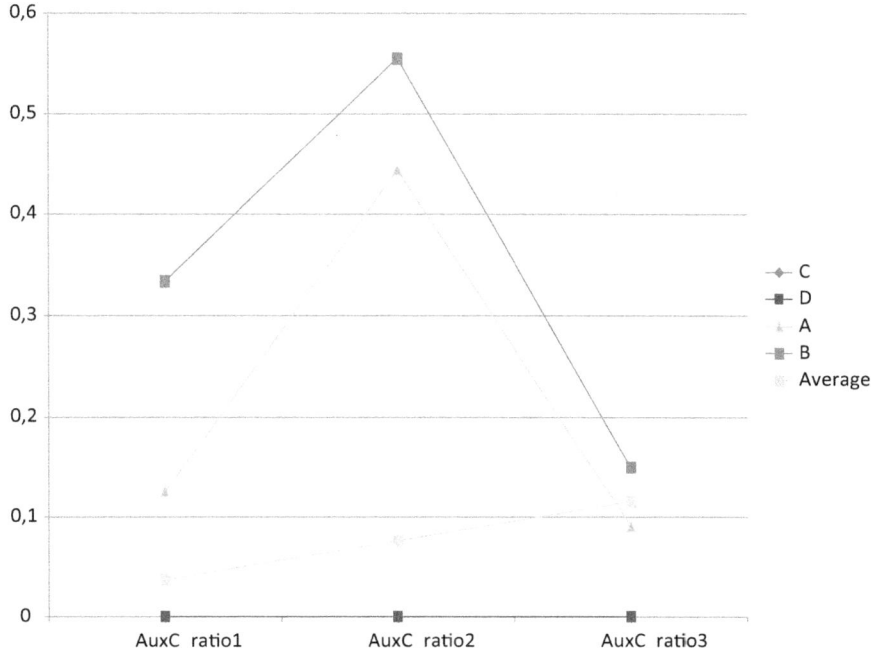

Figure 9.4 *Continued*

from the individual learner profiles, also influenced the final outcome of language development.

Intraindividual variation

From the figures above it is also obvious that the four participants followed different paths of development on all the measures within the three years. Raw scores for each participant on all measures are presented in separate tables (Tables 9.2, 9.3, 9.4 and 9.5). Besides the raw score visual representation of delta values on all three measures (the rate of change from one data collection point to the next) were used to help us identify any sudden changes in the performance of each individual participant. The delta values are provided in the Appendix.

Additionally, the raw scores obtained on the three measures, within the three years, were transformed to z-scores in order to make them comparable across the indices of vocabulary, noun phrase, and verb phrase complexity. This visual data allowed us to conclude which language aspect each participant concentrated on when performing the tasks throughout the three years.

Table 9.2 Raw scores for all three indices at all data collection points for participant A

Participant A	Grade 2	Grade 3	Grade 4
Giraud's index	3.58	4.13	5.30
Det/N ratio	1.5	0.23	0.73
Aux/C ratio	0.13	0.44	0.09

Table 9.3 Raw scores for all three indices at all data collection points for participant B

Participant B	Grade 2	Grade 3	Grade 4
Giraud's index	4.24	5.11	5.13
Det/N ratio	0.57	0.61	0.25
Aux/C ratio	0.33	0.56	0.15

Table 9.4 Raw scores for all three indices at all data collection points for participant C

Participant C	Grade 2	Grade 3	Grade 4
Giraud's index	2.47	2.67	1.79
Det/N ratio	0.00	0.00	0.00
Aux/C ratio	0.00	0.00	0.00

Table 9.5 Raw scores for all three indices at all data collection points for participant D

Participant D	Grade 2	Grade 3	Grade 4
Giraud's index	2.83	2.91	3.13
Det/N ratio	0.20	0.11	0.00
Aux/C ratio	0.00	0.00	0.00

The results are plotted for each individual learner so that the paths of development of all language aspects as well as their interaction can be compared at the same time (Figures 9.5, 9.6, 9.7 and 9.8).

Participant A

Participant A is a male young learner who had the highest score on the vocabulary complexity measure in Grade 4. He attended a city school. During

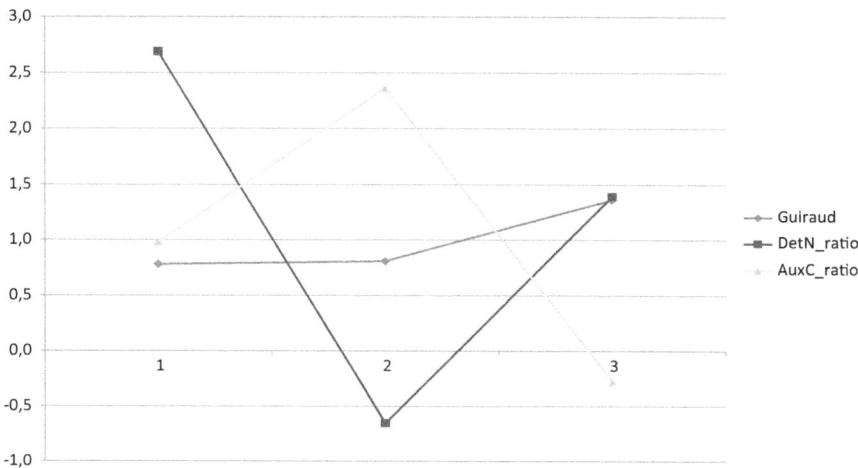

Figure 9.5 Intraindividual variation from Grade 2 through Grade 4 of three indices from the role-play tasks for participant A

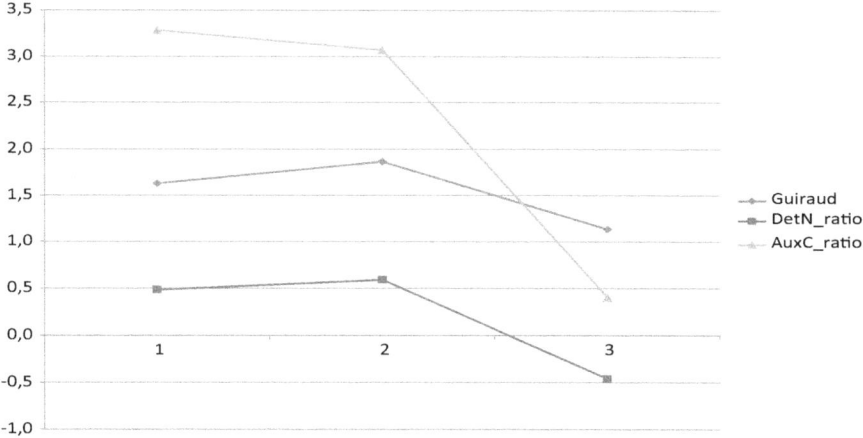

Figure 9.6 Intraindividual variation from Grade 2 through Grade 4 for three indices from role-play tasks for participant B

observations in Grades, 2, 3, and 4, his interest and engagement in the classroom were high. He stood out in terms of his ability to do all the tasks without any difficulty, but at the same time very often he seemed bored with the repetitions in class, at which point he would become restless and disruptive. His teachers identified him as the source of most discipline problems in the classroom. In Grade 2 he reported not liking English. He did not like learning new words in class, but his favourite activities were reading and

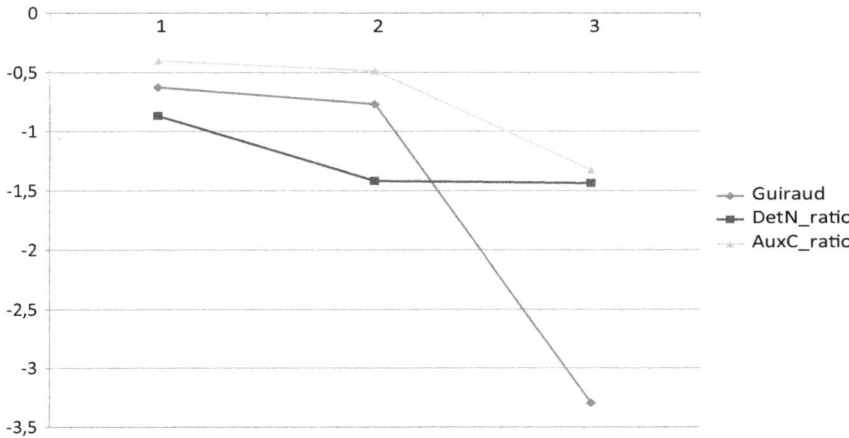

Figure 9.7 Intraindividual variation from Grade 2 through Grade 4 on three indices from role-play tasks for participant C

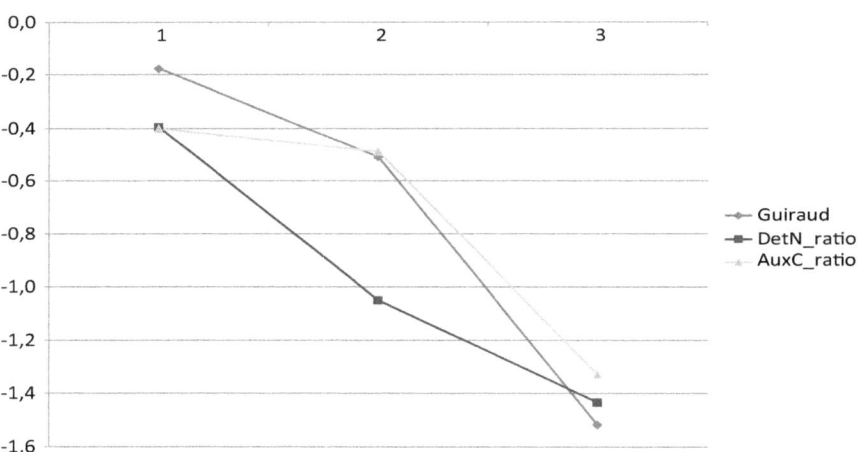

Figure 9.8 Intraindividual variation from Grade 2 through Grade 4 on three indices from role-play tasks for participant D

playing competitive games. In Grade 3 similar data was obtained: he did not like English very much, and his favourite activity was reading. In Grade 4 he was found to have more positive attitudes towards English classes. He reported that speaking was his favourite activity, and cited singing as his least favourite activity, because there were 'no interesting new words'. Reflecting on the level of difficulty of English lessons throughout the three years, he constantly reported that the lessons were easy and that they were repeating the same words over and over again. In Grade 4 he reported taking additional English classes out of school.

In Grades 2 and 3 this participant was able to assess himself as one of the best learners in class, in Grade 3 he concluded that he learned faster than his peers, and in Grade 4 he attributed his above-average success to the English language classes he was attending outside of school.

In Grade 2 he said he had never met anyone who spoke English, but in Grade 3 he reported having met a person who he could speak to in English and he felt great about it. In Grade 4 he mentioned another occasion on which he tried to speak English to a person who did not speak the participant's mother tongue, but he claimed he could not understand the person, as he or she did not speak English well.

In terms of exposure to the English language outside school, throughout the three years he reported his mother helping him with homework upon his demand, and his parents reported having an English dictionary as well as CD/video materials in English, which they shared with him. In Grades 2 and 3 he reported listening to English music, watching movies, and reading story books in English with his parents, and in Grades 3 and 4 he reported using the internet for listening to music and playing games in English for at least an hour a day.

Figure 9.5 shows which language aspects the participant A concentrated on when performing the tasks over the three years. In Grade 2 his highest score was achieved on noun phrase complexity, followed by verb phrase complexity and vocabulary complexity. In Grade 3 his score was the highest on verb phrase complexity, followed by vocabulary and noun phrase complexity, while in Grade 4 vocabulary and noun phrase complexity were the highest. It is obvious that the level of complexity of different language aspects changed from one data collection point to the next.

The actual production clearly shows the relations between different measures of complexity through time. In Grade 2 participant A was not familiar with some words required by the task, but he always used possessives and determiners with the nouns he did produce, and often used the auxiliaries where necessary in the clauses.

Examples from Participant A's production in Grade 2 are the following:

Where is the WC [toilet]?
Where is my food?
Martha, will you please sit down?
Hot.
Food is very cool.
And two...ne znam jabuke [I don't know the word for apple].

In Grade 3 verb phrases often included auxiliaries, and the vocabulary necessary for the task was correctly used, but the determiners were often left out.

Here are examples from Participant A's production in Grade 3:

Where is WC?
Can I have cheeseburger, to my mum?
Why this fish is cold?
Food is fantastic.
Please, can I have some apple, please?

In Grade 4 the participant was familiar with all the vocabulary necessary for the tasks and correctly used determiners with nouns where necessary. Auxiliaries were properly used in affirmative sentences, while in questions they were left out.

Examples from Participant A's production in Grade 4:

(I: interviewer)
I: How old is he?
A: Nine years old.
I: Yes. Is he tall, is he short?
A: He's short, he has short hair, his hair is black, he's happy...
I: Where is this person in the picture?
A: Near the table.
A: What he wearing?
I: He is wearing a blue T-shirt and black trousers.
A: What he has on the his T-shirt?
I: Some kind of yellow circle.
A: What's he doing? A ne, to sam pito. [No. I already asked that!] How old are they boy now?
I: I think he's ten years old.

However, only when looking at the raw scores on different measures of complexity from one data collection point to the next (or from the Delta values shown in the Appendix) can we see at what point in the development significant changes occurred. In the case of Participant A, vocabulary complexity showed linear rise from Grade 2 through Grade 4. However, noun phrase complexity decreased from Grade 2 to Grade 3, and then suddenly increased from Grade 3 to Grade 4. There was an obvious increase in verb phrase complexity from Grade 2 to Grade 3, and again a sudden decrease in Grade 4, compared to Grade 3. We may assume that the initially high noun phrase complexity (in Grade 2) was due to the formulaic use of determiners, but it may also be that the participant's concentration on the apparently increasing verb complexity was at the expense of noun phrase complexity in Grade 3. However, the decrease in verb phrase complexity in Grade 4 is brought about by the more demanding task where he had to use question forms. The decrease in verb complexity is visible through the lack of auxiliaries in obligatory context in questions. The variability in verb phrase complexity points to the changes in his system.

Participant B

Participant B is a female participant who had the second highest score on the vocabulary complexity measure in Grade 4. She attended a city school. During observations in Grades 2, 3, and 4 her interest and engagement varied from average to high in Grade 2, and from low to high in Grades 3 and 4.

In Grades 2 and 3 she neither liked nor disliked English classes. In Grade 2 she liked drawing during English classes and in Grade 3 she liked writing and answering the questions best. In Grade 3 she started taking additional English classes out of school, which she compared to English classes at school and said that the former were more fun even though they used the same textbook. However, in Grade 4 she cited English as one of her favourite subjects, as she was good at it and found it easy. She mentioned learning new things as her favourite activity. In Grade 2 she was not sure whether English was easier for her than for her peers, while in Grade 3 she said she was about the same as the others, and she was able to point to her weaknesses (she had trouble pronouncing some words and had to practise her reading and writing). In Grade 4 she claimed she was better than other pupils, 'but not too much'.

In terms of exposure to English outside the classroom, she repeatedly reported meeting some English-speaking children at her school, and in Grade 3 she reported being able to talk to them and understand them. She felt great about her ability to communicate in English. She was the learner with the greatest awareness of her exposure to English. In Grade 2 she reported that she was exposed to English through films in English, through the English music she listened to on the radio and on CDs, as well as through the fairytales her parents read to her in English. In Grade 3, in addition to music and films, she mentioned spending half an hour a day playing computer games in English on the internet. In the same year she reported taking additional English classes out of school. In Grade 4, she mentioned again all the media through which she was exposed to English; she said she visited English web sites for a few hours a week either to play games or search for information for projects in English.

Figure 9.6 shows that participant B appeared to be most advanced on verb phrase complexity, followed by vocabulary complexity and then noun phrase complexity both in Grade 2 and Grade 3. In Grade 4, she scored highest on the vocabulary complexity measure, which was followed by verb phrase and noun phrase complexity. Her production on all measures on all data collection points were above the average, except for noun phrase complexity in Grade 4.

The actual production shows advanced verb phrase complexity in the form of modals used in polite requests, but also advanced vocabulary and somewhat lower, but still above-average use of determiners before nouns both in Grade 2 and Grade 3.

Examples from Participant B's production in Grade 2:

Where's the toilet?
Can you give me some bread and water?
Pizza is cold.
The lunch is very good.
Can I please, can you please give me two apples?

Examples from Participant B's production in Grade 3:

I will ask somebody where the bathroom?
Can I have some bread and water?
This chicken is cold. Can I get the other one?
This lunch is very good and delicious.
Can you... can I get one more apple?

In Grade 4 she was familiar with all the necessary vocabulary to complete the task. Her production concentrated on detailed descriptions of people, which included advanced vocabulary and various word types. The apparently lower concentration on verb phrase complexity was obviously influenced by the type of task. Since it was an interactive task in which she had no trouble performing, her turns in interaction mostly started with straightforward short answers, and the advanced verb clause complexity was obvious from the part in which the participant had to make questions on her own. However, she often left out determiners before nouns in her production.

Examples from Participant B's production in Grade 4:

I: *Is it a boy or a girl?*
B: *A girl, I think.*

I: *What is she wearing?*
B: *Pink T-shirt.*

I: *What does she look like?*
B: *She has got pink shirt, trousers and she's got straight hair.*

B: *Is she boy or girl?*
I: *It's a boy.*

In terms of her development on each measure across the three years, we see that participant B made substantial progress from Grade 2 to Grade 3 and her very slight increase from Grade 3 to Grade 4 may only be explained by the ceiling effect on the tasks in Grades 3 and 4. Noun phrase complexity was high already in Grade 2 and a slight decrease in complexity was evidenced in Grade 4, when she sometimes left out articles. On the other hand, there was a clear increase in verb phrase complexity from Grade 2 to Grade 3, and the decrease in verb phrase complexity in Grade 4 can be easily explained by higher communicative competence whereby she apparently found full-sentence answers redundant.

Participant C

Participant C was a male learner who had the lowest score on vocabulary complexity at the end of Grade 4. He attended a village school.

From Grade 1 his interest was average and engagement during lessons ranged from low to average. In Grade 2 his interest and engagement were low, and he did not seem to be focused during lessons. In Grades 3 and 4 his attention and participation were mostly low, and there were obvious signs of low comprehension.

However, throughout the four years he repeated that he liked English, but it was his favourite subject only in Grade 1. There was difference in terms of his favourite activities throughout the four years: drawing in Grades 1 and 2, singing in Grade 3, and singing and colouring in Grade 4. In Grade 1 he said he was better at English than his peers, in Grade 2 he was not sure how he was doing in comparison with other pupils, in Grade 3 he said he was doing as well as his peers, and only in Grade 4 did he report doing worse than his peers because he was not studying as much as they were.

In terms of exposure to English, he repeatedly reported never having met anyone who spoke English. At home he did not have any books in English nor access to the internet. Only in Grades 3 and 4 did he report watching films and listening to songs in English. In each year he reported his sister helping him with his English homework, as his parents did not speak English. In questionnaires that were given to parents' to report on their child's exposure to English, his parents expressed their doubts about the usefulness of English for their child and necessity to start learning it at his age.

Participant C scored below average on all measures on all data collection points relative to the whole sample. Actually, he had no scores on noun and verb phrase complexity by the end of Grade 4, and vocabulary complexity, the only relatively linearly increasing variable in the whole sample, had a decreasing tendency from Grade 2 through to Grade 4.

From the actual production in Grade 2 it is obvious that the student was not able to successfully communicate the message in most situations. The only situation in which he gave a suitable answer was the item which required saying, *'Thank you'* and *'Sit down, please.'* In Grade 3 there was no improvement in terms of success on the task. Again, he was successful only in the item where he was required to say, *'Thank you,'* and the slight increase in the lexical diversity came from the item in which he managed to produce the words *apple* and *three*. He was not able to provide any answer to the situation in which he readily offered an obviously prefabricated chunk, *'Sit down, please,'* in Grade 2.

Given that the task in Grade 4 was entirely in English on the interviewer's part, the task required a certain amount of comprehension that was not met by participant C. He was able to understand only a few of the interviewers' questions, and all he provided in the target language was either *yes* or *no*.

Participant D

Participant D was a female learner who had the second lowest score in vocabulary complexity at the end of Grade 4. She attended a village school.

In Grade 1 interest and motivation were high, but engagement and performance was average to low. Though active in whole-class activities, she was restless and easily distracted. In Grade 2 she was very active in easier activities: repeating after the teacher or a recording, but often did not understand teacher's questions or instructions. In Grade 3 there were signs of low comprehension. She didn't understand instructions, her answers were only sometimes correct, she would wait for others to finish and copied from them.

In Grade 1 English was among her favourite subjects, but in Grades 2, 3, and 4 this was no longer the case. Her favourite activities from Grade 1 to Grade 4 were colouring and drawing, singing and playing, singing, and role-play, respectively.

In terms of her learner self-concept, each year, starting from Grade 1, she reported that English was more difficult for her than for her peers.

In Grades 2 and 3, she said she had never met anyone who spoke English, and in Grade 4 she said she had, but she did not try to speak to that person.

Her parents do not speak English, and she reported that her brother helped her with homework in Grades 2 and 3, but no one helped her in Grade 4. At home, throughout the three years of the study, she did not have English language resources, and her parents' claimed she was exposed to English about 2–4 hours a week through English films on TV. However, her parents were concerned about her finding English too difficult, and they seemed to be worried by the bad Grades she got in English. They considered learning English to be very important (as they saw from their own lack of knowledge) but did not think it can be either easy or fun for learners of her age.

From the raw scores presented in Table 9.5, it is already obvious that there was very little progress on vocabulary complexity from Grade 2 to

Grade 4, and no progress on either noun or phrase complexity. Figure 9.8 clearly shows that the participant was regressing on all the measures relative to development of the whole sample as well.

From the actual production we see that the same single-noun utterances were produced in both Grade 2 and Grade 3; in Grade 4 the participant had problems with comprehension, and her production again showed only instances of either single-noun or single-verb utterances depending on whether she was trying to refer to objects or actions.

Examples from Participant D's production in Grade 2:

Water
Sit down
Super
Three...apple

Examples from Participant D's production in Grade 3:

Toilet
Apple
Milk
Please, sit down

Examples from Participant D's production in Grade 4:

I: is it a boy or a girl?
D: yes

D: she il' [or] he?
I: it's a boy

D: er ..stand up ?
I: pitaš me da li stoji ili [you are asking me if he is standing up or]?
sit+ ... ?
ili sjedi [or sitting down]?

There appeared to be very little progress from Grade 2 to Grade 4. If we look only at the development of vocabulary complexity, we may assume that the ratio of word tokens and types increased, but when all the aspects of language development are taken into account at the same time, we see that there was no increase in language competence after all, as the participant was unable to comprehend most of the questions asked by the interviewer at the end of Grade 4.

Conclusion

We have demonstrated that the path of language development in young learners was far from linear. Individual performances exhibited different patterns of development: some regressed and progressed, while some remained unchanged over time.

We found more variation in the developmental paths of learners with increased knowledge levels (in the case of more successful learners), which may prove that variation enables growth in a dynamic system. Some aspects of language development seemed to have stagnated (such as noun phrase complexity) in order to allow for the growth of other aspects of development (such as verb phrase complexity).

The patterns of variation in their development and the interaction of different measures of development found in their production seemed to exhibit characteristics of dynamic systems.

The language did not develop linearly, and it was affected not only by input (the two most successful learners had more intensive input), and positive parental influence, but also by the interaction of subsystems, such as the learners' mother tongue (lack of articles, leaving out of auxiliaries in question forms in the case of better learners), and by the interaction between the development of different aspects of language (at a particular point in time, one language subsystem developed at the expense of other which temporarily backslided). It also seems that the changes within the system were influenced by the individual learner differences, such as their motivation and their learner self-concept, which also changed through time.

All of the aforementioned can be related to the DST postulates outlined in the introductory section of this chapter.

References

Cooper, D. (1999) *Linguistic Attractors: The Cognitive Dynamics of Language Acquisition and Change*. Amsterdam: John Benjamins.

de Bot, K. and Larsen-Freeman, D. (2011) Researching second language development from a dynamic systems theory perspective. In M.H. Verspoor, K. de Bot and W. Lowie (eds) *A Dynamic Approach to Second Language Development* (pp. 5–24). Amsterdam: John Benjamins.

de Bot, K., Lowie, W. and Verspoor, M. (2005) *Second Language Acquisition: An Advanced Resource Book*. London and New York: Routledge.

de Bot, K., Lowie, W. and Verspoor, M. (2007a) A dynamic systems theory approach to second language acquisition. *Bilingualism: Language and Cognition* 10 (1), 7–21.

de Bot, K., Lowie, W. and Verspoor, M. (2007b) A dynamic view as a complementary perspective. *Bilingualism: Language and Cognition* 10 (1), 51–55.

Herdina, P. and Jessner, U. (2002) *A Dynamic Model of Multilingualism: Changing the Psycholinguistic Perspective*. Clevedon: Multilingual Matters.

Larsen-Freeman, D. (1997) Chaos/complexity science and second language acquisition. *Applied Linguistics* 18 (2), 141–165.

Larsen-Freeman, D. (2002) Language acquisition and language use from a chaos/complexity theory perspective. In C. Kramsch (ed.) *Language Acquisition and Language Socialization: Ecological Perspectives* (pp. 33–46). London: Continuum.

Larsen-Freeman, D. (2012) Complexity theory. In S. Gass and A. Mackey (eds) *The Routledge Handbook of Second Language Acquisition* (pp. 73–88). London and New York: Routledge.

Larsen-Freeman, D. and Cameron, L. (2008) *Complex Systems and Applied Linguistics*. Oxford: Oxford University Press.

Van Geert, P. (1991) A dynamic systems model of cognitive and language growth. *Psychological Review* 98 (1), 3–53.

Van Gelder, T. (1998) The dynamical hypothesis in cognitive science. *Behavioral and Brain Sciences* 21 (5), 615–656.

Afterword

The term **Primary English** is used in this book to refer to two related concepts. First, it is used to denote the teaching and learning of EFL which begins during the primary education phase. Second, it refers to the teaching and learning of English as the first foreign language by young learners, i.e. between the ages of 6 and 14.

The chapters in this edited volume throw light on Primary English from several new angles. The findings presented in the book point to the need for a new approach to the complexity involved in the processes of teaching and learning English, suggesting a new dynamics that needs to be addressed. They seem to offer substantial enough evidence of crucial changes that have been taking place in the field during the last few decades, and that merit an attempt to reconceptualize Primary English in today's world.

Language acquisition has, in fact, always been dynamic, as well as idiosyncratic, though this seems to have been often overlooked. Nowadays, the inherent dynamics of English language development is constantly enhanced by the increasing number of external factors impacting this development. For one, the role of English in today's globalized world has contributed to relaxing the rigidity of norms prevailing in, for example, pronunciation and grammatical correctness (we addressed this issue in Chapter 3). The omnipresence of English in everyday life results in different types, degrees and quality of out-of-class experience that the modern Primary English learner has. The EFL learner turns into the EFL user much earlier than it used to be the case. This, together with the generally increasing family support, impacts not only the Primary English learners' affective responses to EFL learning, as illustrated in Chapter 2, but also the cognitive processes they engage in during mastering as well as using, for example, their mental lexicons (Chapter 7), verbal tenses (Chapters 5 and 6) or the concepts and markers of definiteness and indefiniteness (Chapter 4). The impact does not end there but extends to the outcomes of EFL learning, particularly at the level of language reception, as shown in Chapter 8.

The dynamics of Primary English is evident at both the macro and micro levels of EFL development. As clearly shown in Chapter 9 of this volume, young learners' development is definitely not linear. The different patterns of development which involve progression as well as regression, or simply stagnation, reflect high variation of young learners' performance over time. It is suggested that this is the result of interaction between the development of different language subsystems and aspects as well as individual learner differences.

Compared to a few decades ago, the EFL teacher nowadays also faces different challenges. While she herself is more aware of the language acquisition processes and individual learner differences, thanks to more informed teacher education curricula, she needs to be able to cope with growing (and often unrealistic!) expectations of parents, education authorities as well as learners themselves. This is highlighted in Chapters 1 and 2.

We provide an outline of this new dynamics in Figure 1.

As can be seen from the graphical representation presented in Figure 1, three layers are distinguished, with a number of elements that are positioned in each of them. The elements we include are not the only ones that are relevant or possible, but those which the insights based on our findings showed to be salient.

In the centre lies the process of learning, which is embedded in the school context, which in turn is embedded in the socio-educational context. The layers, as well as their salient elements, are characterized by constant changes and interact with each other, creating complex processes that are in constant flux. We will now describe the layers and elements.

THE SOCIO-EDUCATIONAL CONTEXT is the broadest layer that impacts, and is also impacted by, Primary English. It involves **FLL policies** that position English as a school subject at a particular place in the primary **curriculum** and define how it is taught, as well as how EFL teachers are trained for the job. It also involves out-of-school English language **exposure,** which is influenced by the *linguistic landscape* in a particular context, and can be enabled through the *media, extra private lessons,* and the like. All of the above reflect the status of English in the socio-educational context. The **home** is also one of the salient elements which can be an important source of learning support for Primary English learners. The caretakers' *socio-economic status* and their *attitudes* towards EFL are closely connected with the amount of exposure mentioned above – that is, the amount of exposure within the home (through *books,* the *internet,* and *games*) – and therefore play an important role in the learning process.

THE SCHOOL CONTEXT, as the middle layer, comprises the **teacher, syllabus, resources** and **facilities, staff attitudes**, and **peers** as the most salient components. Each of them influences learning by itself as well as through interactions with other components. Some of them are heavily influenced by the outside, socio-educational context (e.g. the teacher by the education she has received, the syllabus by the general curriculum, the resources by the country's economy), and some of them heavily influence the inside, i.e. the learning layer. For example, the teacher's teaching philosophy and classroom behaviour (e.g. *teaching methods, teacher beliefs, relationship with*

216　Early Learning and Teaching of English

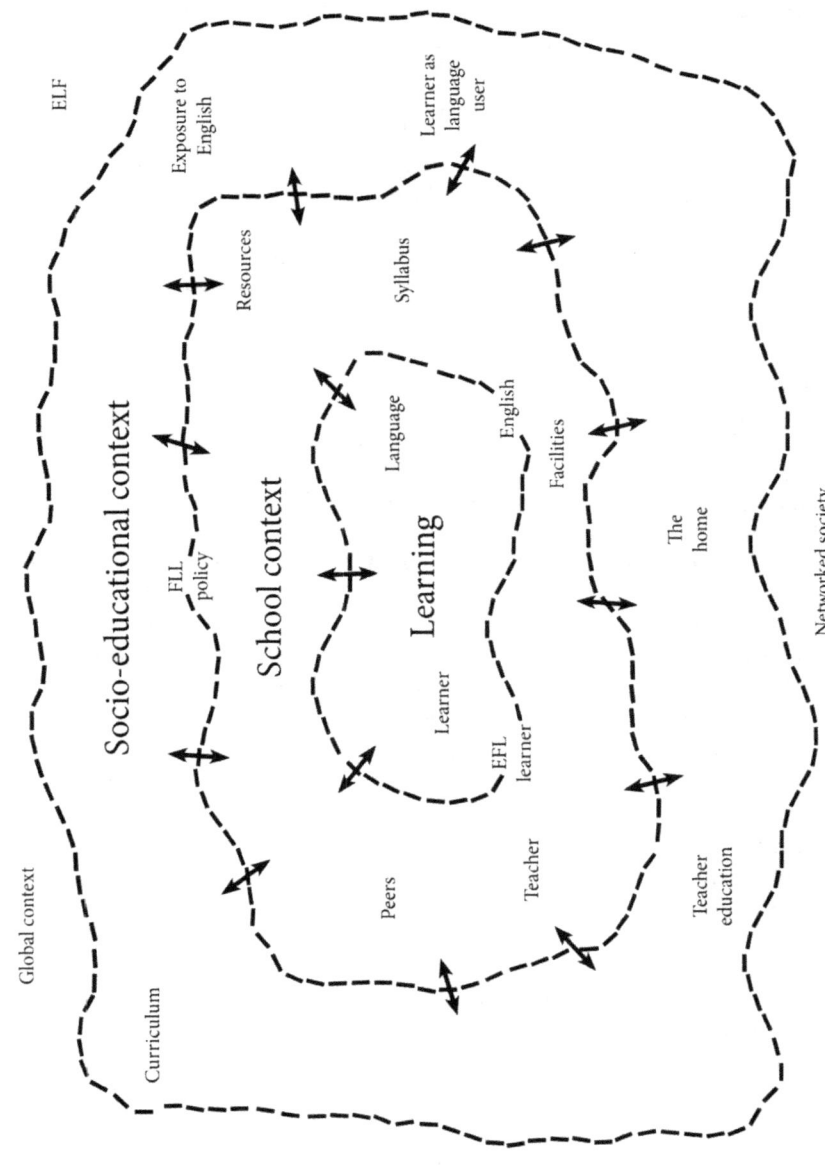

Figure 1 The new dynamics of Primary English

pupils) can very much affect the learning process and the learner. The role of peers is equally influential. The learning and the pupil are also influenced by the available resources, and by the whole atmosphere surrounding early EFL. **LEARNING** is embedded in the two layers described above, and happens as the result of their interactions, but also as the result of the cross-layer and within-layer interactions of their elements. The learning of Primary English takes place in the **learner** who – besides the **English** language itself – constitutes the main element in this layer.

The process of Learning and the Learner are the two key components of EFL learning, and so they are in our view of new dynamics of Primary English. We will conclude this afterword by putting together and stressing once again the most salient findings from the chapters, which, although focusing on different aspects of the learner and the learning process, all point to the new dynamics.

The New Dynamics of Primary English: A Conclusion

Our analyses of the learning process and the learner, performed at the group level, offer evidence, as many studies before, of common trends among primary learners of English in their language development as well as their characteristics. That is why we can talk about Primary English as different, for example, from adult EFL learning.

However, once a closer look is taken at the individual learner level in terms of their cognitive, linguistic, and affective developmental trajectory, it becomes obvious that there exists significant **variability**. When we take a broader, as well as a deeper, look at the learner as an individual, we realize that Primary English is often a highly **complex, dynamic** and **idiosyncratic linguistic process**. It is also a higly complex and dynamic process in terms of EFL **learner language behaviour**. Thus, learner individual characteristics (e.g. language learning ability, cognitive maturity, focusing ability, affective dispositions), which are in constant change, cause different elements to exert influence on their behaviour at different points. When the learner is younger, the teacher plays a pivotal role: the young learner's attitudes to learning English, perception of the immediate learning environment, as well as self-concept, rely heavily on her. At different points during Primary English, the learner's peers enter into the equation because learners increasingly start evaluating themselves against their peers. On the other hand, additional variability is created by the varying degrees to which learners are exposed to English outside the school and the varying degrees of learner digital literacy. Learner behaviour (e.g. ability to be on task) may, in turn, lead the teacher to use specific language forms when addressing the learner, which influences the development of the learner's mental lexicon. Furthermore, two distinct types of primary learners emerged in our research: the **learner as a learner** of English, and the **learner as a user** of English. Our findings show that a primary EFL learner may display different characteristics, and may perform differently, in these two roles. This can, for example, imply a confident learner turning into a user who experiences high language anxiety in a real life communication situation, and avoids the opportunity to use English. On the other hand, a pupil may feel insecure during English lessons, yet communicates successfully in real-life communication situations out of school.

So in the end – going back to the so-frequently-stressed complexity, variability, dynamism and idiosyncracy of the language learning process and the language learner/user – we might ask ourselves whether this really is a new feature of Primary English, or variability and dynamism existed before and we just were not as aware of them as we are today. Variability and dynamism certainly existed because they are inherent features of a complex system and process such as foreign language development is. However, we believe that additional dynamism and variability have been inserted into the system by the recent changes in pupils' out-of-school exposure to English (which differs from learner to learner), and by the changes in the ways in which our increasingly digitally literate learners have access to and process new information.

In the 1991 early language learning project described in Chapter 1, the situation was more uniform – all the learners received the same amount of intensive language instruction per week; all the teachers (although of varying personalities) were similarly trained: they were specifically instructed on how to work with early learners and what classroom atmosphere to create; in all the project schools, attitudes towards early EFL learning were very positive, and out-of-classroom exposure to English was more limited and more uniform than today.

The 'non-project', regular EFL context of today looks quite different from the one just outlined. We have to accept the variability, the flux, and the unpredictable changes within the process of EFL development, keeping in mind the inherent feature of dynamic systems: that, despite all the dynamism and idiosyncracy along the way, if continual and constant energy is put into the system, the outcome of the process will be a predictable one. This energy in the context of Primary English teaching and learning should consist of a sufficient amount of in-school and out-of-school input, good teaching methods, and a positive classroom atmosphere. If this is provided, the predictable and desired outcome will be a higher level of English language proficiency reached by all our learners.

Appendix

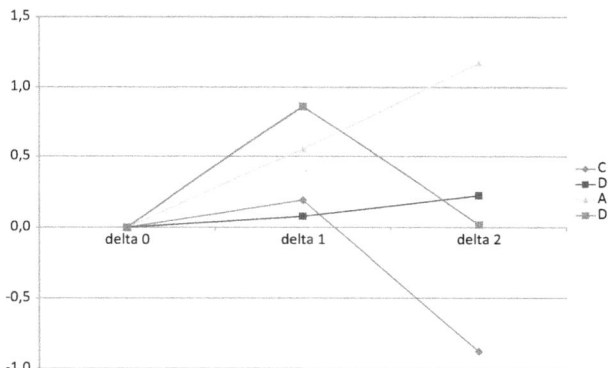

Rate of change for individual participants from one data collection point to the next on the measure of vocabulary complexity (Giraud's index)

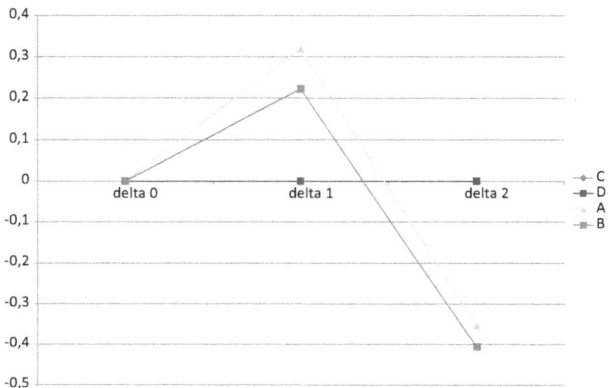

Rate of change for individual participants from one data collection point to the next on the measure of noun phrase complexity

Index

absolute present 84
abstract nouns 77
abstraction 161, 170
accent *see also* listening; pronunciation
   foreign accent signified by non-native word stress 57
adjectives 66
affective factors
   as background for pronunciation 39
   and extreme disfluency 49
   as key to new dynamics of Primary English 214
   and young learners 10–34
age
   declining motivation with age 11, 17, 33
   optimal starting age for FL study 2
   starting age of FL in Croatia 5
Ahn, S.-C. 40
Alderson, C.J. 8
American English vs British English pronunciation 38, 40–41, 50–51, 54–55
Anderson, R.C. 164
Applebee, A.N. 110
articles 66–67, 67–78
aspect *see also* telicity 83, 88
assessment 177
attention 81, 156, 175
attitudes
   case studies 20–32
   in dynamic systems theory 203–204, 207, 209, 210
   group work, and attitudes to learning 17-19
   parental attitudes 189, 199, 205, 209–210, 214–215
   previous studies on 2, 3, 11
   young learners' attitudes 12–15, 17–19

auxiliary omission 101, 197, 199, 205–206
awareness, language 66, 176, 181–188

background knowledge *see* prior knowledge
Bagarić, V. 66
Bakran, J. 40
Bardovi-Harlig, K. 87
Barlow, M. 84
Bauer, P.J. 153
Beaugrande, R. de 144
Biber, D. 86
bottom-up processing 174–175
boundedness 82, 83, 99, 104
British vs American English *see* American English vs British English
Brown, A.L. 153
Brown, G. 175
Burt, M. 2
Bybee, J. 86

Cameron, L. 152, 191
Canadian English 55
case studies of attitudes/motivation/self-concept 20–32
Casenhiser, D. 85
categorization 81, 150, 155–158, 162–169, 170
CEFRL model 105
Cekaite, A. 34
Cergol, K. 55
Chamot, A.U. 175
CHAT (Codes for Human Analysis of Transcripts) 89
chunks
   in child language acquisition 86, 146
   formulaic chunks 146, 165, 182, 210
   memorized chunks of L2 92–93, 96, 175
   multi-word units 146, 157, 159

specific vs schematic multi-word units 159
city vs town learners 60–61, 63, 180, 188
CLAN (Computerized Language
    Analysis) 89–90
classroom arrangements 17–18, 33
classroom discourse *see also* listening
    in L1 111, 116, 146, 176
    and source of past tense examples
        111, 128, 146
    and vocabulary 158, 160
clear vs dark /l/ 41, 55–56
code-cracking skills 175, 189
cognates 152, 163
cognitive approaches 80–86, 105–106,
    111, 149–151, 156, 175, 191
Cohen, A.D. 175
Collins, L. 87
Common European Framework 5
complexity theory 191
comprehensible input 174
conceptualization
    cognitive approaches 80–86, 111
    conceptual transfer 87, 95, 102, 105,
        125–127, 132
    and experience 149–150
    and the mental lexicon 153
    overextension/underextension
        155–156, 163
    and vocabulary networks 161–169
concrete operational stage of cognitive
    development 111, 159, 161
confidence *see* self-concept
confidentiality 8
connected speech phenomena 41, 56–57, 63
consent for the study 8
construal of meaning 80–86, 111, 149,
    151, 164, 170, 184
constructivist approaches 150, 151
content-related teaching 3
context, wider *see also* listening; prior
    knowledge; reading
    contextualized teaching of grammar
        146, 159
    as experience 152
    using context to comprehend temporal
        meanings 112, 113, 116, 122, 125,
        127, 142–144
    contextualized teaching of grammar
        146, 159
continuous present 80, 83, 90–106
Cook, V. 39, 43
Cooper, D. 191

corpus linguistics 86
Coultard, M. 153
countable/uncountable nouns 70–72,
    74–75, 81, 99
critical period 1, 77–78
Croatia, context for the study 4, 56,
    113–114
Croatian *see also* crosslinguistic influence
    count/uncountable nouns 99
    and final devoicing 58
    no definite/indefinite distinction 66, 67
    non-separation of tense and aspect 84
    telicity 102
    as voicing language 40, 48
Croft, W. 80, 81
crosslinguistic influence/L1 influence *see
    also* reading
    awareness of L1 helps with L2 176
    benefits of lower L1 use in classroom 116
    conditioning factors 171 n(3)
    and definiteness/indefiniteness 77
    and dynamic systems theory 192
    and interlanguage 86–88
    L1 literacy affects L2 177
    mental lexicon 153
    morphosyntactic transfer 87–88
    present tense 100–101, 102
    and pronunciation 58
    reducing use of L1 via formulaic
        chunks 146
    and second vs foreign language
        learning 2
    in storytelling 141–143
    and strategic meaning construal 151
    in the time domain generally 88
    unified competition model 151
    using L1 to express past meanings
        124–125, 128–129, 131–132,
        134–143, 144–147
    on vocabulary 158, 162, 163, 164
Cruse, D.A. 80, 81
Crystal, D. 37
Curran, Ch. 3
cyclical nature of early FLL *see* also
    linear vs non-linear language
    development 34

Dabrowska, E. 85
Damon, W. 12
de Bot, K. 191
decoding vs reconstruction (listening and
    reading) 175

definiteness/indefiniteness markers acquisition 66–78
deixis 83
demonstratives 70–78
Deterding, D. 44, 54
determiners 67, 194, 197–198, 205–206
developmental errors (vs formal errors) 102, 105
Diesel, H. 85
digital natives *see also* listening; out-of-school exposure to English; reading
  as key to new dynamics of Primary English 217–218
  and pronunciation 39, 49–50, 62–63
  and vocabulary 169
dimensional theory of feature geometry 40
Dirven, R. 83, 84
disfluency, extreme 40, 46, 49, 60–61, 62, 63
distinctive features, recognising 175
Dörnyei, Z. 12
Dressler, W. 144
Driagina, V. 88
Dulay, H. 2
dynamic systems perspective 34, 191–212, 214, 217

Early Language Learning in Europe (ELLiE) project 4–6, 8, 13
Ecke, P. 171 n(3)
Edelenbos, P. 10–11, 17
EIL (English as an International Language) 38, 43
ELF (English as a Lingua Franca) 37–64
ELLiE *see* Early Language Learning in Europe project
Ellis, N.C. 84, 86, 150
Ellis, R. 77, 118, 146
emergentism 84–85
Enever, J. 6
English
  American English vs British English pronunciation 38, 40–41, 50–51, 54–55
  as aspiration language 40, 48
  English as a Lingua Franca (ELF) 37–64
  English as an International Language (EIL) 38, 43
  exposure to English *see* out-of-school exposure to English
  globalization of English 37, 43, 214
  Inner Circle Englishes 38, 43
  International English 37
  Outer Circle Englishes 54
  as predominant FL 5
  TV and films in English 6, 169, 189, 210
English in Croatia project 8
ergonomy of speech 61
errors
  developmental errors (vs formal errors) 102, 105
  error analysis (data analysis technique) 90
  errors in form 97–102
Eubank, L. 86
experience, as factor in second language acquisition 149–153, 156, 164, 170
explicit teaching of tense (vs gradual acquisition) 114–116, 118
exposure to English *see* out-of-school exposure to English

Fekete, H. 8
fixed expressions 146, 165, 182, 210
form, errors in 97–102
formulaic chunks 146, 165, 182, 210
free speech
  and conceptual transfer 102
  and grammar 111
Freebody, P. 164
FREQ (Frequency), as measure 89–90
frequency of language input 85, 105–106
functional errors 102–104
function-to-form mapping 85
future tenses 114–115, 128, 140

Garvie, E. 110
Geld, R. 151, 152, 156
gender
  and pronunciation 62
  of sample 7
generalized statements 111, 122
Giraud's index 194
globalization of English 37, 43, 214
Goldberg, A.E. 80, 85
Görlach, M. 37
Graddol, D. 37
grades, as measurement tool 61
grammar *see also* morphology
  changing policies on grammar tuition 145–146
  contextualized teaching 146, 159
  definiteness/indefiniteness markers acquisition 66–78
  in dynamic systems theory 194, 197–211

explicit teaching of tense (vs gradual acquisition) 114–116, 118
grammatical correctness vs communication 144–146
morphosyntactic transfer 87–88, 105, 112
present tense development 80–106
temporal meanings in narrative discourse 144–145
verbs often omitted 118
grammaticalization 81
group size 4
group work *see* attitudes
growth, and younger learners 177

Haladyna, T.M. 11
Hall, C.J. 171 n(3)
Hart, D. 12
Harter, S. 12
Hawkins, E.W. 66
Heinzmann, S. 10, 11
Herdina, P. 191
higher-ability learners
  and definiteness/indefiniteness 71, 72–73, 75
  in dynamic systems theory 199–201, 202–209
  and tense development 92, 95, 121
  'user' vs 'learner' 39, 43, 214, 218
Hoey, M.P. 86
holophrases 105
Hudson, R. 154
hyperactive learners 22–23, 29, 32
hypercorrection 58, 100

imperfective vs perfective verbs 82, 84, 88, 102–104
indefiniteness/definiteness markers acquisition 66–78
individual learner differences
  affective factors and young learners 10–34
  and dynamic systems theory 201–211, 212
  idiosyncratic nature of 31, 34, 170, 214, 217
  as key to new dynamics of Primary English 217–218
  and vocabulary learning 164, 167–168, 170
information processing strategies 175
-ing endings 52–53, 83, 102, 118
Inhelder, B. 111
Inner Circle Englishes *see* English

input, language 85
intelligibility, international 37–64
intensive learning 4
interlanguage
  and crosslinguistic influence 86–88
  and dynamic systems theory 192, 195
  and grammatical development 145
  and pronunciation 58
  self-correction as indication of 101
  U-shaped curve 91, 105
International English 37
international intelligibility 37–64
internet and mass media *see also* listening; out-of-school exposure to English; reading
  as key to new dynamics of Primary English 217–218
  and pronunciation 39, 49–50, 62–63
  and vocabulary 169
intonation 41, 56–57, 63, 177
Iverson, G.K. 40

Jakupčević, E. 61
Jarvis, S. 87, 88
Jenkins, J. 37, 38, 39, 41, 47, 48, 51, 57, 61
Jessner, U. 191
Josipović Smojver, V. 39, 43, 63

Kałuza, H. 67
Kachru, B.B. 37
Kaldonek, A. 61
Kalogjera, D. 98
Kellerman, E. 87
Kemmer, S. 84
Kennedy, T.J. 11
Kirkpatrick, A. 37, 63
Klein, W. 87
knowledge, background *see also* listening; out-of-school exposure to English; reading
  and vocabulary development 151, 156, 165, 170
Kolb, A. 12
Kormos, J. 58
Kovačević, M. 118, 132
Krashen, S.D. 174
Kukolja, M. 61

L1 influence/crosslinguistic influence *see also* reading
  awareness of L1 helps with L2 176
  benefits of lower L1 use in classroom 116

L1 influence/crosslinguistic influence *see also* reading (*Continued*)
  conditioning factors 171 n(3)
  and definiteness/indefiniteness 77
  and dynamic systems theory 192
  and interlanguage 86–88
  L1 literacy affects L2 177
  mental lexicon 153
  morphosyntactic transfer 87–88
  present tense 100–101, 102
  and pronunciation 58
  reducing use of L1 via formulaic chunks 146
  and second vs foreign language learning 2
  in storytelling 141–143
  and strategic meaning construal 151
  in the time domain generally 88
  unified competition model 151
  using L1 to express past meanings 124–125, 128–129, 131–132, 134–143, 144–147
  on vocabulary 158, 162, 163, 164
Lakoff, G. 80, 81
Lakshamanan, U. 87
Langacker, R.W. 80, 81, 82–83, 151, 154
language anxiety 49, 78
language awareness 66, 176, 181–188
Language Learning for European Citizenship programme 2–4
language transfer 86–87
Larsen-Freeman, D. 149, 191
Lauš, I. 111
learner language behaviour 217
learner/user concepts 39, 43, 214, 218
'learning optimists' 19
lenition 51
Lenneberg, E. 1
Letica Krevelj, S. 156
Levis, J.M. 38
lexical level *see also* listening; pronunciation; reading; vocabulary
  and American vs British English models 50
  and the critical period 2
  in dynamic systems theory 194–196, 197–211
  vocabulary networks 149–170
  wrong lexical item as result of mispronunciation 57
Lieven, E. 85
Lindgren, E. 6

linear vs non-linear language development *see also* listening, reading, 34, 191–192, 198, 212, 214–215
linguistic system (cognitive linguistics) 81–82
listening 174–190
  accent, hindering listening ability 177
  background knowledge and listening skills 175, 176, 177, 187–188
  clues, in listening comprehension 181–188
  classroom discourse, and listening skills 176
  context in listening 175, 188–189
  decoding vs reconstruction 175
  digital natives and listening skills 189
  interactive model of listening 175
  internet and mass media and listening skills 189
  importance of vocabulary in listening skills 181, 185, 186, 188
  metalanguage awareness about listening 181–186
  motivation for listening to English 189
  prior knowledge and listening skills 175, 176, 177, 187–188
  out-of-school exposure and listening skills 188
  proficiency and listening skills 174
Long, M.H. 149
lower-ability learners
  and definiteness/indefiniteness 70, 71, 74, 76
  and dynamic systems theory 199–201, 209–211
  present tense development 92–93, 99, 102
  and pronunciation 46, 47, 49
Lyons, C. 66

MacWhinney, B. 84, 151
Mandler, J.M. 153
Marschollek, A. 11
Marsh, H.W. 11
Martin, W. 110
McEnery, T. 86
McKay, P. 34, 177
meaning construal 80–86, 111, 149, 151, 164, 170, 184
Meara, P. 164
Medved Krajnović, M. 77, 112, 146
memory 81, 86, 93, 96, 153, 175

mental lexicon 153–154, 218
Mercer, S. 11, 12
metalangauge awareness *see* listening, reading
Mihaljević Djigunović, J. 3, 5, 49, 78, 189
MLU (Mean Length of Utterance), as measure 89–90
monophthongisation, inappropriate 41, 54
morphology
  awareness of temporal verb endings 132
  and the critical period 12
  and past/present verb forms 111–112
  present tense development 80–106
  verb endings often omitted 118–120, 125–127
morphosyntactic transfer 87–88, 105, 112
motivation *see also* listening, reading
  as background for pronunciation 39, 42–44
  case studies 20–32
  declining motivation with age 11, 17, 33
  and dynamic systems theory 192, 203–204, 207, 209, 210
  previous studies on 2, 34
  and the role of experience 151
  stability of 11
  study into young learners' motivation 12–17
motivational evolution 12
multi-word units *see also* chunks 146, 157, 159
Muñoz, C. 6

Narančić Kovač, S. 111, 112
narratives 3, 110, 112, 125, 128, 134, 140–143
Nation, P. 152
native-like pronunciation *see* pronunciation
negative constructions 100
Nikolov, M. 11, 17
nouns
  countable/uncountable nouns 70–72, 74–75, 81, 99
  and definiteness/indefiniteness 66–67, 70–78
  nominal predications 82
Nunan, D. 174
Nuttall, C. 175

Odlin, T. 87, 88
O'Malley, J.M. 175

Optimality Theory 58
oral production
  of definiteness/indefiniteness markers 70–73
  lack of complete sentences 118–120, 125
  preferred by learners to writing 39
  using past tenses 127–134, 144
out-of-school exposure to English *see also* listening; reading
  in affective factors case studies 20–32
  in Croatia generally 6
  differing self-concepts in-school and out-of-school 32, 43, 205, 218
  and dynamic systems theory 199, 205, 207, 209, 210
  as key to new dynamics of Primary English 214, 215, 218
  measurement of 14–15
  and pronunciation 64
  real-life usage of English 32, 43–44, 218
  TV and films in English 6, 169, 189, 210
  and vocabulary 154, 160–161
overextension/underextension, conceptual 155, 153
Oxford, R. 175

parasitic learning strategy 171 n(3)
passive vs active language users 174
past continuous tense 122
past tense development 110–147
patterns of use 81, 84–85
Pavlenko, A. 87, 88
peers, influence of 215, 217
perception 81
Perdue, C. 87
perfect (past) tense 110–111
perfective vs imperfective verbs 82, 84, 88, 102–104
personal pronouns 70–78
'person-in-context' 32
Phillips, S. 176
Piaget, J. 111
Pienemann, M. 87
Pinter, A. 19
plurals, irregular 53
Polunenko, A. 88
possessives 70–78
pragmatics
  connected speech phenomena 41, 56–57, 63
  and definiteness/indefiniteness 66
  and tense 83

Pranjković, I. 66, 84
present tense
  present tense development 80–106
  temporal meanings in narrative discourse 110–147
  in vocabulary exercises 159
  vs need for past tense for e.g. storytelling 110–111
prior knowledge *see also* listening; out-of-school exposure to English; reading
  and vocabulary development 151, 156, 165, 170
proficiency *see also* higher-ability learners; listening; lower-ability learners; reading
  and dynamic systems theory 192–193
  links to pronunciation 44–45
  measurement of 13
  relationship to affective factors 33
  school grades, as measurement tool 61
progress, measurement of 62
progressives 83
pronunciation *see also* digital natives
  /ɜː/ mispronunciation 39, 47
  /æ/ as /e/ mispronunciation 39, 44–47, 57–58, 59–60, 62, 63
  allophonic variation [l] - [ɫ] 41, 55–56, 63
  alveolar *t* and *d* 1, 41, 52, 57–5
  American English vs British English pronunciation 38, 40–41, 50–51, 54–55
  aspirated consonant pronunciation 40, 47–48, 59–60, 62, 63
  British English vs American English pronunciation 38, 40–41, 50–51, 54–55
  core features 39–41, 44–51, 63
  and the critical period 1
  dark [ɫ] 41, 55–56
  dental fricative /θ/ and /ð/ 1, 41, 52, 57–58
  diphthongisation, inappropriate 41, 54
  and English as a Lingua Franca 37–64
  English as an International Language (EIL) 38
  final devoicing 58
  and gender 62
  final tensing 56, 63
  flapped /t/ 41, 51, 61–62, 63
  /g/ final 52–53
  glottal pronunciation 40, 47–48
  intervocalic /t/ (flapping) 41, 51, 61–62, 63
  lingua franca core pronunciation 38
  long vs short vowel distinction 40, 48–49, 58, 59–60, 62, 63
  and morphological errors 99
  mispronunciation affects grammatical words more than lexical 45–46, 54
  native-like pronunciation vs international intelligibility 38, 61, 63
  non-core features 41, 51–57, 63
  non-rhotic pronunciation 38, 49–51
  plural ending, mispronunciation of 41, 53
  post-alveolar /r/ 56
  pre-fortis clipping 40, 48
  tense-lax contrast in vowels pronunciation 40, 48–49, 58, 59–60, 62, 63
  velar merger 52–53
propositional simplification 118, 125
prosody 41, 52, 56–57, 61, 177
prototypicality 81, 82
psycholinguistics 175, 191
psychological approaches *see* cognitive approaches

quantifiers 70–78

rhoticity 38, 40, 49–51
Radden, G. 81, 83, 84
Randall, M. 175
reading 174–190
  background knowledge and reading skills 175, 176, 177, 187–188
  clues, in reading comprehension 181–188
  context in reading 175, 188–189
  decoding vs reconstruction 175
  digital natives and reading skills 189
  interactive model of reading 175
  internet and mass media and reading skills 189
  importance of vocabulary in reading skills 181, 185, 186, 188
  metalangauge awareness about reading 186–188
  motivation for reading English 189
  out-of-school exposure and reading skills 188

prior knowledge and reading skills 175, 176, 177, 187–188
proficiency and reading skills 174
using L1 to express reading comprehension 186–187
real-life usage of English *see also* out-of-school exposure to English
and self-concept 32, 218
and 'users' vs 'learners' 43–44
Received Pronunciation 38
receptive learning 3
relational predications 82
relative present 84
Renandya, W.A. 174
Richards, C.J. 153, 174
Ringbom, H. 86
Robinson, P. 86
rote-learned sentences 165

sample (whole study) 7–8
Schmidt, R. 153
school context, for learning 215–216
school grades, as measurement tool 61
Scott, A.W. 176
second language acquisition
cognitive approaches 84–86, 105–106, 111, 149–151, 156, 175, 191
constructivist approaches 150, 151
dynamic systems perspective 191
innateness vs experience debate 149–150
integrated model 152
second language vs foreign language 2
Seidlhofer, B. 37
selective attention 156
self-concept
case studies 20–32
differing self-concepts in-school and out-of-school 32, 43, 205, 218
idiosyncratic nature of individual learner differences 31, 34
previous studies on 11–12
study into young learners' self-concept 12–15, 19–20
self-correction 101, 104, 121
Selinker, L. 86, 87
semantics
meaning construal 80–86, 111, 149, 151, 164, 170, 184
present forms with past meanings 125–127, 132
temporal meanings in narrative discourse 110–147

Sharwood-Smith, M. 87
Silić, J. 84
simple present 80, 82, 83–84, 90–106, 111
Sinclair, J. 86
Slobin, D.I. 85
Smiley, S.S. 153
socio-economic status 14
socio-educational context 56, 215
songs and lyrics, as vocabulary source 169
speaking
definiteness/indefiniteness markers 70–73
lack of complete sentences 118–120, 125
preferred by learners to writing 39
using past tenses 127–134, 144
Stanojević, M.M. 39, 43, 63
storytelling 3, 110, 112, 125, 128, 134, 140–143
strategic construal 156, 162
stress (prosody) 41, 56–57, 61, 177
structuralist approaches 174–175
substitution
of articles 67, 72, 75
lexical 162, 163
morphosyntactic transfer 87–88, 105, 112
phonemic 39, 44, 47–48, 52, 54, 58, 59
of present forms for past 112
syllabic rhyme 52
Szpotowicz, M. 153

Talmy, L. 150
Taylor, J.R. 81, 85
teachers
Croatian context 6
greater teacher input needed at younger age 17–19, 217
influence on affective factors generally 11
influence on motivation 2, 3, 11
modern challenges for 215
pivotal role for younger learners 217
present forms with past meanings 125
specially trained for young learners 4
spontaneous use of past forms 114, 118, 124–130, 133
teaching of tense 115–118, 122–123
using L1 to express past meanings 124–125, 128, 130, 135–143, 144–147
telicity 82, 88, 102–104, 105

tense
  in cognitive linguistics 83 84
  explicit teaching of tense (vs gradual acquisition) 114–116, 118
  present tense development study 80–106
  temporal meanings in narrative discourse study 110–147
  young learners and their clues 113–124
thematic organisation of vocabulary 152–153
Thomas, G.P. 11
time
  conceptual transfer 88, 105
  conceptualisations of 82–83
  present tense development study 80–106
  temporal meanings in narrative discourse study 110–147
'time out' 143
to be 97–99, 100–101
to have 100
token frequency, as measure 85
Tomasello, M. 80–81, 84, 85
top-down interpretation view 175
topological schematization 150–151
total emotional response (TER) 3
town vs city learners *see* city vs town learners
transcription of data 8
transition between primary stages 5, 31, 33
Trenkić, D. 67, 75
triangulation of data 15
TV and films in English 6, 169, 189, 210
type frequency, as measure 85

underextension/overextension, conceptual 155, 163
unified competition model 151
usage theory/emergentism 84–85

'user' vs 'learner' 39, 43, 214, 218
Ushioda, E. 12, 32

Van Geert, P. 191
Van Gelder, T. 191
viewing frames 83
Vilke, M. 1–2, 2–4, 5, 11, 37, 111, 118, 145, 146
vocabulary *see also* listening; reading
  in dynamic systems theory 194–196, 197–211
  vocabulary networks 149–170
voiced vs aspirated consonants 40, 47–48
VOT (voice onset time) 40
vowel reduction 38, 56–57
Vrhovac, Y. 2, 3
vulnerability, of younger learners 177

Widdowson, H.G. 112, 174
wider context *see also* listening; prior knowledge; reading
  contextualized teaching of grammar 146, 159
  as experience 152
  using context to comprehend temporal meanings 112, 113, 116, 122, 125, 127, 142–144
Wilson, A. 86
Wolter, B. 164
word order 100
written production
  of definiteness/indefiniteness markers 73–76
  oral production preferred by learners to writing 39
  present forms with past meanings 126

Ytreberg, H.L. 176

Zergollern-Miletić, L. 66, 67, 77

For Product Safety Concerns and Information please contact our EU Authorised Representative:

Easy Access System Europe

Mustamäe tee 50

10621 Tallinn

Estonia

gpsr.requests@easproject.com